W9-BTB-775

Just Words

Just Words

Lillian Hellman, Mary McCarthy,
and the Failure of Public
Conversation in America

ALAN ACKERMAN

Yale

UNIVERSITY PRESS

New Haven and London

Yale University Press books may be purchased in quantity for educational, business, or promotional use. For information, please e-mail sales.press@ yale.edu (US office) or sales@yaleup.co.uk (UK office).

Set in Minion type by Westchester Book Group.
Printed in the United States of America.

Illustration credits: xii, Sam Falk/*New York Times;* xiii, copyright Carlos Freire, photographer, Paris

Library of Congress Cataloging-in-Publication Data

Ackerman, Alan L. (Alan Louis)
    Just words : Lillian Hellman, Mary McCarthy, and the failure of public conversation in America / Alan Ackerman.
        p.   cm.
    Includes bibliographical references and index.
    ISBN 978-0-300-16712-2 (clothbound : alk. paper) 1. Hellman, Lillian, 1905–1984—Trials, litigation, etc.   2. McCarthy, Mary, 1912–1989—Trials, litigation, etc.   3. Dick Cavett show (Television program)   4. Trials (Libel)—New York (State)—New York—History—20th century.   5. Television talk shows—Political aspects—United States.   6. Libel and slander—United States—History—20th century.   7. Freedom of speech—United States—History—20th century.   8. Politics and literature—United States—History—20th century.   I. Title.
    KF228.H45.A25 2011
    346.73′034—dc22
    2010052126

A catalogue record for this book is available from the British Library.

This paper meets the requirements of ANSI/NISO Z39.48–1992 (Permanence of Paper).

10 9 8 7 6 5 4 3 2 1

For Andrea Most

Contents

Acknowledgments

In completing this book, I have been a beneficiary of a research grant from the Social Sciences and Humanities Research Council of Canada. I am also grateful for the support of the University of Toronto, Department of English, and particularly for the guidance of Brian Corman and Alan Bewell.

Andrea Ewing was an exceptional legal research assistant and an extraordinary teacher of law at this project's early stages. Other students and research assistants at the University of Toronto—Sarah Kriger, Jane Iordakiyeva, and Anna Gallagher-Ross—also contributed to this work. Dean Rogers at the Vassar College Libraries assisted me in exploring and reproducing key items from the Mary McCarthy Collection. Thanks as well to Marguerite Perry for stress-free technical assistance and to photographer Carlos Freire.

At Yale University Press, Sarah Miller nurtured this project from its earliest stages and offered shaping criticism. Laura Jones Dooley was a patient and painstaking manuscript editor. Cynthia Crippen ably assisted with the index, and Karen Gangel provided valuable proofreading assistance.

This book about the failure of public conversation was forged in exceptionally rich and productive private ones. I gratefully acknowledge my debt to the friends, colleagues, and family members whose generosity illuminates every word. In fact, many of the words in these pages are theirs, though responsibility for the flaws is mine. Sarah Wilson's sharp intelligence, warm sense of humor, and friendship informed this project from start to finish. Jonathan Warren, Pamela Klassen, John Marshall, Andrew DuBois, Elspeth Brown, Arthur Ripstein, Lisa Brownstone, Benjamin Zipursky, and Jeremy Feinstein read chapters and offered vital criticism and instruction. Peter Ackerman, James Berkman, Richard Berkman, and Richard Rabinowitz read selections at formative stages and taught me to speak a more engaging and less "academic" language. I greatly appreciate the kind attention and insights of Dick Cavett, Carl Rollyson, Stephen Gillers, Floyd Abrams, Reuel Wilson, Rita Wade, and Joan Mellen. My old friend Neal Dolan deeply shaped my understanding of the rigors of civil discourse, liberalism, and the challenge of navigating between reason and passion. I thank Andrea Slane and Simon Stern for reading drafts and for inviting me to present versions of two chapters at the University of Toronto Faculty of Law. Thanks also to members of the law and literature symposium. I am grateful to Mona and Jacques Kornberg, Mark Stabile, Greg Beiles, Karen Weisman, Joshua Fogel, and Joan Judge for their friendship and contributions to my thinking about a wide range of social issues, historical concerns, and public policy questions. The collegiality and keen insights of Charlie Keil, Martin Puchner, Michael Cobb, Matt Smith, David Savran, and Joyce Antler have also made this work possible. Louis Sokolov, Karen Beattie, and Richard Macklin have shared legal insights, a passion for civic and familial life, and countless meals. Elaine Scarry and Philip Fisher offered invaluable support and advice. Graeme Taylor has given me the benefit of his analytical rigor and wisdom.

I dedicate this book to Andrea Most, to whom I am indebted beyond words for our life of shared words. She has been my best reader and most compassionate critic, a brilliant teacher and constant conversationalist. My kids, Max and Alice, continual arguers and vivid inspirers, have shaped this book's central concerns, from pedagogical theory to moral decision-making. I grew up in a milieu dominated by vigorous conversation on public and private subjects, politics, history, literature, and just plain gossip. The life of the Republic, I believe, depends upon the dinner table. My parents, Alan and Barbara Ackerman, my brother, Peter Ackerman, and my sister, Elizabeth Kaiden, have influenced this work profoundly. I also wish to pay tribute to the memory of my remarkable grandmothers, Esther Ackerman and Selma Berkman, co-generationists of Lillian Hellman and Mary McCarthy. My grandmothers were not public figures, but in key ways they resembled the subjects of my book and shared their America. My close relationships with them made Hellman and McCarthy intimately familiar to me. Without them I doubt that I would have become interested in these histories.

Lillian Hellman teaching at Yale, 1966

Mary McCarthy at a conference on her writing,
Centre Pompidou, Paris, 1977

Introduction

By privacy, I mean a person's power to control what
others can come to know about him or her.
—Stephen Breyer, *Active Liberty: Interpreting
Our Democratic Constitution,* 2005

Jenny said, "*Schweigen vor dem Kind,*" and
everybody was silent.
I said, "I will go to bed now so you won't have to
Schweigen vor dem Kind and I've known what that's meant
since I was three years old."
"You're smart," Jenny said, "but if you were smarter you
wouldn't have told us that."
—Lillian Hellman, *Pentimento: A Book of Portraits,* 1973

*J*ust *Words* emerges from the libel suit that author Lillian Hellman filed in 1980 against critic Mary McCarthy, who said on the *Dick Cavett Show* that every word Hellman wrote was a lie, "including 'and' and 'the.'" The lawsuit became a cause célèbre that illuminated the arguments—and the passion for argument—of their generation. As the social critic Irving Howe wrote, "It's not just two old ladies involved in a catfight. The question involved—of one's attitude toward communism—is probably the central political-cultural-intellectual problem of the 20th century. I think for many of us those disputes were the formative passions of our lives—for good or bad, it's made people what they are today."[1] Although Howe oversimplified this clash of personalities (and McCarthy would disagree vehemently with this interpretation of the case),[2] debates about communism throughout the twentieth century served as a lightning rod for more general debates about free speech, reputation, and moral responsibility. Hellman and McCarthy each contributed personal histories of their times, and the lawsuit was about those competing narratives.

The story of libel from the 1920s to the 1980s traces an arc in the life of American society. What it means to defame someone depends on how a society regards fame. New media, including "talking pictures" and broadcast television, changed the way people understood private life and what was "newsworthy." More public space made for more celebrities, which made for more conflicts over reputation and raised questions about the legal consequences of telling stories. A culture of mass advertising emerged as a defining force in American life. As journalist Walter Lippmann put it in his 1922 book *Public Opinion,* it had become impossible to check the facts of every story, and no public figure ever told the whole truth anyway: "Great men, even in their own lifetime, are usually known to the public only through a fictitious personality."[3] After the publication of Hellman's best-selling memoirs, many leveled the charge that her claim to fame was largely fictitious, and that was what McCarthy had in mind when she called Hellman a liar. A critic and satirist, McCarthy thought "thirst for fame . . . just as dangerous to self-respect as the thirst for alcohol."[4] But Lippmann, one of America's premiere public intellectuals at the time, had been making an argument about the failure of modern citizens to engage critically in public conversation. As the audience grows larger, he insightfully commented, "the number of common words diminishes."[5] This diminishment of shared words, suggested by McCarthy's glib attack on Hellman's *every* word," is at the core of what this book regards as failures of American public conversation. Only in acknowledging that facts are invariably shaped by opinion, Lippmann explained, can citizens become truly tolerant. The Hellman-McCarthy libel suit raised pointed questions about the limits of tolerance, as well as about relations between fact and opinion, words and actions, the personal and the political, that continue to reverberate today.

Born in New Orleans in 1905, Lillian Hellman was an only child and, by her own estimation, a difficult one. When she was about six, her father Max's shoe business failed, and he moved the family to New York City. He became a traveling salesman, and Hellman spent the next ten years between New York and New Orleans, lonely and off balance. By 1924, having lost interest in classes at New York University, she landed a job with Horace Liveright's publishing firm. There she worked in advertising and publicity, read manuscripts, and entered the orbit of literary celebrity. Though she lacked

conventional beauty, the shapely, auburn-haired office girl excited the interest of the editors. She attended their wild parties, full of liquor, "lush girls," and "almost-actresses."[6] At the
age of twenty-one, Hellman knew the world of public opinion. She briefly worked as a press agent for a musical revue,
The Bunk of 1926, before turning her hand to book reviews—
the vocation at which the young Mary McCarthy made her
name in the 1930s. Barely three years after the appearance of
the first commercially successful talking picture, *The Jazz
Singer* in 1927, the twenty-five-year-old Hellman moved from
New York to Hollywood. Her husband, Arthur Kober, had
secured a job as a screenwriter for Paramount. Feeling out of
place, bored, and drinking hard, Hellman hated Hollywood.
Moody yet glamour-hungry, she got a job as a reader at MGM,
where she sat at a desk in a large room full of other readers for
fifty dollars a week. In the fall of 1930, she met the detective-
novelist Dashiell Hammett. He was tall, thin, famous, and
eleven years her senior. Hellman initiated the affair when she
spotted him one evening across a restaurant, asked who he
was, rose quickly from her seat, and grabbed him on his way
to the men's room. By 1932 she had divorced Kober. Soon she
too became a scriptwriter. In 1934, she became famous with
her first major Broadway hit, *The Children's Hour*. During the
following two years, Hellman campaigned vigorously to organize the Screen Writers Guild. Her long career and her life
were thus intimately connected to mass media. Living in a
world of celebrities, she hung out with William Faulkner and
F. Scott Fitzgerald. Her friends in the 1930s included the Ger-
shwins, Darryl F. Zanuck (producer of *The Jazz Singer*), writers such as Nathanael West, S. J. Perelman, and Dorothy
Parker. In 1984, her funeral was attended by Warren Beatty,
Carly Simon, Norman Mailer, Mike Nichols, and others who

flew in from both coasts. Throughout her life, Hellman both craved publicity and guarded (or misrepresented) the details of her private life.

The genres Hellman chose, drama and memoir, indicate her lifelong concerns with exposure and privacy. "Privacy" has diverse meanings under the law, which include a person's power to control what others can come to know about him or her, a right not to be represented in a way that places one in a "false light" before the public, and a constitutional right to make important decisions about marriage, contraception, and abortion without undue interference by the state. Although from a legal point of view, an invasion of privacy is not the same as an injury to reputation, Hellman shows that on a personal level they are closely related. Her plays, such as *The Children's Hour* (1934), *The Little Foxes* (1939), *The Autumn Garden* (1951), *The Lark* (1955), and *Toys in the Attic* (1960), center on what people should or should not say in public, and they speak directly to Hellman's personalized histories, *An Unfinished Woman* (1969), *Pentimento* (1973), and her memoir of the communist witch hunts, *Scoundrel Time* (1976). The House Un-American Activities Committee (HUAC), before which Hellman appeared in 1952, made a spectacle of asking witnesses to name people they knew to be communists; it systematically destroyed reputations. Starting in 1947, HUAC held hearings into alleged communist influence in the film industry that led to the blacklisting of hundreds of directors, actors, and screenwriters, including Hellman. In her hearing, Hellman insisted that she would speak about herself but not about "people who in my past association with them were completely innocent of any talk or any action that was disloyal or subversive."[7] Her performance before HUAC (and her use of it in memoir) was a signal instance of the way in which she protected her privacy while courting publicity.

In 1977, Hellman was lionized at the Academy Awards by Jane Fonda. On prime-time television, the aging author, in a shimmering silver gown and helmet of blonde hair, presented the award for Best Feature Documentary. Three years later it was McCarthy's comment on the *Dick Cavett Show,* rather than a similar remark that had appeared in print, that prompted Hellman's libel suit. Although television sets became available in the 1930s, by 1960 only 50 percent of households owned one. By the mid-1980s, cable television had appeared, providing a new home for off-beat hosts such as Dick Cavett, whose dry wit and penchant for conversation kept him popular but took him to the margins of the mainstream. His PBS program ended in 1982, midway between the offending episode with McCarthy and Hellman's death in 1984, which brought the libel suit to an end. By that point 99 percent of American households had at least one television; most had more than one. In 1980 it was typical for an old woman like Lillian Hellman, whose deteriorating health and vision made it impossible to read, to turn on the tube and listen to talk shows as a way of putting herself to sleep.

This book takes a particular interest in the television talk show, specifically as conducted by Cavett, who was central to several important conflicts of the 1970s before he was named as a codefendant with McCarthy in 1980. Considering Cavett's significance as a talk-show icon of the 1970s, a close friend from his days at Yale remarks that intellectualism was his commodity. His shows centered on conversation. As he has said, "It is just that I want to hear good people talk about important things." Nonetheless, when asked in his deposition for the Hellman-McCarthy case to describe his profession, he replied, "I guess I'm a performer."[8] As host of a television program, he trafficked in the intimate experience of celebrity.

McCarthy's put-down of Hellman was, as Hellman argued in her libel suit, an attack on her reputation rather than a conversation about public issues. Cavett's show played an instrumental role in blurring the boundary between the public and the private, politics and entertainment, fact and opinion. In conjunction with the rise of mass media and celebrity culture, along with the increased presence of "personal" issues in public conversation, Hellman and McCarthy's generation shaped and was shaped by the reformulation of notions of the public and the private. One area in which these ideas underwent significant revision was the law of libel or defamation. In broad terms, the common law of defamation imposed liability on a speaker who (1) communicated to a third party (2) a defamatory statement (3) about the plaintiff that (4) was likely to cause (5) damage to the plaintiff's reputation. A speaker could be held liable for a defamatory statement even if he or she actually and reasonably believed it to be true. The common law mitigated the harshness of this regime by recognizing a number of privileges, such as the doctrine of "fair comment," which protected statements of opinion about matters of public concern (including books and works of art that were offered to the public), so long as the underlying facts were true. However, privileges like fair comment were *qualified* privileges that could be defeated by showing malice on the part of the speaker. This is how the law stood until 1964, when the Supreme Court ruled for the first time on libel in the landmark case *New York Times, Inc. v. Sullivan*. In this famous case, the Court held that the common law of defamation, including the defense of truth, failed to provide adequate protection for the right to criticize public officials. In doing so, it made libel a constitutional issue and initiated a debate that continued over the following decades about, among

other things, the meaning of "malice" and what constituted a
"public" concern. Ensuing cases extended the ruling on public officials to suits brought by *"public figures"*—those who are
not public officials but who play a prominent role in the society or take an active role in public controversies—and then to
private figures libeled on matters of *public concern*. In short,
the Court addressed the increasingly heated debate, of which
the Hellman-McCarthy case was to be symptomatic, about the
proper balance between free speech and the interest in protecting individual reputations. At the same time, although
the Constitution protected freedom of expression under the
First Amendment and the right to remain silent under the Fifth,
there was no constitutional right to privacy until the *Griswold
v. Connecticut* birth-control case of 1965. While the *Griswold*
and *Times* cases were not immediately related under the law,
they indicate overlapping concerns with defining the language of privacy and deeply interrelated aspects of experiences in the lives of women such as Hellman and McCarthy.

Mary McCarthy was born in Seattle in 1912. In 1918 she
and her three younger brothers became orphans when their
parents died in the global influenza epidemic. Sent to Minneapolis to live with a cruel aunt and uncle from her father's
Catholic side of the family, "poor Roy's children" endured five
miserable years of which McCarthy gives a vivid account in
Memories of a Catholic Girlhood (1957).[9] Like her autobiographical fiction, from "Ghostly Father, I Confess" to *A
Charmed Life,* McCarthy's memoirs, which also include *How
I Grew* (1987) and *Intellectual Memoirs* (1992), subject her own
life and her faulty memory to unsparing analysis. As she often
suggests, transparency, precision, and accuracy are not only
the hallmarks of compelling prose but also a blow for truth
against tyranny and injustice. In 1923, when the McCarthy

children were split up, Mary moved back to Seattle to live
with her maternal grandparents (her grandfather, a prominent Republican lawyer, was Episcopalian and her grandmother was Jewish). In 1929, she left for Vassar College. When
she graduated in 1933, she moved with her first husband, actor
Harold Johnsrud, to New York City.

As a critic, McCarthy launched her career in 1935 with a
series of slash-and-burn articles for the *Nation,* entitled "Our
Critics, Right or Wrong," dubbed later in the *New York Times*
"a St. Valentine's Day massacre of reviewers and critics" (the
gangster Dutch Schultz had been killed the day the first was
published).[10] She acquired thereafter a reputation for unsparing bluntness, if not meanness. Alfred Kazin, another
prominent critic and memoirist, who met her in Provincetown,
Massachusetts, in 1940, found her critical intensity uncomfortably zealous. Her self-confessed obsession for detail often
seemed motivated by something more than rigorous objectivity, though Kazin acknowledged her "brilliance in putting
down friends, enemies, and various idols of the American
tribe."[11] He himself wrote a memorably detailed if unsympathetic portrait of their first meeting in the summer of 1940:

> I met Mary McCarthy through [Bertram] Wolfe,
> and all the time she spoke to some friends with her
> fluent style and her nervous laugh, inching her
> way from personality to personality over boulders
> of well-chosen words. . . . Wolfe and his wife, on
> principle, avoided personalities; Mary McCarthy
> dealt in nothing else. She had, I thought, a wholly
> destructive critical mind, shown in her unerring
> ability to spot the hidden weakness or inconsis-
> tency in any literary effort and every person. To

this weakness she instinctively leaped with cries of
pleasure—surprised that her victim, as he lay torn
and bleeding, did not applaud her perspicacity. She
seemed to regard her intelligence as essentially impersonal; truth, in the person of this sharply handsome twenty-eight-year-old Vassar graduate, had
come to pass judgment on the damned of Provincetown. Though she was often right enough about
the small specific absurdities that she felt compelled to point out about themselves to her friends,
she despised the world in which she moved.[12]

McCarthy's novels and stories, often thinly veiled accounts of
her personal acquaintances, have been read as acts of malice.
After reading *The Oasis,* her satire of the intimate crowd at
the literary-political journal *Partisan Review* (where she
served as an editor and drama critic in the late 1930s), the
founding editor and her former lover, Philip Rahv, was so enraged that he went to a lawyer and threatened to sue, only to
be dissuaded by their mutual friend Dwight Macdonald, who
said, "You realize, Phil, in order to win this lawsuit, you have
to prove that you are Will Taub. Are you prepared to make
that kind of jackass out of yourself?"[13]

   McCarthy reached the crest of her fiction-writing career
and her celebrity with the popular success of her 1963 roman
à clef, *The Group,* which detailed the adventures of young
Vassar graduates in the 1930s. But, as she told Cavett, she
hated its "bestsellerdom" and disliked fame. Moreover, in the
1960s she had found herself at odds with a new generation of
intellectuals. Susan Sontag, who had taken over what had
once been McCarthy's theater column at *Partisan Review,* described her condescendingly in a 1962 journal entry: "Mary

McCarthy's grin—grey hair—low-fashion red + blue print suit. Clubwoman gossip. She is *The Group*. She's nice to her husband."[14] (McCarthy married diplomat Jim West in 1961 in Paris. By 1979 the couple lived for most of the year in an apartment on the rue de Rennes.) The New Left and Old Left acted like family members in an oedipal drama. McCarthy, one of the Old Left's central figures, expressed anxiety about Sontag in letters to Hannah Arendt: "When I last watched her [Sontag] at the [Robert] Lowells', it was clear that she was going to seek to conquer you. Or that she had fallen in love with you—the same thing. Anyway, did she?"[15] Beyond acknowledging Sontag's powers of intellectual seduction, McCarthy betrays her awareness that the mantle of physical attractiveness, a quality that had been essential to her own persona in the 1930s, had been assumed by another, more striking woman.

McCarthy had never liked Hellman, but she became increasingly irritated by the fact that Hellman's star had grown yet brighter in the late 1970s following her heroic self-portrayal in *Scoundrel Time*. Hellman's Soviet sympathies and her public-relations coup before HUAC were particular targets of McCarthy's ire and became central to the lawsuit. McCarthy, a liberal anticommunist, was outraged that a former Stalinist (as she considered Hellman) would pose as an advocate for personal freedom and free speech. She resented that Hellman took the protection of the Fifth Amendment, without acknowledging it, and regarded her invocation of privacy as a sign of guilt. This hostility, as Howe rightly observed, dated back to the political and sexual feuds of the 1930s, when a generation of women and men treated self-exposure and personal attack as the hallmarks of significant civic discourse. As Diana Trilling, essayist-reviewer, wife of literary critic Lionel

Trilling, and sometime friend of both McCarthy and Hellman, later wrote, "Ours was, in fact, a cruelly judgmental society, often malicious and riddled with envy."[16]

McCarthy and Hellman were at the center of a crowd known as the New York intellectuals, a group, mostly born in the first two decades of the twentieth century, which was radicalized in the early 1930s and split over Soviet communism a few years later. The fiction and criticism they produced was often a transparent extension of their lives. They wrote for the *Partisan Review* and later for *Commentary, Dissent,* and the *New York Review of Books.* They were largely but not exclusively Jewish. Irish-Catholic novelist James T. Farrell was from Chicago. For WASPs and Yale men Dwight Macdonald and F. W. Dupee, radicalism was an extension of personal restlessness. Many of the others were educated at the City College of New York and the moderately more privileged—such as Lionel Trilling, art historian Meyer Schapiro, and communist agent and author Whittaker Chambers—at Columbia University. In the 1930s, Trotskyite, socialist, and Lovestonite students at CCNY gathered in dark niches of the lunchroom with their books, pamphlets, ragged overcoats, and cheese sandwiches to argue and shout slogans, contending with the more numerous and powerful Stalinists. To one degree or another, all the New York intellectuals were shaped by ideological battles over Marxism. Their hopes and disappointments in the Soviet Union, the crisis of the Spanish Civil War, and John Dewey's Commission of Inquiry into the Charges Made against Leon Trotsky in the Moscow Trials in 1937 were, however, also interconnected with passionate advocacy of the modernist avant-garde. Their parties in hot Manhattan apartments were characterized by heavy drinking, arguments over formal purity in painting, Stalinism, and socialism, and they resulted in personal feuds and competitive publication. These men and women were imbued with a sense of their historical importance. Trilling, who became a professor at Columbia University and the foremost literary critic of his day, was less overtly ideological but shared this group's moral perfectionism and the belief that the hard work of interpretation was an ethical obligation. As McCarthy wrote of one raucous party at a Lexington Avenue apartment during the split in Marxist allegiances of the late 1930s, "I could hardly understand them as they ranted and shouted at each other."[17]

The Ukrainian-born Philip Rahv and William Phillips founded *Partisan Review* as a publication of the American Communist Party in 1934 before breaking with the party and reconstituting the journal with McCarthy, who came into the journal's orbit as "Philip's girl." She was the sole woman on the editorial board. She left the masthead in the spring of 1938, shortly after she left Rahv, though she continued to be one of the magazine's most valued contributors. She was an incisive theater critic. "There was a vivid shine on everything she wrote," commented Diana Trilling, "and whatever she wrote was always a statement of her sense of her own power."[18] With her vivid smile, long brown hair, and bohemian dress, McCarthy was *Partisan Review*'s sexy fresh face. Though living with Rahv (who was married to another woman), she served as bait to lure Edmund Wilson, the preeminent critic of his generation, then stout and middle-aged, to be a contributor. Her coeditors, including Rahv, urged her have dinner with the great man. When McCarthy woke up at the Chelsea Hotel the next morning, having passed out the night before, she cried, "Oh, God, oh, God, I've disgraced *Partisan Review*."[19] She split with Rahv and married Wilson (the second of her four

husbands), by whom she had a son, Reuel Wilson, in 1938. Like
most of her cohort, McCarthy was not a feminist and later expressed disdain for feminism. She believed in marriage, and
married often.

In 1941 Hannah Arendt immigrated with her husband,
Heinrich Blücher, moved into an apartment on West Ninety-
Fifth Street with her mother, and later settled into a dark
Morningside Drive flat. Arendt's work began to appear in
Partisan Review in 1944. She encountered McCarthy first at a
Murray Hill bar in Manhattan, accompanied by art critic
Clement Greenberg, with whom McCarthy was having a dis-
agreeable affair (while married to Wilson). Then in the spring
of 1945 at one of Philip Rahv's parties (Rahv was then married
to McCarthy's former Vassar classmate Nathalie Swan), they
met again, and McCarthy made a provocative remark about
the Nazi occupation of Paris. She felt sorry for Hitler, she said,
because he absurdly longed for the love of his victims. Arendt
took offense: "How can you say such a thing in front of me—a
victim of Hitler!"[20] Within a few years of crossing paths and
working together on Dwight Macdonald's new journal *politics,* they had not only patched up their disagreement but also
discovered a deep intellectual sympathy. "Let's end this nonsense," Arendt said to McCarthy one evening on a subway
platform. "We think so much alike."[21] Thus began an enduring friendship, characterized by shared interests and mutual
admiration. In a brief note to McCarthy in 1949, Arendt wrote
that her novella *The Oasis* was "a pure delight . . . a veritable
little masterpiece."[22] McCarthy responded with even greater
enthusiasm to Arendt's *Origins of Totalitarianism* (1951) and
The Human Condition (1958). In their twenty-five years of
richly intimate correspondence, McCarthy expresses herself
with a passionate sincerity to her "Dearest Hannah" (as she is

"Dearest Mary") conspicuous in the writing not only of these women but also of anyone else in their group. Along with other refugees such as Arthur Koestler and Nicola Chiaromonte, Arendt brought a flavor of European intellectual life and galvanized the *Partisan Review* crowd in its postwar antitotalitarian direction, as energies turned from hot war against Nazis to cold war against Soviets.

After World War II, this group of former Trotskyites fully integrated into American culture, taking up residence in universities and propagandizing against the Soviet Union on lecture tours sponsored by the US government, through advocacy groups such as the Congress for Cultural Freedom and in journals such as *Encounter,* covertly subsidized by the CIA. McCarthy, an instructor at Bard College and Sarah Lawrence, as well as a frequent lecturer in the United States and abroad, and the more moderate among them represented what historian Arthur Schlesinger would call *The Vital Center.* Some among the New York intellectuals, such as philosopher Sidney Hook and *Commentary* editor Irving Kristol, turned much further to the right. They became the godfathers of neoconservatism and were later welcomed into the Reagan White House. Others split on the subject of McCarthyism, for which Hellman bitterly (and unfairly) assailed them all in *Scoundrel Time* and was in turn attacked by Irving Howe, sociologist Nathan Glazer, Hook, and, of course, McCarthy. These strong-minded people shared more in their moral assumptions and worldview than they might acknowledge, yet for that very reason, intellectual, political, and sexual competition among them was intense.

Much has been written of the men in the group. *Just Words* focuses on the women. I am indebted to the useful biographies of both Hellman and McCarthy by authors William

Wright, Carl Rollyson, Joan Mellen, Carol Gelderman, and Carol Brightman, among others. But *Just Words* takes a different approach to these women's lives. It aims to provide a human window through which to examine key questions about what we can and cannot or *should not* say in public. The rise of libel as both a cultural and constitutional concern since the mid-twentieth century indicates a failure of liberal virtues—reflective judgment, self-restraint, sympathy, and toleration—that are necessary for healthy public conversation. The Hellman-McCarthy case is emblematic of that failure, and their lives illuminate the genealogy of the current crisis. Because their dispute was nominally about "every word," *Just Words* uses life stories to reflect on our failures to forge a shared public discourse and on increasingly vituperative accusations of truth and lying in America. Hellman and McCarthy's relationship to issues such as sexual freedom, the right to privacy, female reproduction, and equal rights was deeply intertwined. They bequeathed to second-wave feminists an ambivalent legacy. In 1970, McCarthy wrote to Arendt of meeting fashionable people in London, "including the current Women's Lib idol, an absurd Australian giantess [Germaine Greer] who made remarks like 'We must make them understand that fucking is a *political* act.'"[23] But McCarthy herself had brandished her sex life like a torch, describing her own adventurism in graphic detail, turning it into provocative words, without perhaps fully understanding what she had illuminated. Hellman's lawsuit, which ended with her death in 1984, also raised questions about relations between the personal and the political that reverberate today.

In 2009 Elizabeth Edwards, wife of former senator and presidential candidate John Edwards, aired the family's dirty laundry in her memoir *Resilience: Reflections on the Burdens and Gifts of Facing Life's Adversities,* which, she told talk-show hosts Oprah Winfrey and Matt Lauer, she wrote for her children. Her affecting (and potentially libelous) stories of personal loss, physical suffering, and marital infidelity aim to teach readers larger life lessons that bridge the private-public divide.[24] They also stake her claim to a history apart from that of her politician husband. Like the Hellman-McCarthy case, Edwards's story continues the American tradition of heated civic discourse about personal character, the notion that the health of the Republic depends on the private virtues of its citizens and that personal flaws can cause real harm to the society. North Carolina lawyer Andrew Young, who specialized in concealing John Edwards's deceptions on the campaign trail, said on *Good Morning America* that "virtually every word that came out of his mouth was a lie."[25]

Libel is an area of law that is itself characterized by conflict over problems that have proven impossible to resolve, such as the status of the "truth," the definition of "malice," and what does or doesn't count as "public." In 1919 Justice Oliver Wendell Holmes wrote that the best test of truth is the power of the thought to get itself accepted in the marketplace of ideas and that the notion that ideas compete freely and openly is the basis of the liberal public sphere. But America has never had a public sphere characterized purely by reason or by openness. The supposedly neutral press carried libelous language long before the founding of the Republic, as Benjamin Franklin complained in his *Autobiography.* Thomas Jefferson, while vice president to John Adams, allegedly paid a journalist to denounce both Adams and former president Washington, who was called "a traitor, a robber, and a perjurer." That's George Washington—a liar! As Justice Lewis Powell recognized, more than a century and a half later, "some falsehood"

needs to be protected "in order to protect speech that matters."
How much depends on specific, local factors. Libel is, therefore, inextricably linked to the development of media from the
printing press to television to the Internet.[26]

In speaking of the story of libel, moreover, I want to
draw attention to the idea that narrative and dramatic forms
are not neutral or separate from the real-life stories. Those
stories—about real and fictional characters—are of conflicts
in which people sometimes behave irrationally and dishonestly, in which they don't always play by the same rules or express themselves openly and fairly. The characters include not
only Hellman and McCarthy but also John Kerry and Swift-
Boat Veterans for Truth leader John O'Neill (who debated
Kerry on Cavett's show in 1971), Norman Mailer and Gore
Vidal, who also appeared on the *Dick Cavett Show*, Whittaker
Chambers and Alger Hiss, Dashiell Hammett, Dorothy Parker,
Edmund Wilson, Diana Trilling, Harry Truman and Richard
Nixon, as well as Stanley Kowalski and Blanche DuBois and
many other historical and fictional figures. Every word one
person says may seem like a lie to another. But that's not all.
Although this list includes the real and the fictional, I do not
eschew that distinction or suggest that, because facts are not
independent of values, there are no facts or that dishonesty
does not involve guilt. Nor do I believe that any interpretation
is as good as any other. People's lives, even the well-being of
American society, depend on whose story you believe and on
who has the force (rhetorical, financial, or political) to compel
belief.

At the end of *Scoundrel Time*, Hellman announces that
the true scoundrels of the Cold War were not Joseph Mc-
Carthy and Richard Nixon, whose villainy was widely acknowledged, but the liberals who disliked their methods but agreed

with their aims and failed to stand up to them. She remained angry, she said, in 1976. "Such people would have a right to say that I, and many like me, took too long to see what was going on in the Soviet Union. But whatever our mistakes, I do not believe we did our country any harm. And I think they did."[27] This line was calculated to enrage a certain group of readers, and it did. "Lillian Hellman could not be more mistaken!" exclaimed Howe. "Those who supported Stalinism and its political enterprises, either here or abroad, helped befoul the cultural atmosphere, helped bring totalitarian methods into trade unions, helped perpetuate one of the greatest lies of the century, helped destroy whatever possibilities there might have been for a resurgence of serious radicalism in America. Isn't that harm enough?"[28] Many more furious responses followed. In the decades since her death, Hellman biographers have also expressed the concern that her iconic status has been harmful to America and that setting the record straight will restore a measure of sanity to everything from labor relations to foreign policy. They have asked whether her "outsized legend" was justified—with predictably mixed results—and aimed to reduce her stature because of her "mendacious and totalitarian politics" and her alleged distortions of history.[29] Hellman also still has passionate defenders and apologists. Some insist on the need for a more nuanced picture to counter what they perceive as a lack of generosity. My aim is neither to diminish nor to enhance the legends of Hellman or McCarthy but to illustrate the failure of public conversation in America by attending to the history of their dispute.

I take the title of my book, *Just Words,* from the Democratic presidential primary of 2008. A paid advertisement for Senator Hillary Clinton asserted: "When all is said and done, words aren't action. They are just words."[30] The line became

central not only to Senator Clinton's campaign against Senator Barack Obama but also to Obama's campaign against
Clinton—this after the widely noted corruption of political
language by the malapropistic George W. Bush, the culmination, I wish to suggest, of a crisis in American moral discourse that dates back to the 1930s. It has become a truism of
academics that words do not just describe a world *out there*
but that they perform actions; they bring our world into being. But in an ordinary sense, we can understand what Senator Clinton meant in seeking to distinguish her actions from
Senator Obama's eloquence. She was referring to her experience enacting public policy and contrasting it with his as a
law professor and writer of autobiographies. In the abstract,
she was neither right nor wrong to distinguish her actions
from his words. But, of course, we do not understand language in the abstract. It is not incidental that it was the first
woman to be a serious candidate for her party's nomination
for president who made the claim that words are not actions.
This book will show why. On the one hand, I use the title *Just
Words* to deflate the idea that words give us access to a universal truth. On the other, "just words" indicates my sense that it
is only through the hard work of taking each other's words
seriously—including "and" and "the"—that we can hope for
justice.

   Although *Just Words* is about a particular author, a particular critic, and a particular conflict, a libel suit, this book is
also about authors and critics more generally, as well as about
the author and critic each of us carries within us. In a 1946
New York Times article, "Author Jabs the Critic," Hellman
commented that the critic-writer relationship is both too large
and too small a subject to bear up under quick generaliza-
tions. She complains that authors and critics speak different

languages: "Critics use many words that working writers do not understand: perhaps they are not meant for writers to understand." Beneath the polite rhetoric about preserving the "great tradition" of disagreement between writer and critic is the personal hurt and anger that Hellman cannot express directly in the newspaper. "It's always so noble to put things on larger grounds," she writes, thinking of the criticism she might advance, "and the opening sentence goes this way: 'Now, my dear, it isn't that I mind what you say about me, it's that such talk is a major defect in your own nature.'"[31] *Just Words* focuses on defects in the nature of private individuals—as well as attempts to hide or expose them—and explores what they can teach us about the larger dynamics of American public discourse.

Hellman's name comes up most often these days with the accusation of fraud in autobiography, a phenomenon that seems to have become increasingly common. On the one hand, more and more readers seek intimacy with authors through televised book clubs, as well as through new autobiographical technologies such as personal webpages, blogs, Facebook, and Twitter. On the other, investigative media have become more intrusive in private lives since Louis Brandeis and Samuel Warren developed the notion of "the right to privacy," in an 1890 *Harvard Law Review* article of that name, to protect people from "instantaneous photographs and newspaper enterprise."[32] As Justice Stephen Breyer notes, rapid changes in technology have prompted Americans to engage in a democratic conversation about the values implicated by our interest in privacy.[33] In recent decades, television hosts, from Cavett to Winfrey, have introduced readers to real-life authors who have shared their own stories on air and raised the old concern about the foundations of liberal democracy in the quality of its citizens. Although every life has gaps, Hellman's both excited and intentionally provoked intense criticism. It is useless to continue asking whether she told the truth. Certainly she invented stories and intentionally fashioned the historical record in a way more favorable to her reputation. She came to represent the power of lies, the fragility of truth telling, the shaping pressure of public opinion, and the vulnerability of reputation from her first dramatic work in 1934 to her last memoir, *Maybe*, in 1980 (not to mention the posthumous *Eating Together: Recollections and Recipes,* cowritten with Peter Feibleman), diverse genres that represent complementary and equally crucial aspects of American civil discourse. These subjects also preoccupied McCarthy for fifty years, and her wide-ranging body of work continually manifests the tension between critic and author dramatized by her fight with Hellman. *Memories of a Catholic Girlhood,* in which she confesses to being a "problem liar" at an early age and "a walking mass of lies," is a self-consciously conflicted book in which chapters of memoir alternate with italicized critical essays that take the author to task for lapses of authenticity, historical fact, and truthfulness.[34] The author and critic are two voices of one person.

        In unraveling the twisted knot of the Hellman-McCarthy dispute, it becomes possible to advance more general claims about how we have arrived at the current stalemates of public conversation in America not only about education, abortion, and foreign affairs but also about the appropriate degree of self-exposure in the media. Their libel suit spoke to questions of who was or was not a public figure (Hellman insisted that she wasn't, for legal reasons; McCarthy that she was), about the balance between society's power to educate liberal subjects and the exercise of personal freedom, about tensions between constitutional protections of free speech and of self-incrimination, about whether principle or pragmatism ought to guide decision-making in personal and political cases, and about how libel, lies, and life stories have come to define America's civic landscape. The following chapters will examine each of these important subjects, showing how they radiate from the legal battle like spokes of a wheel. Chapter 1 recounts details of the case and demonstrates how the idiom of libel and the autobiographical impulse became intertwined in twentieth-century America. Chapter 2 contrasts the philosophies that governed language instruction when Hellman and McCarthy were growing up. Chapter 3 turns to the overlapping vocabularies of biological and literary reproduction and to the ambiguous meanings of "the right to privacy." Chapter 4 discusses models of moral language that shaped political disputes during the Cold War. Chapter 5 examines distinctions and connections between defamation and literary criticism.

In 2009, the New York Senate, composed of equal numbers of Democrats and Republicans, was deadlocked and unable to carry out the business of the state: marshals could not enforce financial judgments; property tax bills could not be sent to homeowners; local officials could not issue bonds to balance municipal budgets. "In their intense self-regard," the *New York Times* reported on June 8, 2009, "these men failed to notice that they were no longer even in office."[35] The intensity of individual citizens' self-regard, the collapsing and reinforcing boundaries of public and private life indicate that it is impossible to write or tell an impersonal history. That problem was the major preoccupation of both Lillian Hellman and Mary McCarthy. Their late-life conflict brought to a head tensions between privacy and self-expression, freedom and restraint in language that not only characterized the central public issues of their day, from debates about liberal education to the application of the right to privacy to sexual freedom, but also continue to inform the failures and successes of American public speech.

I
Libel and Life-Writing

One need only pick up any newspaper or magazine
to comprehend the vast range of published matter
which exposes persons to public view, both private citizens
and public officials. Exposure of the self to others in
varying degrees is a concomitant of life in a civilized
community. The risk of this exposure is an essential incident
of life in a society which places a primary value on freedom
of speech and press.
—Justice William Brennan, *Time, Inc. v. Hill,* 1967

I feel enraged at this drunken, foul-mouthed, degenerate
bitch and I think of letters to write and things to
say denouncing her.
—Arthur Kober, commenting on Tallulah Bankhead,
Kober's diary, 1940

L ibel is woven into our everyday language. It springs from a complicated set of motivations: vanity, envy, and resentment. Although many of us utter actionable slanders every day, libel suits are relatively rare because they require a huge investment of energy, time, and money. In general, you have to be rich to protect your reputation through litigation, and you need to be prepared to expose your private life to public scrutiny. As writers, publishers, broadcasters, and ordinary citizens increasingly discovered in the 1970s and 1980s, it is hard to know when the telling of stories will have legal consequences.

In 1980, Dick Cavett and the Educational Broadcasting Corporation (hereafter PBS) were listed as codefendants with Mary McCarthy in a libel suit brought by Lillian Hellman in the state of New York. Cavett, the son of an English teacher, long had a reputation as America's most literate talk-show host. He remains best known as the host of the late-night show on ABC, which ran from 1968 to 1975, opposite Johnny Carson's *Tonight Show*. But Cavett never matched Carson's mainstream appeal, and he moved to PBS in the fall of 1977. Like Carson, Cavett was raised in Nebraska and was interested in magic.[1] After graduating from Yale in 1958, he moved to New York, where he hoped to find a job as a writer; he was hired at NBC after waiting in a corridor and thrusting some of his work into the hands of Jack Paar (Carson's predecessor). Mary McCarthy appeared on Paar's *Tonight Show* in 1963 to pitch her novel *The Group*. In 1961 Paar needed a translator for one of his guests, the German Miss Universe. With his college German, the slender, twenty-six-year-old Cavett got big laughs; it was his first network television appearance. As his former Yale roommate and PBS producer Christopher Porterfield says, "The literary, the dramatic, the philosophical and psychological—these pretty well defined Dick's academic orbit. But his greatest facility was in languages."[2]

Witty and urbane, Cavett hosted John Lennon, Jimi Hendrix, Janis Joplin, Groucho Marx, and Katharine Hepburn. But he also had a gift for interviewing writers. From 1968 through the 1980s, his guests included Tennessee Williams, *New Yorker* humorist S. J. Perelman, the poet Richard Wilbur, critic Stanley Kauffmann, the mutually admiring John Cheever and John Updike, and, in a notorious episode, the feuding Norman Mailer and Gore Vidal. A *Life* review of late-night television in 1972 described Cavett's work as a "continuing moral inquiry almost unique on commercial television and certainly unique among TV talk shows." Cavett often handled provocative combinations, though he rarely booked guests himself. Georgia governor and white supremacist Lester Maddox stormed off the set after a conversation about segregation with novelist Truman Capote and football star Jim Brown in 1970. Brown had asked Maddox if he had had any trouble "with the white bigots because of all the things you did for blacks." After a commercial break Cavett rephrased Brown's question: "Mr. Brown asked if you had any trouble with your white admirers." Maddox shot back, "He did not say admirers!" "No," agreed Cavett, "he said bigots." Maddox angrily said that this was "another example of how words are twisted against me," demanded an apology, and then walked out. During the next break, Cavett ran after him into the street, but the governor would not return. As the *Life* reviewer commented, Cavett "follows and develops a conversation rather than driving it, like a dune buggy on an ego trip, into pits stops for a cheap laugh or a snide comment. . . . As a result the Cavett show has become almost a form of diplomacy, an open negotiation among acts, ideals, and attitudes, a nightly witness." On PBS, in a half-hour format, he returned to his strong suit: one-guest interviews.[3]

On October 18, 1979, McCarthy had gone to the WNET-TV studio in New York to which Cavett had moved in 1977. Hellman herself had appeared on Cavett's PBS show with Richard Wilbur in 1977. Unlike Hellman, whose late career writing personal histories of herself and others in *An Unfinished Woman, Pentimento,* and *Scoundrel Time* had brought her critical acclaim, new invitations for public appearances, and considerable new wealth, McCarthy, who had been editing the letters of her dear friend Hannah Arendt, had been largely out of the public eye for the past decade. She told Cavett that the loss of Arendt in 1975 made it hard to know whom to talk to anymore. Cavett repeatedly emphasized that her visit to his show was a *rare* television appearance.[4] As Hellman's secretary Rita Wade archly put it, McCarthy "was a has-been."[5] But McCarthy continued to produce not only political journalism on subjects ranging from Vietnam to school bussing but also novels and literary criticism. Although her writings on Vietnam, collected in *The Seventeenth Degree* (1974), scarcely made a dent, she also covered the Watergate hearings for the *Observer* of London and published *The Mask of State: Watergate Portraits* in 1974. She went to Cavett's studio that autumn morning to pitch her new book *Cannibals and Missionaries,* a novel about the psychology of terrorism, for an episode that would air three months later. Cavett had first encountered her in the 1950s at Yale as a guest lecturer who "managed to seem entirely charming while wickedly making fools of the academics who questioned her from the floor."[6] That was the Mary McCarthy he wanted for his show.

No longer slim, increasingly gap-toothed, McCarthy had cut the hair she once wore long. When she entered Cavett's studio in a pleated green wool dress, stepping gingerly in new pumps, she showed the signs of age. She had been treated for breast cancer in the mid-1970s, and the hands with which she gestured as she talked were gnarled and white. However, though she acknowledged that the "decay of the organism is not pleasant," she rarely complained of her health. Her hair, pulled to the right by a tortoiseshell barrette, gleamed silver beneath the klieg lights. When Cavett asked her why, as she had earlier claimed, she did not like being old, she replied simply: "I don't like the way I look any more, and I used to like the way I looked." She added, however, that if as a result of age her writing had slowed, it was only due to a more strenuous perfectionism, and the conversation turned to American culture's lost facility with language or, as McCarthy put it, the inability to "find the word that fits."

Two days before taping the interview, McCarthy had met with a member of Cavett's staff in New York to discuss topics of conversation. She was game for a lively interview, but her answers also indicate the naïveté with which she entered the talk-show forum. McCarthy did not have a television in her Paris flat. Though she had always enjoyed the verbal jousting of public discussion, she eyed newer media with a mixture of irony and skepticism, even distaste, as recorded by a Cavett show staffer:

> [My] first few questions got a simple "yes" or "no." But when I asked if she'd like to discuss which writers are overrated and which are underrated and suggested that it could be like a game, she was delighted and asked, "Who'll go first?" . . . She stopped me at the word women, saying, "Don't ask me about women." It seems that people are always

asking her about women and she is bored by
them. . . . The only other topic she does not want to
discuss on the show is the Pope's visit to America.
First of all she wasn't here for it, and second she
became "turned off" by him last January or February when she was in Rome. She thinks he has become innocently obsessed with the power of the
media. . . . She seems to be genuinely fond of you
[Cavett] and has refused to do any other T.V. interview. She told me about a wonderful lunch she and
her husband had with you in Washington when
she was covering the Watergate hearings for the
Observer.[7]

The patronizing staffer noted that McCarthy got "corny"
when talking about love and marriage. She also gave Cavett a
reading list, which included an unsympathetic *Paris Metro*
interview of McCarthy. It begins with a pointed contrast between the iconic Lillian Hellman, as portrayed by Jane Fonda
in *Julia,* and the dowdy McCarthy, dressed in pearl gray like a
widow. When asked pointedly about Hellman in that interview, McCarthy replied, "I can't stand her. I think every word
she writes is false, including 'and' and 'but.'" As she made the
remark, the interviewer reported, a "full grin" spread across
her face.[8] Cavett had been briefed on other current aversions,
and in his introduction he listed the three intellectual traits
that McCarthy herself had cited as her touchstones: wit, lucidity, and indignation.

After Cavett's introduction to the first part of the two-
episode conversation and McCarthy's slow entrance, they
took their positions on an elevated stage decorated in muted
colors with a Persian carpet, potted plants, and leather arm-

chairs. With the cameras rolling, Cavett posed leading questions, his fingertips pressed together before his sharp-featured smile, and McCarthy kept up the pleasant banter on verbal usage errors with words such as "ilk" and "eke" and the failures of reviewers of her books to check the facts. She twirled her right hand in the air for emphasis. The conversation proved unexceptionable. Opening the second episode—a continuation of the single taping session—Cavett referred again to the rarity of McCarthy's appearance on television and noted that "truth-telling like hers can sometimes make one uneasy." He proceeded to question her about religion and about the sincerity of those who claimed to be "born-again," and then turned to the Kennedys, Ted Kennedy having recently launched a bid for the presidency. She said that they were "typical U.S. Catholics." They were great "P.R. people," extremely ruthless, a Tammany clan, but in her opinion they were not Christians. Cavett said, "Now this is a provocative statement," and McCarthy cheerfully interrupted, "Do you think it's libelous?" The audience laughed, as Cavett replied, scratching his head and smiling, "Let's see, I don't know who the burden of proof is on in this case. . . . No, no, I don't think it is." He asked her about a negative review she had written of John Hersey's Pulitzer Prize–winning book *Hiroshima* and whether she might have a tendency to be contrary simply because she liked to be adversarial. McCarthy carefully explained her judgment of Hersey's take on the atom bomb and graciously allowed that she might have been wrong; she acknowledged too a tendency to be contrary in her younger days but hoped that her reason and judgment were stronger than anything contrary in her nature. When the conversation shifted to her criticism of US policy in Vietnam, she added, "I hate to talk on the television."

Then he asked her what contemporary writers she thought
were "overrated, and we could do without, given a limited
amount of time."

On January 25, 1980, shortly after 8:30 p.m., Lillian Hellman, nearly blinded by glaucoma and partially paralyzed by
multiple strokes, with emphysema, arthritis, an enlarged
heart, and a voice deepened by decades of whiskey and cigarettes, watched or listened to the television in her Manhattan
apartment at the fashionable East Side address of 66th Street
and Park Avenue. It was a cold, clear night. Hellman was tiny,
deeply wrinkled, and frail. Yet she too remained a formidable
figure. Her former friend Diana Trilling, no slouch at literary
infighting, commented that Hellman was "the most powerful
woman I've ever known, maybe the most powerful *person* I've
ever known."[9] She had nurses around the clock but went to
dinner almost every night either to a restaurant or to someone's house. That evening she had been out to dinner with her
nurse. She never allowed her health to interfere with her social life. Often she was painfully uncomfortable, alternately
cackling, coughing, complaining, and gasping for air. When
they came home, the nurse undressed her for bed, and they
walked—Hellman shuffled—across the hall to her office,
where she kept the television set. Hellman followed this rou-
tine every night. She had trouble sleeping, and the talking on
the television was a soporific. When she was ready for bed, the
nurse would turn off the television and walk her back to her
bedroom. On that Friday night, the nurse turned on the set
just as Cavett was chatting with Mary McCarthy about herself. She heard McCarthy say, "Everything she writes is a lie,
including 'and' and 'the,'" and she laughed. When her secretary, Rita Wade, came in the next morning, Hellman said that
she had already spoken with her lawyer, Ephraim London, a

leading free-speech advocate and a close friend. She was going to sue.[10]

McCarthy and Hellman had crossed paths only occasionally, but over the decades they had shared intimate friends and had assumed conflicting political positions. In her *Intellectual Memoirs* and later in her deposition to Hellman's lawyers on August 12, 1981, McCarthy claimed that she first met Hellman in 1937 at one of the many Upper West Side dinner parties at which smart, successful, New York leftists socialized. She describes such a gathering in her story "The Genial Host": "Every dinner was presented as a morality play in which art and science, wealth and poverty, business and literature, sex and scholarship, vice and virtue, Judaism and Christianity, Stalinism and Trotskyism, all the antipodes of life, were personified and yet abstract."[11] The two women's first public interaction was via an open letter ("A Statement by American Progressives") published in 1938 in the *New Masses,* a monthly magazine that supported Stalin and the Soviet Union. The letter signed by Hellman and numerous other writers, editors, and artists urged McCarthy and her cohorts to resign from the American Committee for the Defense of Leon Trotsky and to stop publishing "reactionary propaganda" and sowing confusion as to the "real meaning" of the Moscow Trials. In 1967, Hellman, always a big letter-signer, was also signatory to "A Statement on the CIA" in *Partisan Review,* protesting the US government's covert funding of nominally independent publications. From this letter, which includes the names of most of McCarthy's closest associates and friends—Hannah Arendt, Dwight Macdonald, Philip Rahv, et al.—McCarthy's own name is conspicuously absent.

In 1948 they met at a dinner party at Sarah Lawrence, where McCarthy was teaching and Hellman had been invited

to give a talk. As McCarthy walked into college president
Harold Taylor's sunroom, she heard Hellman telling students
how the author John Dos Passos had "sold out" in the Spanish
Civil War. McCarthy was incensed at "hearing those lies so
smoothly applied to him," as she told her lawyer years later, in
1980, and she interrupted Hellman to say that what she was
telling the students was "just a slander."[12] Hellman had been
much on her mind in 1978–79 because of a fracas over the
Spanish Refugee Aid Advisory Committee, on whose board
McCarthy refused to serve because Hellman had been invited
to join as a sponsor. Ironically, one of McCarthy's chief gripes
was that it was Hellman who was always defaming others. In
a letter to Dwight Macdonald in 1979 about Spanish Refugee
Aid, she complained that Hellman's "habit of slandering opponents can't be broken, for if she were truthful she would
have to face the fact that she was not more moral than they
but rather the contrary."[13]

Although McCarthy had liked Hellman's first play, *The
Children's Hour,* in 1934, she had written disparagingly of
Hellman's later work. In a 1944 article for *Town and Country,*
McCarthy had remarked of *The North Star,* the pro-Soviet
propaganda film produced to encourage America's wartime
alliance, for which Hellman had written the script: "The picture is a tissue of falsehoods woven of every variety of untruth."[14] Hellman did not really disagree. She never liked the
movie, over which she exercised little control, but McCarthy's
remarks indicate the particular sharpness between them. In a
1964 interview with the *Paris Review,* Hellman was asked
about McCarthy.

> INTERVIEWER: Mary McCarthy wrote in a review
> that she gets the feeling that no matter what hap-

pens, Mr. [Tennessee] Williams will be rich and famous.

HELLMAN: I have the same feeling about Miss Mc-Carthy.

INTERVIEWER: She has accused you, among other things, of a certain "lubricity," of an over facility in answering complex questions. Being too facile, relying on contrivance.

HELLMAN: I don't like to defend myself against Miss McCarthy's opinions, or anybody else's. I think Miss McCarthy's fiction is often brilliant and sometimes even sound. But, in fiction, she is a lady writer, a lady magazine writer. Of course, that doesn't mean she isn't right about me. But if I thought she was, I'd quit. I would like critics to like my plays because that is what makes plays successful. But a few people I respect are the only ones whose opinions I've worried about in the end.[15]

Hellman did not often respond to the published criticism of her work, but when she did, she could be vicious. In 1980, at the end of her life, subject to frequent rages (even more frequent, that is, than in her younger days), as she listened to the interview on television, something snapped. To be sure, a desperate sense of physical decline, impotence, and wounded pride contributed to Hellman's reaction to the *Dick Cavett Show* on that winter night. The boundaries between her life and the work, never clear to begin with, had become more tenuous. Peter Feibleman, Hellman's last lover and her heir, wrote that there was nothing surprising in what followed between Lillian Hellman and Mary McCarthy:

I thought Lillian ought to overlook it and I told her
what she would have told me: forget it and get on
with your life.
"What life?" she said. We argued about it for
an hour or so and I gave up.[16]

However, what transpired is more than a story of petty
grievances or the end of Lillian Hellman. Unlike the libel suit
of Alger Hiss and Whittaker Chambers in 1948, Hellman's
and McCarthy's did not overtly raise questions about national
security, but it was no less the trial of a generation. Friends
and enemies took sides accordingly. Like many libel suits,
Hellman's was ill-judged. It arose not from rational deliberation but from an excess of passion, which is only to say that it
was typical of American public expression, illustrating the
degree to which intemperate, highly personal, and potentially
defamatory language is woven into our discourse. The lawsuit
was about the validity of their personal histories and the nation's political life. It represents a clash between two models
of language: one, as McCarthy saw it, that reports transpar-
ently on matters of fact and one that is self-consciously rhetorical or shaped by desire.

Lillian Hellman was a bundle of contradictions. Despite
her rhetoric of truthfulness (as in her famous refusal to tailor
her conscience for the House Un-American Activities Committee, to whom she wrote of "homely things that were taught
to me: to try to tell the truth, not to bear false witness"), even
those who loved her found her a constant liar.[17] One good
friend, Lee Gershwin, called her the "biggest liar in the
world. . . . She would lie about anything—a man, a woman, it
could be anything—for what we used to call 'a pretty good
story.'"[18] She wrote movingly of Sophronia, the black nurse

who raised her in New Orleans, and of her maid Helen, who accompanied her from New York to Harvard after Dashiell Hammett's death. Yet she tyrannized her domestic staff. The seventeen-year-old Rosemary Mahoney, hired to help Hellman at her Martha's Vineyard home in the summer of 1978, was dismayed to find that the decrepit old woman wasn't "nice," that she had a terrible temper, that she cheated at Scrabble, lied, yelled, swore like a sailor, and insulted people.[19]

From early childhood, Hellman was driven by what she described in *Pentimento* as "the rampage that could be caused in me by anger."[20] Anger defined her. "What made her angry, and continually angry," her friend Jules Feiffer reflected, "were the sorts of things that other people, including fellow radicals, learned over time to accept. . . . She was very bad at letting things pass."[21] She became enraged when novelist William Styron put too much salt on the black-eyed peas and when Elizabeth Taylor asked her not to attend rehearsals of *The Little Foxes*. The journalist John Hersey, her neighbor in Martha's Vineyard, eulogized her anger:

> Most of us were startled by it from time to time. Anger was her essence. It was at the center of that passionate temperament. It informed her art: the little foxes snapped at each other, we could see their back hairs bristle, we could smell their foxiness— they were real and alive because of the current of anger that ran through them, as it did through so many of Lillian's characters. . . . She was very, very angry at death—and not just at the end.

She was an exasperating friend with a deep capacity for friendship. Susan Sontag, who thought it outrageous that

Hellman should sue McCarthy for a blatantly hyperbolic remark, nonetheless felt closer to Hellman. She recalled, "I don't
think Lillian was any less of a monster than Mary—in fact
she may very well have been more of a monster—but she was
a warm monster. She was a touchy-feely kind of monster. I
responded to that."[22] She could be not only funny and charming but also intimate in ways that McCarthy never could,
though both loved to cook and to entertain. Hellman also
relished the fame of those she knew. She shopped with Clau-
dette Colbert, socialized with diplomat Averell Harriman,
and dined with Franklin Delano Roosevelt. Norman Mailer
called her "a celebrity fucker. . . . She was one of those people
taken with high political figures."[23] Playwright and professor
William Alfred met her in the summer of 1954 at a Harvard
symposium on verse drama. He found her funny, even girlish,
and honest about her feelings. "You'd take her out for a steak
dinner," he recalled, "and you'd think she'd never had one
before. She always gave a sense that you and she and some
other friends belonged to a closed group that was really rather
wonderful to belong to."[24] Despite a large nose and, in her
view, the curse of a skinny ass, she made men fall in love with
her, and she rewarded them with loyalty in her fashion. With
her husband of seven years, Arthur Kober, she maintained a
long and devoted relationship, yet she barely wrote about him
in her memoirs. Of Hammett, whose legend she carefully integrated into her own, she wrote, paradoxically and disin-
genuously, "I cannot write about my closest, my most beloved
friend."[25] Hellman's loyalty to Hammett's radical and rigid
political commitments says more about her idiosyncratic notion of integrity than her contradictory public positions. She
supported both the totalitarian Soviet Union and civil rights

activism in the United States, enjoyed friendships with communists and with financiers.

Hellman was often a staunch advocate of freedom of expression. In 1970 she founded the Committee for Public Justice, a national organization of writers, lawyers, and "socially interested persons," formed to protect constitutional rights and liberties, focusing on threats posed to the "basic rights of speech."[26] But she bullied and abused its staff. In 1973, with two congressmen and a professor of international law, she was honored by the American Civil Liberties Union for "outstanding contributions to civil liberties."[27] In 1975 she joined the Reporters Committee for Freedom of the Press and others in a lawsuit against former president Richard Nixon that sought to secure the release of the Nixon White House papers and tapes, arguing, among other things, that at that point Nixon was a private individual and therefore had no right to impose restrictions on the material.[28] Yet her biographer Carl Rollyson has written, "Although Hellman dramatized herself as a great democrat, she had an authoritarian personality. She believed in controlling access to information about herself and her friends." He concludes, "The myth of Lillian Hellman depended on censorship."[29] Of course, all myths—in fact, all reputations—depend to some degree on censorship, if censorship means the suppression of objectionable speech. More difficult is to determine what kinds of information and what contexts—for instance, public or private—legitimate people's desire to keep some things under wraps.

What infuriated McCarthy, more than what Hellman exposed, was what she omitted. Her memoirs are, in fact, extremely short. McCarthy stopped contributing to the ACLU when it became apparent to her that it was showing "not the slightest concern with the two and a quarter million dollar suit brought against me by Lillian Hellman, who, if I'm not mistaken, was a sworn enemy of the ACLU ('insufficiently radical') while I had been a long-time supporter."[30] Whatever her motives in the McCarthy case, Hellman had long initiated crucial, often angry debates about the status of protected speech. Like Rollyson, many critics complained that she only posed as a supporter of free speech. She was hypocritical. She ruthlessly curtailed the rights of others, they say, to speak freely about her. In acknowledgments to his biography *Lillian Hellman,* William Wright, whose project Hellman tried to sabotage, expresses both thanks and sympathy to those who spoke up, "for permitting their privacy-protecting impulses to give way to a desire to see an important story told correctly."[31] So, when McCarthy began to dig for inconsistencies and falsehoods in Hellman's autobiographies, she had a lot of help. Martha Gellhorn, the former wife of Ernest Hemingway and a reporter during the Spanish Civil War when Hellman went to Spain in 1937, combed the historical archive to show that Hellman was a liar and, worse, an "apocryphiar," an intentional and strategic creator of false tales that people take for true. "Nothing excuses apocryphism by anyone about anything," Gellhorn announced self-righteously in her 1981 article. "No good comes of it. It is cheap and cheapening. The world would be a far far better place if people—especially writers and politicians—stuck to fact or fiction."[32] Much writing about Hellman aims to fill in the gaps in the accounts of her life. That is what McCarthy aimed to do in her legal defense. Her argument hinges on whether particular versions of history harm the nation.

Hellman and McCarthy's generation of writers, which came of age during the Depression and became centered for the most part in New York, wrote, as historian David Laskin says, with "intense awareness of one another."[33] When during the taping Cavett asked McCarthy about contemporary authors who were overrated, Hellman, whom she had attacked in recent correspondence and a published interview in *Paris Metro*, was on her mind. Nonetheless, at first she seemed to demur, saying that these days there were sensationalist hacks, on the one hand, and books that were either "witty or serious but that have some real merit," on the other. But she did not think that the "inflation phenomenon" still persisted in the literary marketplace. It was an uncharacteristically diplomatic pose, and Cavett pressed on: "We don't have overpraised writers anymore?" McCarthy considered and replied that there were a few "holdovers" from an earlier generation, such as John Steinbeck and Lillian Hellman, "who I think is tremendously overrated, a bad writer, and [a] dishonest writer." Cavett asked, "What is dishonest about Lillian Hellman?" "Everything," McCarthy answered, grinning broadly as the audience "ooohed." She explained: "I said once in an interview that *every word she writes is a lie, including 'and' and 'the.'*" Now there was a laugh from the audience, and Cavett half-smiled and stroked his forehead: "I'm sure she would write you and correct that, but you wouldn't believe it if she did." He wiped his eyes with his slender fingers and asked, "Have you run into Miss Hellman lately?" McCarthy recalled their meeting in 1948 but acknowledged that they barely knew each other. The discussion of Hellman was over; it had appeared to pass innocuously, as Cavett, who had read that *Paris Metro* interview, later reported: "After the taping, the network's lawyer—paid to anticipate litigation—did not utter even his occasional 'Dick, we may have a problem.' Instead, he said, 'Nice show.' "[34] Following the discussion of Hellman, Cavett and McCarthy had turned to more abstract and seemingly unrelated questions of literary style. McCarthy praised lucidity and perspicuousness. Beauty, she said, is part of transparency. Yet it was a lack of transparency, though she didn't say so on the program, that most troubled McCarthy about Hellman.

During breakfast the morning after the show aired, Cavett's assistant called. "Have you seen the papers? Hellman is suing Mary McCarthy, PBS, and you for two and a quarter million." Another phone rang. It was Hellman: "Why the hell didn't you defend me?" she demanded. "I guess I never thought of you as defenseless, Lillian," Cavett answered. "That's bullshit. I'm suing the whole damn bunch of you."[35] Cavett, who had once been a guest at her home, was sorry that she was taking it so hard and asked her if she would like to respond to McCarthy's remarks on television. Although the offer may simply have been a courtesy, it would also have made sound legal sense, recognizing that public figures have the capacity to defend themselves because the media give them both attention and time to speak. This was an approach to which Hellman was strategically averse. Thinking perhaps of Richard Nixon's 1973 self-defense after the Watergate break-in ("I am not a crook"), Hellman replied that there would be no point in appearing on television to say that she was not a liar.[36] Two weeks later Cavett was named codefendant in the libel suit. It must be noted that Cavett's account of his conversation with Hellman in his deposition for the trial differs in key details— when, where, and who called whom, etc.—from that of his 2002 *New Yorker* article, quoted above. In those recollections, two decades later, he sided with McCarthy, whose health and finances, he suggested, were ruined by the suit. He said that he felt sorrier for her than for "Old Scaly Bird." Yet he wondered if he hadn't been set up by both of these titans to provide publicity for their fading careers.

Public opinion and the courts had become less friendly to the media since a landmark Supreme Court ruling fifteen years earlier. In 1964 the *New York Times v. Sullivan* case had initiated a debate at the highest judicial level about the proper balance between the value of free speech and the interest in protecting individual reputations. That lawsuit, filed by L. B. Sullivan, a Montgomery, Alabama, city commissioner against the *Times,* used defamation law to intimidate the press. The *Times* had run a privately funded editorial advertisement entitled "Heed Their Rising Voices" for the Committee to Defend Martin Luther King and the Struggle for Freedom in the South, which aimed to raise money to defend King against an Alabama perjury indictment. In addition to being signed by prominent figures ranging from Marlon Brando and Sidney Poitier to Eleanor Roosevelt, the advertisement alleged specific forms of police brutality and institutional racism in Montgomery and contained factual errors. Sullivan wasn't specifically named, but he claimed that, as city commissioner, he was the victim of false statements. The circuit court of Montgomery County found in his favor, the jury awarding half a million dollars in damages, a decision affirmed by the Alabama Supreme Court on August 30, 1962. At the same time, as Anthony Lewis has reported, many other libel cases were pending against news organizations in southern states, effectively restricting the freedom of expression in the cause of civil rights by accusing the media of lies.[37] This ruling had such important ramifications for the freedom of the press and civil rights that it was appealed all the way to the Supreme Court. The Court was asked to rule on the extent to which constitutional protections for speech limit a state's power to award damages in cases of libel.

In reversing the Alabama courts' decision, the Supreme Court raised new questions about the limits of libel in regard to issues of public concern and issues that are not of public concern. The decision, as it played out in other cases over the next two decades, made it much harder for a public figure to claim defamation because it raised the burden of proof; it also led to difficult questions about the public or private status of the plaintiff. A further challenge for plaintiffs was to prove that the defendant intentionally made a false and defamatory statement with knowledge of its falsity. The most significant aspect of the *Sullivan* decision was the recognition that defamatory statements—statements that harm someone's reputation, whether written (libelous) or spoken (slanderous)—may be protected by the First Amendment. Before 1964, they were said not to have "free speech" protection. Along with this First Amendment protection for speech, the Court's decision permitted the encroachment of federal constitutional law on state defamation law, or the application of the First Amendment through the Fourteenth Amendment to the states. In the wake of *Times v. Sullivan* and subsequent cases, Hellman's libel suit indicated that defaming people on the relatively new medium of television would also raise questions about First Amendment freedoms. Although I concentrate in this book on the cultural, literary, and political meanings of the Hellman-McCarthy dispute, the significance of their case is intimately related to the difficult legal problem of defining distinctions between the public and the private, fact and opinion, terms of law that also permeated—if in altered forms—the public conversation.

The *Times v. Sullivan* ruling profoundly affected the way Americans thought about libel and reflected a variety of deep changes in contemporary culture. Cases that followed included new questions about who qualified as a "public figure," about the distinction between "fact" and "opinion," and about balancing the protection of free speech against the increasingly astronomical costs of defending libel suits. In raising these issues, libel has become a way of describing the legal consequences of telling stories. Hellman's complaint alleged that the "making and broadcast of the Statement" damaged her "name, reputation, and standing."[38] It was regarded by the Court as libel rather than slander because McCarthy's statement, though oral, was televised, and ultimately the judge dismissed the case against Cavett because he played no role in editing the program. Though nominally a feud between two private individuals, *Hellman v. McCarthy* showed the extent to which debate about "reckless disregard" for the truth, advocacy in the media, and the rights of reputation, had come to pervade public conversation. As Robert Kraus wrote in a satirical article for *Harper's* in 1983, "If you can't call Lillian Hellman a liar on TV, what's the First Amendment all about?"[39]

Hellman's lawyer filed suit in the Supreme Court of the State of New York on February 14, 1980, roughly two weeks after the episode aired. It listed $1.75 million for "mental pain and anguish" and for Hellman's being "injured in her profession," and $500,000 in punitive damages.[40] McCarthy had $63,000 in savings and a bayside house in Castine, Maine, where she and her husband lived when they weren't in Paris. She learned of the lawsuit on February 15, when Herbert Mitgang, a reporter from the *New York Times,* telephoned her at a hotel in London, where she was delivering lectures.[41] At first, she laughed it off. On April 21, 1980, in her Paris apartment, she received a summons with the complaint alleging that her statement was "false, made with ill-will, with malice, with knowledge of its falsity, or with careless disregard of its truth, and with the intent to injure the plaintiff personally and professionally." Cavett and PBS were listed as codefendants. It was alleged that all "acted in concert in producing and broadcasting Cavett's interview" and that "Cavett and the Station approved and acquiesced in the Statement."[42] On September 23, 1980, Cavett's company, Daphne Productions, which produced the show, was added as a defendant.

The lengthy pretrial process known as "discovery" took more than three years. In this phase, each party requests evidence from others. Through written interrogatories and oral depositions lawyers seek to obtain information about what the witnesses will say if the case comes to trial. In response to an interrogatory on October 20, 1980, McCarthy said that her comment had not been a statement of fact but of her opinion that Hellman was a bad writer. Hellman's lawyers asked that she set forth the substance of each published and unpublished statement ever made by Hellman that she knew to be untrue. McCarthy objected that to do so would be unduly burdensome and that her files were at her Paris residence. But she provided limited examples of Hellman's dishonesty that revolve around her view that the "only hero or heroine whom plaintiff allows posterity to honor is plaintiff herself." In her answers to the "First Interrogatories" set forth by Hellman's lawyers in 1980, McCarthy insisted that Hellman's memoirs "distort events which are part of the history of the plaintiff's time, distort and aggrandize her relationship to those events, and are harshly unfair to many individuals."[43]

McCarthy's lawyers wanted to keep the case out of court and made a motion for summary judgment. They argued, first, that Hellman was a public figure and therefore open to criticism, barring "reckless disregard of the truth," and, second, that McCarthy was exercising her right of free speech as a literary critic, that she was expressing *opinions* protected by the First and Fourteenth Amendments. Filing jointly, Cavett, Daphne Productions, and PBS also moved for summary judgment on the basis that Hellman was a public figure and that they were protected by the doctrine of "neutral reportage."[44] The motion asked the judge to dismiss the case on these questions of law. On May 15, 1984, the judge ruled for Hellman that the conduct of McCarthy, PBS, and Daphne Productions (but not of Cavett, the interviewer) *might* rise to the level of clear and convincing evidence of actual malice. In denying the motion, the judge simply ruled that the question as to whether Hellman was a public figure was a fact question for the jury. The case was set to move to trial. On June 12, 1984, McCarthy's lawyers filed a notice of appeal of the summary judgment. On June 30, 1984, Lillian Hellman died, and the case file ended with a notice of her death a week later. A defamation claim does not survive death.

The Hellman-McCarthy case has been ably recounted in numerous biographies of both women, dealt with in countless articles, and turned into a Broadway musical, Nora Ephron's *Imaginary Friends* (2002), which draws on the lawsuit and other documentary evidence and presents a final meeting between the two women in Hell. "I didn't want you to die," Mary tells Lillian in the play. "I was very disappointed there was no

trial. I wanted you to lose in court."[45] What interests me is that
the suit has come to define Hellman's life, ending when she
did, without settlement, and that it has become implicated in
the political, literary, and personal conflicts for which she was
famous. Her libel suit illuminates central tensions in American liberalism—raising questions about who is a public figure,
what is "a false idea," what a "calculated falsehood," what an
"honest utterance." Most important is not the question of
whether libel was an appropriate route for Hellman to take but
the fact that, at that moment in history, it is the route she *did*
take. In focusing on lies and hyperbolically precise words, it
raises vital questions about language and the potency of life-
writing. "For speech concerning public affairs," stated Justice
William Brennan in *Garrison v. Louisiana,* "is more than self-
expression; it is the essence of self-government."[46]

Central to the criticism of Hellman, of which McCarthy's is only the most famous, was the idea that she had violated the rules of open democratic debate, and there is merit
to this charge. In 1977, her autobiographical story "Julia,"
about smuggling cash to antifascist forces in Germany, was
made into a movie. Jane Fonda played a glamorous "Lillian
Hellman," and key details of her history seemed dubious. Articles began to appear that denounced Hellman's personal
and historical writings as fundamentally untrue. *Pentimento:
A Book of Portraits,* in which "Julia" was published, had appeared in 1973. The Italian word *pentimento* refers to the aging of old paint on a canvas and implies that the artist
repented. In considering this term, most critics draw attention to what they perceive as the author's hypocrisy, her refusal to repent old misdeeds, but not to the medium (the
paint, the flatness of the canvas, or the language), as if the two
could be separated. "Lillian Hellman enjoys a wide reputa-

tion," wrote philosopher and communist-hater Sidney Hook. "Students pay her homage, reviewers praise her books. She is also a brilliant polemicist, skilled in moralizing even at the expense of truth, honor, and common sense. And she has spun a myth about her past that has misled the reading public of at least two countries."[47] In the same year, Gellhorn published her bitter and detailed refutation of Hellman's account of the Spanish Civil War.[48] Professor Samuel McCracken's "'Julia' and Other Fictions by Lillian Hellman," in *Commentary*, argued that Hellman's memoirs were so inaccurate that they have had a "contaminating effect on knowledge in our times."[49] I acknowledge elements of justice in these claims while also showing that tendentious, simplistic, and hyperbolic responses to Hellman have both inflated the least important aspects of her work and neglected her sophistication and true significance.

It has been convincingly argued that Hellman stole or plagiarized key aspects of the "Julia" story from the life of another woman, Muriel Gardiner. She made things up, got facts wrong (German train schedules of 1937 don't match up). Yet the story begins with and refers often to *The Children's Hour*, Hellman's play about lies and libel, and centers on a childhood friendship. "Childhood is less clear to me than to many people," Hellman writes, and "the tales of former children are seldom to be trusted."[50] The "truth" of the story ultimately revolves around the life of a lost child that would prove everything. Real-life hunters of Julia's baby have been legion. But the child, for which Hellman herself insists she searched, was never found. The missing baby also reflects more broadly on Hellman's autobiographical project, for Lillian Hellman herself was literally Julia's baby—Julia being her mother's name. The chapter concludes with reference both to the baby

and to a lawsuit that began with the 1954 fraud investigation
of Aristotle Onassis for violating citizenship laws. The man
discussing the case is the son of Julia's lawyer. He says he
never knew anything about Julia's baby, to which she angrily
replies, "I don't believe you," a line echoed less self-consciously
by her readers. Hellman did not sue anyone other than Mc-
Carthy, Cavett, and PBS for libel, but she knew the relative
power of the different media.

Hellman and McCarthy's generation was peculiarly
characterized by high-profile libel suits. The sheer number of
them increased dramatically between the late 1950s and the
1980s, and as legal historian Norman Rosenberg notes, the
"remarkable inflation in the size of defamation judgments
undoubtedly made the gamble of victory more tempting."[51]
Celebrity suits during this period involved figures such as
Johnny Carson, Norman Mailer, Carol Burnett, General William Westmorland, and William F. Buckley Jr. The cases of
Westmorland v. CBS et al. and [Ariel] *Sharon v. Time* were
making their way through the New York courts simultaneously with the Hellman-McCarthy suit. Both were brought by
generals who believed that their roles had been grievously
misrepresented, to the harm of their nations as well as themselves. As Renata Adler comments, the lawyer for CBS aimed
at "nothing less than to rewrite in court the whole history of
the [Vietnam] war to conform with what the broadcast said
'CBS Reports has learned.'"[52] Again, the courts were being
asked to weigh in on historical judgments. As noted free-
speech advocate Floyd Abrams remarks, the military men,
like Hellman, "believed that the narratives critical of them
warranted severe legal penalties."[53] Those cases, too, were
about public attitudes toward telling the truth. From a legal
perspective alone, McCarthy's comment and Hellman's law-

suit bear scrutiny primarily, First Amendment scholar Rodney Smolla argues, as an illustration of the threat to free expression posed by the inflexible application of the fact versus opinion distinction.[54] Each seems to epitomize its author's most unfortunate qualities: McCarthy's put-down is a concise expression of her glib meanness, and Hellman's outraged reaction indicates the passionate intensity of her narcissism. Stephen Gillers, a law professor who met Hellman in 1971 when he became executive director of the Committee for Public Justice, which she founded, reports, "She asked me on the last visit if I thought the suit against McCarthy was a mistake. I did and tried to tell her that gently. I think she was having second thoughts."[55]

But the questions on which the suit depended also illuminate changing attitudes about the media, the protection of privacy, and debates about the hazards and necessity of self-censorship. As Smolla remarked in 1986, "Had the case gone to trial and then to a jury, there is an excellent chance in today's legal climate that Lillian Hellman would have won a substantial jury award."[56] Hellman and McCarthy's behavior was remarkable, therefore, but equally so was the judge's ruling that a jury could take McCarthy's statement literally. A public uproar ensued. In "An Appeal to Lillian Hellman and Mary McCarthy" published in the *New York Times,* Norman Mailer lamented the quarrel between two American writers he most respected, complaining that "the awfulness of the attack was matched . . . by the recklessness of the lawsuit." To say that Hellman was dishonest, Mailer said, is "blarney" because no writer is ever honest, but the lawsuit was a disaster. Hellman's libel suit was in his view an abuse of the judicial system, and it indicated that the law and popular culture had reached a dangerous crossroads.[57]

Hellman's first play, *The Children's Hour* (1934), is about a libel suit filed by two female teachers accused of having an "unnatural relationship." "We're standing here defending ourselves," says one of the defamed schoolteachers, "and against what? Against a lie. A great awful lie."[58] The 1936 Hollywood movie *Libeled Lady*, about a wealthy society girl, played by Myrna Loy, who is falsely accused of breaking up a marriage and sues the *New York Evening Star* newspaper, indicates the place of libel in the popular culture. In discussing the rise in civil defamation suits between World War I and the Cold War, Rosenberg remarks, "Demographic and journalistic trends have expanded the absolute number of cases. Put most simply, more journalists have produced more 'newsworthy' people than ever before. Inevitably this has meant . . . that the potential for libelous statements and comments has been immense."[59] *Libeled Lady* bears a close connection to Hellman's life, for only two years earlier Loy, the actress in the title role and Hellman's exact contemporary (both born in 1905), had appeared in her most famous role, Nora Charles, a character based on Hellman, in *The Thin Man* by Hellman's lover Dashiell Hammett.

Hellman fostered the impression that the feud with McCarthy was political, that there had been a rift between them dating back to the Spanish Civil War. McCarthy strongly denied this description of the affair, insisting in letters to her lawyer that it was "strictly personal" and "professional."[60] It was on this basis that her legal team sought a summary judgment and hoped to avoid a full trial. However, in ruling that the case could proceed, New York State Supreme Court Justice Harold Baer Jr., who had been elected to the bench only in 1982, spoke to two questions. First, Justice Baer ruled that McCarthy's statements were not, strictly speaking, "literary criticism," and therefore constitutionally protected, but that they fell "on the actionable side of the line . . . outside what has come to be known as the 'market place of ideas.'" Second, to establish the applicable standard of proof, the judge needed to determine whether Hellman was a public figure. McCarthy urged the constitutional privilege to criticize public figures in the absence of malice. In a controversial ruling, Justice Baer wrote: "There is no question that the plaintiff is widely known and indeed widely read. The linchpin of public-figure status in libel cases, however, is not simply synonymous with notoriety. . . . Public figure status . . . is appropriate when, coupled with some general notoriety, the language complained of was used by the defendant in the context of plaintiff's participation in a public issue, question or controversy."[61] Gillers, a legal ethicist who esteems both Baer and Hellman, finds this aspect of the decision particularly unconvincing. He comments: "Lillian was certainly a public figure and under *New York Times* and later cases she would have had to prove by clear and convincing evidence that McCarthy's statement would be understood to say that Lillian made things up (was a liar)—that it wasn't just hyperbole—and that McCarthy made her statement knowing it was false or without any regard for its truth or falsity."[62] By virtue of writing books and being a famous author, as well as by founding the Committee of Public Justice, Hellman would seem to be a public personality, yet it is still possible to defame a public personality by calling that person a liar. It is probably true that Justice Baer committed a legal error by failing to rule that Hellman was a public figure and that she would therefore have to establish actual malice to win the case; it is almost certainly true that New York's appellate courts would have rejected his analysis of the public figure issue. However, this point is not essential to the question of whether the case should have proceeded to trial, because it is clear that Justice Baer would not have granted summary judgment even if he had categorized Hellman as a public figure. "Even if the plaintiff was found to be a public figure," he wrote, "the inquiry is just begun."[63]

Baer indicated later in the same opinion that he believed there was sufficient evidence of McCarthy's malice to go to trial even if Hellman were a public figure: "Conceivably, Ms. McCarthy's remarks casting doubt on Ms. Hellman's honesty and veracity might rise to the level of reckless disregard and indifference. The record reflects that Ms. McCarthy had only limited exposure to the works of the prolific Ms. Hellman. Moreover, her repetition of the remark which appeared in the PARIS METRO tends to negate innocent error and may evidence ill will, which, while not necessary to prove 'actual malice,' is some proof of it."[64] Baer appeared to view Hellman's case against McCarthy as reasonably strong. He seemed to think there *was* evidence that McCarthy made a statement about Hellman broad and strong enough that she actually knew that what she was saying about Hellman was false (or was reck-lessly indifferent to whether it was true or false). Although it has been subjected to criticism, particularly by McCarthy's friends and attorneys, Justice Baer's assessment of the question of whether there was enough evidence of actual malice to go to the jury was at least defensible.[65]

The other argument for summary judgment—as to whether McCarthy's statement was nonactionable opinion—was technically independent of the public figure issue. Hellman could have won summary judgment on the fact versus opinion argument even if she was not categorized as a public figure. Yet Baer's analysis of that issue was also provoca-tively pro-plaintiff. Floyd Abrams, who had successfully defended the *New York Times* in the Pentagon Papers case, says, "The words spoken by McCarthy on the *Cavett Show* were a paradigmatic example of what is referred to as rhetorical hyperbole—language that no one could have understood to be offered as literally true and thus not subject to a defamation action." Abrams was retained by McCarthy's legal team shortly after the decision on summary judgment. In his view, this aspect of Justice Baer's ruling was incorrect and likely to be reversed by a higher court. Nevertheless, Justice Baer's view was arguably vindicated as defensible six years later by the ultimate authority on the question, the Supreme Court (in *Milkovich v. Lorain Journal Co.*), because the very same defamatory statement was at issue—a defendant's calling a plaintiff a liar—and the Court used the statement as the paradigm of something that did not deserve special "opinion" protection. Abrams writes, "I'm reluctant to say that Hellman abused the legal system by suing: Everyone has a right to sue and the system did not suffer because she did so. [But] I do think that by suing she acted inconsistently with her professed role as a defender of civil liberties and certainly inconsistently with the norms that usually govern the behavior of those who use their own free speech in a vibrant and outspoken manner."[66] Without entering further into the pros and cons of Hellman's libel suit and its recklessness, we can still see how the language of defamation as well as the controversy over whether Hellman was a public or private person and whether McCarthy's statement was a form of literary criticism illustrate a crisis in public discourse.

In regard to the question of opinion, McCarthy had been asked in discovery, and by Baer's ruling would have been asked by Hellman's lawyers in court, had the case gone to trial, to set forth the substance of each published or written and unpublished statement made or written by Hellman that she knew to be untrue, a nearly impossible task. It might be argued, as Irving Howe has, that Hellman's account of "the [Joseph] McCarthy years is simple, self-serving and, untrue"; but every word?[67] On the other hand, under *Times v. Sullivan* and later cases Hellman would have had to prove by clear and convincing evidence that McCarthy's statement would be understood to say that she made things up—that it wasn't just hyperbole—and that McCarthy made her statement knowing it was false or without any regard for its truth or falsity. That would have been a hard case to make. In her deposition, McCarthy sought a tenuous balance between the burdensome, if not impossible, task of proving every word a lie and drawing on the research of Gellhorn and McCracken and her own close readings of Hellman's memoirs in order to offer a much more lively critique of instances of Hellman's "intellectual dishonesty" than she had on Cavett's program. In memos to her lawyer, moreover, she insisted on distinguishing between outright false statements and "instances of intellectual dishonesty." McCarthy was willing to grant that most of the statements in Hellman's memoirs were true, yet she denied that they added up to the books' often tacit political conclusions, such as that Finland had been a fascist country. Most infuriating to McCarthy was what Hellman did not say, "a worse lie, because more specious and evasive than a direct lie."[68]

The difficulty of sorting the fact versus opinion and public versus private distinctions that Hellman provoked continues to trouble her critics, but most of that criticism fails to recognize the vital interrelationship between these categories, often veering into fierce attacks on Hellman's sex life or her physical appearance under the guise of political critique.[69]

McCarthy hated Hellman, as she acknowledged, but a judge forced her, for better or worse, to analyze relationships and make distinctions between fact and opinion, public and private. Although emotions, such as the "moral indignation" McCarthy described to Cavett, play a vital role in democratic politics, and anger (as Hellman wrote of her own political motivations) commonly leads to the discovery of injustice and demands for redress, some passions tend to have a parochial and self-reinforcing character. These negative passions, which have increasingly contributed to the dynamics of American politics, can prove dangerous to the democratic process.[70] McCarthy's hatred of Hellman did not threaten American pluralism, but Justice Baer reacted to what he perceived as a need to defend public expressions of critical argument. It would have been left to the jury, had the case gone to trial, to decide in a broad sense if McCarthy's hatred of Hellman truly threatened the public sphere (technically the jury would have been asked only whether Hellman had proven the elements of her tort and whether she met the constitutional standard applied to the case). In compelling McCarthy to defend her remarks about Hellman's language, Justice Baer raised questions central to both law and literary criticism: What is the source of interpretive authority? Is it grounded in objectivity or is it free? The law's answer to both questions is vague.

A statement of fact in one context may be treated as a statement of opinion in another, which is not to say that everything is relative or that interpretation is arbitrary or that it just depends on who has the power to impose what can be said, though Hellman provokes us to wonder about each of these possibilities. It was the particular style of Hellman's self-presentation as much as her positions on the public events

of the day that most angered McCarthy. But how does a critic
assess a mendacious style in a literary text, apart from specific
instances of mendacity? The critical sense can seem capri-
cious and subjective, but, even given a degree of subjectivity,
it comes down to the wisdom a person acquires from a lifetime of learning and reading. McCarthy would have thought
of it as judgment, a notion she understood partly through her
reading of Kant, a philosopher who actually appears in the
final pages of her novel *Birds of America,* "a small man,
scarcely five feet high, in an unbuttoned twill jacket with a
white stock."[71] In the late 1970s, after the death of Hannah
Arendt, McCarthy turned to editing Arendt's New School
Lectures on Kant's idea of judging. Kant's *Critique of Judgment* (and specifically *The Critique of Aesthetic Judgment*) describes the judgment of the beautiful with a paradoxical turn
of phrase; this kind of judgment is "subjective universal,"
which implies that it is not absolute but that other people
ought to be led to agreement through common sense *(sensus
communis),* a term that particularly attracted Arendt in her
attempt to reconcile the ethical and the aesthetic.[72] Judgment
in this sense subverts the legal categories of fact and "pure
opinion." Personal narrative always includes a fictive aspect,
literary critics generally agree, and they conclude that in
reading autobiographies we should be concerned not with
factual but with figurative truth. As *New Yorker* writer Nancy
Franklin wrote in a review of *Secret Diary of a Call Girl* (a
television show based on a book supposedly by a high-end
prostitute), the writing can seem "not just fictional but false,"
offering instances in which neither the style nor the content
passes the "smell test."[73] McCarthy made a similar point in
her deposition, without withdrawing the accusation of lying,
when she conceded that the majority of Hellman's facts were

true but that the work as a whole had a tone of falsity: "I don't mean literally nothing when I say 'Nothing in her writings rings true.' I don't mean, of course—say perhaps seventy per cent of factual statements are probably true—I don't mean that."[74]

In a 1960 essay, "The Fact in Fiction," McCarthy expresses one of her abiding concerns, that contemporary novelists had lost interest in facts: "The distinctive mark of the novel is its concern with the actual world, the world of fact, of the verifiable, of figures, even, and statistics."[75] "I have this fanatical obsession with accuracy," she remarked to her publisher William Jovanovich in 1975.[76] In *Memories of a Catholic Girlhood,* which recounts the death of her parents and the misery she and her brothers endured with Dickensian foster parents in Minneapolis, McCarthy situates the formation of her critical mind. "Like all people who have been mistreated," she writes, "we were wary of being taken in." She describes the propaganda with which her Irish-Catholic relatives sought to discredit her Protestant and Jewish relations in Seattle. In the language of the 1940s, she describes her wicked aunt's regime as "totalitarian," which meant that "she was idealistically bent on destroying our privacy."[77] As a result, Mary herself became both a gifted liar and highly sensitive to the coercive fabrications of the powerful. A lifelong student of languages— Latin, French, Italian, German—McCarthy was "passionate about language," as Gelderman notes, "and [was] most critical of those writers who compose carelessly."[78] Moreover, like the heroine of one of her autobiographical stories, she felt that "you could not treat your life-history as though it were an inferior novel and dismiss it with a snubbing phrase."[79] But McCarthy was obviously exaggerating in her snubbing phrase about Hellman. (And Hellman composed with a great deal of

care.) What she really meant was a "general tone of uncon-
vincingness." At the core of her interpretation of Hellman's
memoirs was the problem of implication, of unstated meanings, such as Hellman's failure to mention others who stood
up to the House Un-American Activities Committee or that
she took the Fifth Amendment to protect herself from self-
incrimination. These omissions are among McCarthy's key
examples of falsehood. They draw attention to Hellman's
elliptical style, a provoking suggestiveness, a resistance to
representation that her books represent figuratively in characters who are liars, secretive, or untranslatable (because they
speak other languages), in the missing valise of her grandfather's letters in "Bethe," or Julia's lost baby, objects that would
prove everything but can't be found. In one sense McCarthy
succumbs to this provocation; fanatical precision turns into
its opposite—imprecision.

American law is partly to blame for this paradox. "If this
judge's main point was that H. isn't a public figure," McCarthy
wrote her lawyer, "this can be most effectively contested by
confronting her political persona: the appeals she signed or
initiated, the mass meetings she addressed and sometimes, I
believe, organized, her 'Committee for Public Justice.'"[80] In
libel law, however, the definition of what is "public" is slippery
and contradictory. On the one hand, a defamatory statement
need not even be "published," in the sense of being made public; it is enough that it is communicated to a third party, someone (even one person) other than the plaintiff, provided the
plaintiff is damaged by it. On the other, the courts have used
the language of the "public" to define libel, finding that libel
involves exposing the plaintiff to "*public* contempt, ridicule,
aversion or disgrace, or induc[ing] an evil opinion of him in

the minds of right-thinking persons, and to deprive him [or her] of their friendly intercourse in society."[81] The legal definition of "publication," therefore, is very broad, and it does not necessarily accord with the conception of "publicity" that is applied to the distinction between public and private figures.

So the law employs two concepts of "public" for these two different elements of defamation: the first means "to make one's private thoughts public," and the second is closer to a concept of a public sphere (as opposed to the private sphere of home, family, and individual). But defamation grants all individuals—public or private—a remedy against false communications that harm their reputation. In considering the formation of a defense committee for McCarthy in 1980, Diana Trilling, who suspected that her recent book contract with Little, Brown (Hellman's publisher) had been derailed by Hellman because it contained remarks critical of *Scoundrel Time,* speculated that "the aim of such a committee couldn't be to raise money but to mobilize sentiment on Mary's behalf and extrude Lillian from the community of the fair-minded."[82] McCarthy was appalled by that idea, too, and was against the whole idea of "trying the case in the court of public opinion."[83] She did not want to be taken up as a cause, like the Scottsboro Boys, and scuttled the idea of a defense committee (though she was less averse to a defense fund). It would be for the courts to decide if her critical remarks were defamatory.

Throughout their works and lives, McCarthy and Hellman repeatedly examined the ability of language to accommodate conceptions of "truth." The libel suit brought this challenging, philosophical problem to a head in personal terms. Their antagonism gives shape to the key literary, social, and legal question of their day: whether a text means what its author meant. Both authors' intentions were in question: McCarthy's in the alleged libel (was she malicious?), and Hellman's in her memoirs (was she a conscious liar?). The case highlights the fact that literature is a social institution and that language, its medium, involves inextricable relationships between facts and metaphors, the literal and the figurative. *A Charmed Life,* McCarthy's satirical novel of 1955 about an artists' and writers' colony in a New England village, which features thinly veiled portraits of her ex-husband the critic Edmund Wilson as Miles Murphy and McCarthy herself as the brilliant yet peculiarly literalistic protagonist Martha Sinnott (a philosophy PhD), explores the trendy critical terms of the day. The painter Warren Coe, who is comically incapable of grasping artistic theories, paints bewildering portraits based on uncritical readings of works selected by Miles; both believe that "all painting is literary." At first, influenced by science and philosophy, "the poor fellow could not get the idea of proof out of his noodle," but when he discovers that logical proof does not apply easily to his own work, he falls back despondently on the idea that everything is false: "His work, he had discovered, was a lie, just as big a lie, he said bitterly, as Rembrandt or Titian, who at least *thought* the world they were painting was real. . . . He realized he was a faker and illusionist and probably ought to be put in jail." This revelation makes him sick, but then he is cured by relativity: "He thought about outer space and reasoned that a lie could be true there, just the way parallel lines could meet. Miles had not the heart to gainsay him. What was the use of explaining to him that a lie existed only in discourse." In outer space, where there are no people, it is possible that either everything or nothing is true, positions that are the "absolute topsy turvy" of each other, and, we are told, Warren's work "takes a leap into freedom, or a plunge into necessity," entering a domain in which "you could not tell whether it was good or bad." But, the narrator informs us, *people* give words their meanings, an insight we can extend to recognize that even "and" and "the" do not have meanings apart from the people who use them. Understood this way, Hellman and Mc-Carthy's legal battle can seem like an allegory of language in struggle with itself, contending with the demand for accuracy, immediacy, certainty, the problem of translation from one idiom into another, and endless questions of interpretation and moral life, self-knowledge and sociability. Disagreements cannot always be resolved.[84]

American constitutional law grants more freedom to public discourse from controlling norms of civility than other national legal systems. It is largely up to individuals to negotiate relations between public and private, moral and aesthetic, formal and historical elements of their shared words; so, people need to be generous, to constrain their own freedoms in order to balance a right to disagree with a fair-minded attempt to understand each other's purposes. However, the fact that other points of view are available does not make them equally legitimate. In her deposition, McCarthy attempted to assert the validity of her interpretation; in the "public" sphere of the *Dick Cavett Show,* when she wasn't legally constrained, she did not. The fact that McCarthy spoke hyperbolically does not mean that her comment was not a calculated falsehood or that Hellman did not dangerously distort history in her memoirs. But the curiously imprecise precision of Mc-Carthy's statement about "every word" reflects on the law that is called to adjudicate its meaning, the intention behind it, and its effect. Defamation cases themselves, like all areas of judge-developed law, depend on murky, even obfuscating language, in spite of the courts' best efforts to segregate the figurative and the literal.[85] The Hellman-McCarthy case, which arises from a statement, a joke really, about an impossible standard for linguistic precision, also highlights the fact that judges make their language impossible to define in universal terms in order to promote forms of interpretation that depend on particular contexts, intentions, and responses. It is impossible to define a "calculated falsehood" or an "honest opinion" without taking into account intentional and affective factors. McCarthy's emphasis on the objectivity of words belies an anxiety, spawned in part by the catastrophic demagoguery of the 1930s and 1940s, about the shaping power of both political personalities and emotional responses in the construction of meaning.

Though McCarthy insisted that her remark on the *Dick Cavett Show* "wasn't political overtly or covertly," the conflict centers not only on an author's supposed obligation to be honest but also on public language ("every word") more broadly.[86] McCarthy knew that larger political issues depend upon the most nuanced aspects of the way we use language. The idea that certain forms of literary criticism are inseparable from certain forms of politics clearly motivated her long career, as it had motivated the *Partisan Review* editors and contributors. Hellman's and McCarthy's was an emblematic Cold War controversy not because it was about Stalinism but because it was about the pros and cons of a right to privacy (and a related right to publicity) and the way such a right defines our identity as political subjects. Assaults on privacy and truth not only by totalitarian regimes but also by the CIA, and the subversion of language by propagandists, spies, and liars, from Klaus Fuchs to Alger Hiss, led to extensive reflections on what linguists of the 1950s called "meta-language," language about language, in works of American culture from Lerner and Loewe's *My Fair Lady* to Nabokov's *Lolita*.

Hellman's writing continuously reflects on its own language and rhetorical form, on the political double-talk of the Cold War and Watergate, on acts of imperfect translation, and on the "stylish, *épater* palaver" of the smart theater set.[87] One of Hellman's most penetrating biographers, Joan Mellen, has warned readers not to rely on Hellman's details because the more detailed her prose, the more likely that she was lying.[88] But Hellman herself had already warned readers to be distrustful, while at the same time calling for a specific kind of close reading. In dramas and memoirs, Hellman offers numerous parables for the invasive act of reading a written life. In one of the many diary entries in *An Unfinished Woman*, for instance, she vividly describes her experience on a trip to the Soviet Union in 1944, though in the previous chapter she warned that her diaries included nothing important: "In those five months I kept diaries of greater detail and length than I have ever done before or since, but when I read them last year, and again last week, they did not include what had been most important to me, or what the passing years have made important."[89]

Both Hellman and McCarthy are deeply concerned with rhetoric and particularly with the fine line between persuasion and deception. Privacy, the ability to control information about oneself, can protect the innocent, but it can also shield the guilty. Hannah Arendt, who, like McCarthy, could appear both aloof and inclined to fight, once wrote to her that the "discrepancy between public image and actual person is greater in your case than any other I know of."[90] It was a similar, though in her view more hypocritical, discrepancy that McCarthy found intolerable in Lillian Hellman. These two women not only fought within the public discourse of their time but also represented competing notions of discourse itself. They spoke different moral languages, each with its own characteristic concepts and modes of reasoning. The following chapters show how they acquired their power to persuade (or not) by situating them within the larger frameworks of understanding from which they drew.

II
Language Lessons

Latin, that hoary old man of the Requirements, is still on trial. Denounced last year by [Harvard] President Conant, his case is now being investigated by the Committee on Admissions. . . . If Latin needs compulsion to help it win proselytes, it doesn't deserve them. But Latin is far from being the dead language it is usually called. It still has enough vitality and allurement to win scholars by its own powers. Thus the only course of wisdom is to kill the crippled Latin requirement, the last vestige of the tyranny of the Roman Empire.
—*Harvard Crimson,* November 19, 1935

When I was twelve I was working out in the fields, and that same year I taught myself Latin and French. At fourteen I was driving mules all day and most of the night, and that was the year I learned my Greek, read my classics, taught myself—Think what I must have wanted for sons. And then think what I got. One trickster, one illiterate.
—Lillian Hellman, *Another Part of the Forest,* 1946

Whan Mary McCarthy said that "every word" Lillian Hellman wrote was a lie, "including 'and' and 'the,'" she provoked a fight about language itself. In a basic sense, their differences stem from the ways they learned languages as children. Language lessons in public and parochial schools shaped their worldviews, and this chapter tells the story of their formative years and of how Americans have thought about childhood and language acquisition more broadly. In their work, Hellman and McCarthy often reflected on how to teach languages and on the instruction they received as children. Examining historical attitudes toward education also indicates how language lessons in America have been related to shifting ways of understanding the private lives and public responsibilities of teachers.

Schooling Lillian Hellman

In 1920, at age fourteen, Lillian Hellman, a moody, narrow-shouldered girl with a strong chin and a downward turning, thin-lipped mouth, entered Wadleigh High School for Girls on West 114th Street near Seventh Avenue. Wadleigh was the first public high school for girls in New York. The massive H-shaped schoolhouse, built of red brick and buff Indiana limestone, had terra-cotta trimmings, a great peaked roof of light green slate, and a tall tower rising from the inside western corner of the front courtyard. Hellman later characterized the building as a "large, smelly, unpleasant dump."[1] It housed nearly three thousand girls and was, in fact, the epitome of Progressive Era urban, educational architecture, economically constructed yet providing expansive space for large laboratories, gymnasiums, and theaters, in one of which Hellman performed the villain in the school play, "improvising a dazzling scene, which fattened up her own part by a number of showy remarks" when the stage door stuck.[2] Operating on a departmental system of instruction analogous to the modern department store (Macy's moved to its nine-story Thirty-Fourth Street location in 1902), Wadleigh High School included a two-story assembly hall in addition to a large bicycle storage room, teachers' dining rooms, a kitchen, and, of course, lecture halls and classrooms with large windows. Its construction in 1902 was part of an enormous investment in New York public education in the decade before Hellman's birth in 1905, somewhere around fifty million dollars, mostly toward secondary education. As the educational historian Lawrence Cremin has remarked, a "revolution in American secondary education" had taken place in the years between two seminal studies, the Committee of Ten report in 1893 and the *Cardinal Principles* report of 1918: "From an institution conceived for the few, the high school became an institution conceived for all. From an adjunct to college, the high school became the pivotal point in the public school system, one which carried forth objectives yet unfinished by the elementary school and opened new vistas leading on to the college."[3]

As the shape of American society changed, so did the shape of liberal education and pedagogical theory. As building blocks of brick and stone rapidly fell into place, so too metaphorical building blocks, specifically the study of language, drew new critical attention. Hellman's best subjects at Wadleigh were English, grammar, history, and Latin. Textbooks announced that Latin courses, still at the center of American education through the 1920s, sought to provide the structure of both a language and a civilization upon which young

American students of the Progressive Era could build.[4] Without Latin, a student could not get into Harvard, Yale, Princeton, or countless other private and public universities in America, let alone study medicine or law. As historian William Wraga has noted, "During this period, classical education seemed almost to wax and wane simultaneously. While, for example, both the sheer number and the proportion of adolescents studying Latin increased dramatically, education theorists increasingly questioned the value of the classics in the school curriculum for a modern industrial democracy."[5]

Hellman, whose family had only partially moved to Manhattan when she was six, split the year between New York and New Orleans. She never mastered a second language. The fact that she studied Latin, did well in it, but never progressed beyond a rudimentary level typified the experience of countless American high school students of her day. But, as a peripatetic adolescent, Hellman's education was also atypical in a way that deeply colored her thinking about school. Although on the surface she scarcely resembles the patriarchal autodidact Marcus Hubbard in her play *Another Part of the Forest,* she too disdained institutional schooling, considered herself largely self-taught, and came to regard language learning—perhaps because she had so little of it herself—as an essential sign of a specific form of pragmatism and of self-reliance. To learn multiple languages enables one to move between value systems, to question the objectivity of each, and to assert one's own with peculiar force.

To study an ostensibly foundational language, such as Latin, is, in theory, to discover the very idea of foundations in languages and in morals. The editors of *Allen and Greenough's New Latin Grammar* (1903) make this clear in their introduction to the part of the book dedicated to syntax, where they provide a brief narrative of the history of spoken language from the time when, as they imagine, "word-forms were no doubt significant in themselves, without inflections, . . . just as to a child the name of some familiar object will stand for all he can say about it," to the last stage when inflections were developed to express *person, tense, case,* and other grammatical relations "resulting from our habits of mind."[6] Such an ungrammatical way of thinking about language learning and human cognition—that individual words are significant in themselves and that habits of mind exist before grammar—were to be completely undermined in the next fifty years by philosophers of language such as Ludwig Wittgenstein and linguists such as Noam Chomsky. As in the models of language explored by her contemporaries in other fields, in Hellman's writings, language learning dramatizes relationships between practical language use and habits of mind, or the ability through words to make one's own view of the world, and one's own values, the world and values in which and by which others live.

A stubborn and temperamental only child by her own account, Hellman refused to submit to discipline and never felt comfortable in school but read novels voraciously on her own. She recalls those awkward years in *An Unfinished Woman:*

> When I was about six years old my father lost my mother's large dowry. We moved to New York and were shabby poor until my father finally settled for a life as a successful traveling salesman. It was in those years that we went back to New Orleans to stay with my father's sisters for six months each year. I was thus moved from school in New York to

school in New Orleans without care for the season
or the quality of the school. This constant need for
adjustment in two very different worlds made a formal education into a kind of frantic tennis game,
sometimes played with children whose strokes had
force and brilliance, sometimes with those who
could barely hold the racket. Possibly it is the reason I never did well in school or in college, and why
I wanted to be left alone to read by myself.[7]

The Hellmans lived on West Ninety-Fifth Street between Riverside Drive and West End Avenue. Max and Julia
Hellman's sending Lillian first to Public School 6 on the East
Side, where the Marxes, her rich maternal relatives, lived, reflected the center of gravity of the family's social life and, possibly, their economic aspirations. But the effect on Lillian of
the "constant need for adjustment," of feeling that learning
was a game in which she was sometimes overmatched and
sometimes dominant, was that she assumed a pragmatic understanding of truth. The words "pragmatic" and "truth" in this
context refer to a particular way of thinking, given expression
most famously by the American philosopher William James
in his 1907 book *Pragmatism*. James asked what concrete difference an idea or belief's being true might have in anyone's
actual life. "*True ideas,*" he wrote, "*are those we can assimilate,
validate, corroborate and verify. False ideas are those we cannot.*"[8] Hellman, like James, would be skeptical of more abstract and less expedient definitions not only of "truth" but
also of how language works. This is not to say that she believed
that nothing was true (or false) or that she was cynical. But it
does condition and circumscribe what she and her characters
mean when they speak of ideals or principles. For Hellman,

an ideal is not something that is injected from without; rather, ideals arise from an appreciation of the meaning of what is actual.

Hellman grew into a New Yorker, albeit a southern one. She never grew into school, but education would become an important subject of her work, and she would go on to teach at America's elite universities, at MIT, Yale, and, a couple of times, at Harvard, where she talked constantly about teaching with members of the English department such as William Alfred and department chair Walter Jackson Bate. During her 1961 stint at Harvard, Bate, an intimidating scholar who was then completing his biography of John Keats, found Hellman's insistence on lunch meetings and frequent demands for help with "how to teach" exasperating. But students appreciated her careful attention. She wrote brief, incisive comments in the margins of their papers and stories. One student in her fiction-writing seminar reported suggestively to Carl Rollyson that she pressed him to clarify what his narrator meant by the term "moral code."[9] Her courses often focused on adaptation, or the way stories can be translated into other stories. At Yale she taught her own adaptation of Voltaire's *Candide*. She took a maternal interest in the students and brought sweets to class. She encouraged argument and informality. Hellman urged Jerome Wiesner, president of MIT, to implement a rigorous curriculum in literature. At her funeral Wiesner said: "Lillian taught for a time at MIT. At first she did this with some misgivings, asking what she could teach young scientists whose language she didn't understand." But, he concluded, she won them over, and "her public lectures were among the best attended the school had ever seen."[10]

Hellman's deep interest in education and her works suggest a philosophy of education that, though not explicitly progressive, indicates a pragmatist's sensibility, shaped as it was (and not unlike that of William and Henry James) by her peripatetic educational experience. It is not possible to say whether Hellman read William James, whose historic home on the Harvard campus she would have passed on her walks to the English department, but she certainly read, taught, and, in her plays, stole from his brother, Henry, whose fiction offers complex studies of school-age children, who provoke and elude final judgment. Hellman's school years and the schooling of her characters will not enable us to decide if Mary McCarthy was right in saying that every word she wrote was a lie, including "and" and "the," but they help to explain her self-consciousness about language. Her memoirs refer to people who don't like her English or to the patois French that New Orleans taught her and of which she is ashamed.[11] Yet in an important sense the figurative creole of Hellman's work turns out to be a rich blend of moral vocabularies. Reading it this way, in the light of her education, can illuminate the quality and significance of the ethical questions raised by what many regarded as her "bad" language.

Mary McCarthy's Catholicism and "Crude" Citizenship

Mary McCarthy was a particularly keen Latin student, starting at the age of six in 1918, when she became an orphan after her parents died in the flu pandemic. McCarthy spent five years in Minneapolis, the home of her father's relatives. There she endured a grim existence under the supervision of her middle-aged, penurious, and small-minded Aunt Margaret and Uncle Myers and attended a parochial school where Latin both offered an "aesthetic outlet" in the "words of the Mass and the litanies and the old Latin hymns" and fostered a sense of "crude 'citizenship.'"[12] The crudeness was subsequently refined and the sense of citizenship challenged during her days at the elite, Francophilic Sacred Heart Convent in Seattle, where she moved to live with her maternal grandparents, the more affluent, non-Catholic Prestons, in 1923. She spent her final three years of high school at the majestic Annie Wright Seminary, a private Episcopal school, situated on a lovely ten-acre campus overlooking Commencement Bay in the north end of Tacoma, Washington. There she studied Latin privately with the unfashionable, dyspeptic, and rigidly upright Highland Scotswoman Miss Ethel MacKay (basis for Miss Gowrie in *Memories of a Catholic Girlhood*), to prepare for Vassar, which at that time required three years of Latin for first-year students.

McCarthy liked the angular and awkward MacKay, who at that point was in her late thirties, "a Celt, like me," wrote McCarthy, with a "literalist mind." MacKay inspired her with revealingly contradictory passions: on the one hand, for Caesar, "just laconic, severe, magnanimous, detached—the bald instrument of empire who wrote not 'I' but 'Caesar.' The very grammar was beautified for me by the objective temperament that ordered it, so much so that today I cannot see an ablative absolute or a passage of indirect discourse without happy tears springing to my eyes." On the other hand, as a member of the high school Latin club, McCarthy played the rebel Catiline, "adulterer, extortioner, profligate, bankrupt, assassin, suspected wife-killer, broken-down patrician, democrat, demagogue, thug" in a production of *Marcus Tullius* written by MacKay. In Catiline, too, McCarthy found a figure with whom she identified deeply: "Catiline was not only a hero—he was me." The judicious Caesar and the defiant, untrustworthy Catiline are figures for two sides of McCarthy that came to dominate not only her memoirs, like her opposed chapters of reminiscence and self-criticism in that book, but also all of her writings.[13]

At Vassar (1929–33), McCarthy took ten Latin courses, more than in any other subject but English. The fact that as an adult she saw herself and was characterized by her friends as a Latin student bears significantly on her curious animosity to Lillian Hellman, her suggestion that "every word" Hellman wrote was a lie, and Hellman's own litigious response.[14] In a 1972 essay written in the context of the Watergate hearings and expressing the sense that "people have become so practiced in evasion, euphemism, circumlocution, and all the forms of lying that they would not know how to tell the truth if an occasion favoring truth-telling should arise," McCarthy complains that everyone misuses prepositions because nobody studies Latin in school anymore:

> One reason for the loss of clarity in our current speaking and writing must be the fact that the classical languages are no longer taught in schools. In fact, the loss of control over prepositions—the articulate parts of speech—seems to have coincided with the disappearance of Latin as a "subject" in public high schools. Up through the war, at least in New England, in the mill towns (not just in Boston), Latin was still taught—Greek sometimes too—by vigorous unmarried old ladies. When they died or retired, it went. In New England, in former days, the teaching of Latin was considered indispensable to a truly civic educa-

tion; it was thought to form democratic habits of mind. Whether it did or not, the dropping of it from the program of free universal education certainly deepened the chasm between the classes. And whatever it did or did not do toward conserving democratic habits, Latin surely promoted clear, analytic thinking and helped us in our language to distinguish the relations between members of a sentence.[15]

That vigorous, unmarried old ladies rendered Latin indispensable to the public sphere is a curious development both for the ladies and for Latin since the days of the Roman Republic, when Latin was alive and women were relegated to private life, as McCarthy well knew. More noteworthy in McCarthy's prewar parable is the place of those unhitched old ladies, whose unmarried status enables them to act as joiners who compel their citizen-students to distinguish relations not only between elements of a sentence but also between members of a society. It is the function of language to join and to separate, as McCarthy suggests by her use of the adjective "articulate," from the Latin *articulatus,* which means "distinctly jointed." It would be Hellman's articulate forms of speech, the conjunction "and" and the article "the," that McCarthy singled out hyperbolically as lies without, she said, meaning it literally. But Hellman did take her literally (at least in court). Latin lessons help us understand why.

In McCarthy's essay, teaching Latin seems to bestow two contradictory results. On the one hand, Latin lessons instill democratic habits of mind, a virtuous but, insofar as they are habitual, unreflective way of behaving. On the other hand, Latin lessons promote clear, analytic thinking. How can Latin do both of those things? The teaching and learning of languages, and especially of Latin, in America revolved around that question for more than two hundred years, and it is a subject that McCarthy, Hellman, and their contemporaries explicitly interrogate. In his 1961 essay "What Is English?" the poet Archibald MacLeish, who in addition to being Hellman's close friend had been Librarian of Congress and, during World War II, director of the War Department's Office of Facts and Figures and the assistant director of the Office of War Information, wrote of his experiences on being appointed to the Boylston Professorship of Rhetoric and Oratory at Harvard. What exactly, he wondered, was he to teach in this role?

> When letters were first taught in the Colonial colleges they were taught in Latin with Latin manuals and Latin and Greek examples. The teaching of composition in the vulgar tongue had begun, it is true, before the Revolution, but the extraordinary debate which preceded and accompanied that event was conducted with the classical modes and models in mind. . . . John Quincy Adams, the first Boylston professor, signalized his installation by delivering an inaugural address in which the word "English" never once occurs. It was not London to him, nor Stratford, from which the great tradition flowed but Athens and Rome. "Novelty," he told his audience, "will not be expected; nor is it perhaps to be desired. A subject which has exhausted the genius of Aristotle, Cicero, and Quintilian can neither require nor admit much additional illustration."[16]

Adams's subject had been rhetoric and oratory, the title of his chair, but MacLeish, who was also responsible for bringing Hellman to Harvard in 1960 to give the Theodore Spencer Memorial Lecture on Drama and then to teach a regular course in the English department in January 1961, situates his concern within an institutional history. The subject of English instruction cannot be "texts as texts," an approach that destroyed the classics in American education by turning them into objects of rote learning and led a generation of graduate students to study "biographies of poets, economic and sociological interpretations of novels, literary history—anything but the texts themselves." Language and literature instructors continued to swing between two extremes. The revolution that had privileged biography and sociology led to a counterrevolution of "new critics . . . reading words as words," leaving MacLeish and his postwar contemporaries somewhere in between, always with "one foot in the text and the other in the world so that the two, text and world, are made to march together."[17]

For MacLeish a crucial difference between his relationship to rhetoric and classical languages and that of Adams has to do with a historic transformation of the public and, by extension, the private sphere. "'English,' we think today, is something more than the reading of words as words but something less also, surely less, than the teaching of the private life the words came out of."[18] It is a romantic notion that words come out of private lives, or that we are the origin of words and not the other way around, but the idea that words detached from private lives are inanimate and inert recalls the ancient prejudice that privileges speech over writing. MacLeish, who had taken a rigorous prep-school course in languages at Hotchkiss in the 1890s, including four years of

English, Latin, and French, and three of German, not to mention ancient history, assumes a hierarchy with the speech of
private life at the top and inert words on the page at the bottom, with the teacher and students someplace in between. It
is a position that recalls that of Socrates and his pupil Phae-
drus. In Plato's famous dialogue on pedagogy and pederasty,
Socrates both discusses rhetoric's necessary relationship to
truth and critiques writing, which, he claims, does not allow
the student access to the teacher's soul. The teacher's own private life must then be regarded as a source of words. That
idea, which has inflamed debates about teachers' sexuality
and politics in contemporary America, is one that both Hellman and McCarthy examine intently and at length.[19]

The question of what to teach, content or form, knowledge of "culture" or methods of analysis, is the basic question
of liberal education. Since the late eighteenth century, liberal
educators have sought to move beyond the Latin, text-based
curriculum of their medieval forebears. Students must be
shaped to take their place in civil society. To do so, some argue, they need to have a base of knowledge—what E. D.
Hirsch Jr. calls "cultural literacy"—as well as analytical skills
with which to process information and think critically and
creatively. But, then, do they act creatively on culture or does
culture act creatively on them? The two sides in this debate,
both focused on the generic or ideal child in the middle, are
still much in force. Hellman and McCarthy give us insight
into forms of acculturation through language study and
into the emerging matrix of popular and professional dis-
courses that contributed to producing a new model of "the
child" in the 1930s. Language lessons were central to early-
twentieth-century debates about the formation of the "liberal" subject.

Latin and Liberalism

The Hellman-McCarthy antagonism suggests a conflict in languages of American public conversation. McCarthy advocated a language that registers fact but doesn't color it; language in this sense is a neutral form that conveys an empirical or rational truth. Hellman, in contrast, treated language as both form *and* content, the manner of presentation and what is presented. Language is protean, always colored by perspective, and therefore, so is the truth. These two ways of thinking represent divisions in American liberalism that center on a seemingly esoteric part of the curriculum, the teaching of Latin.

Compulsory education in Latin was a serious bone of contention in American colleges and high schools in the 1920s and 1930s, when Hellman and McCarthy were completing their formal studies and publishing their first works. In 1933, Harvard required three years of Latin or two of Greek for all entering freshmen who wanted to receive the A.B. degree, a requirement that not only set the standard for other colleges around the country but also trickled down to secondary-school curricula, particularly at selective schools in New England, where students enrolled in the hope of gaining admittance to such colleges. In 1935, in his second annual report, the forty-year-old chemist-president James Bryant Conant, himself a graduate of Roxbury Latin School in Boston, called for the elimination of the Latin requirement for the A.B. degree, a decision that prompted vehement opposition, including a letter of protest entitled "Omnibus ad quos hae litterae pervenerint Salutem" and signed Harvard '22, Harvard '28. The Latin—"Those to whom these letters come"—refers to those who would have the high-status letters (A.B.) after their names—that is, diploma Latin. The address to Conant plays on the irony of Latin being the medium of conferring degrees that do not require Latin (in 1961, when Harvard switched to English diplomas, privileging communication over grandiosity, about four thousand students protested in the "diploma riots").[20] But questions about the value of Latin and the teaching of ancient languages had long been central to debates about liberal education in America and would continue to be for years to come not only in practical curricular terms, as the Latin requirement all but disappeared from American public schools, but also in more broadly symbolic and ideological ones. Delivering the Vassar Commencement Address in 1976, McCarthy said, "If the quality of high-school education could be improved, brought back to what it used to be in the old New England Latin Schools or what it is today in Europe, then college could become the equivalent of today's graduate schools but accessible to greater numbers."[21]

In 1936, Walter A. Jessup, president of the Carnegie Foundation for the Advancement of Teaching, noted that the nineteenth-century college curriculum left much to be desired: "Its core was language and language and more language. Not only were undergraduates limited to this type of instruction, but they were orally and publicly examined," and he acknowledged that it did seem that with changing times students ought to have better knowledge of science and practical subjects. "Nevertheless," he added,

> our own founders, the signers of the Declaration of Independence and the designers of the Constitution, were for the most part college graduates who during their immature years in college were fed a steady and exclusive diet of languages which

for practical purposes were almost as dead then as now. Yet these graduates . . . led a political revolution that rocked the world. They studied Latin, Greek, Hebrew, literature, history and philosophy, rather than material recommended by a Social Science Commission. They defended their right to graduate by disputation in Latin rather than by participating in open forums on social problems, as advocated so convincingly by our contemporaries. They resulted and risked their necks thereby. They set up a constitutional government that has outlasted any of its time.[22]

The facts are true enough, but the inference that the study of Latin, Greek, and Hebrew caused or enabled a revolution may seem more dubious, and in fact, since the American Revolution, the question of whether the study of ancient languages has much to contribute to a modern republic has been regarded skeptically, even by the founders, who were themselves schooled in those languages and deeply conscious that the idea of (the very word for) a *republic* itself is rooted in Latin. Thomas Jefferson, who loved the classics and thought they added beauty to life, did not think that the learning of Greek and Latin was necessary for a healthy republic. "To whom are these [classical languages] useful?" he wrote. "Certainly not to all men. There are conditions of life to which they must be forever estranged, and there are epochs of life, too, after which the endeavor to attain them would be a great misemployment of time."[23]

In 1828, the Yale Report (officially entitled "A Report on the Course of Liberal Education"), by Yale president Jeremiah Day and classics professor James L. Kingsley, inquired into the expediency of restructuring the liberal education curriculum with the possibility of dropping the classical course of study based on "dead languages."[24] This important document, which came down in favor of retaining the classical curriculum, continued to raise debates more than 150 years later. The authors recommended the study of Latin and Greek not as a return to an idealized past but as a way of disciplining the mind, and it was in this sense that they emphasized the study of rhetoric in order to develop the art of speaking. Critics, however, worried that the "report's doctrine of mental discipline left liberal education without a focused moral direction" and that the ship of liberal education, as a consequence, "was set adrift in the nineteenth century on the swirling waters of pluralism, individualism," and so on.[25]

Latin lessons, promoted by some as a model of intellectual and moral seriousness, have been seen by others as promoting an ethic of self-interest, rhetoric in all its pejorative associations, and moral relativism. In James Joyce's *Ulysses*, Stephen Dedalus remarks: "I teach the blatant Latin language. I speak the tongue of a race the acme of whose mentality is the maxim: time is money. Material domination. *Domine!* Lord! Where is the spirituality?"[26] Yet by and large, the rhetorical, pragmatic, liberal view of Latin has been treated more sympathetically by American authors. Adopting a typical attitude toward those practical Romans, Kenneth Burke, the most prominent left-wing political theorist of the Depression era, finds in the Stoic administrator Marcus Aurelius an "incipient pragmatism." Reading the Roman emperor and philosopher from the standpoint of his own "grammatical" way of regarding human motives as forms of verbal action, Burke expresses a preference for utilitarian aspects of classical education. Law and justice, Burke writes, are fundamentally related to "matters of form in art."[27] In 1893 then president of Harvard Charles W. Eliot published the findings of the Committee of Ten charged by the National Council on Education to recommend high school sequences of study. This influential report also retained Latin in its core course of study but fostered liberalization, classifying Latin with a "scientific" course of study, in opposition to modern languages.[28] Characterizing her own mind in her memoir *How I Grew*, Mary McCarthy would write that "clear, concise Latin was always more natural to me than Greek with all its 'small, untranslatable words.'"[29]

Whatever particular philosophy animates a desire to return to the classics, however, American democracy is, all agree, radically unlike its classical precursors, in size and diversity alone. Alexis de Tocqueville made this point in offering his own view that literary Americans should study classical languages but that schools should not teach them, focusing instead on science, commerce, and industry. At the crux of Tocqueville's analysis is his recognition that ancient and modern democracies held radically different conceptions of public and, by extension, of private life. For the ancients, private life, the sphere of women and children, was a site of privation, whereas for us, for better or worse, it is the source of our most basic freedoms and satisfactions. To formulate an ethical and realistic philosophy of education, therefore, to assess our putative need for a shared moral language, a lingua franca or Latin of the public sphere, we must first formulate a clear understanding of the place, or the freedoms and limitations, of the private sphere, and the degree to which that language is translatable from the one to the other.

For proponents of liberal education, language assumes an importance that it did not have in earlier philosophies of

education, for to study language is to study our ways of living
or how we arrive at warrantable beliefs and how we can improve those beliefs in shared discourse.[30] Hellman and Mc-
Carthy direct their attention to schools, with their internal
hierarchies, social microcosms, and porous borders, their organization of a curricular culture and their inability to censor
fully the culture of adults (as corrupting books, cigarettes, and
sex sneak in), their lying children, and their uneasy combination of the public and private spheres. The child is a crucial
point of intersection of public and private interest, perhaps
the key point of intersection, a citizen in whose physical well-
being and acculturation the state takes an active and expen-
sive role and on which it will depend.

Few topics can raise the pitch of a political conversation
or a marketing campaign as that of children can, an intensity
that comes with the sense that the society's health or disease
can be traced directly to how children are acculturated. Neil
Postman's influential book *The Disappearance of Childhood*
(1982) asserted that the category of childhood eroded in the
age of mass media, and specifically of television. Postman argued that "childhood" arose with the invention of the printing
press out of a need to censor information that could thereby
become accessible to society's youngest members.[31] Against
the notion that childhood has been undermined by new media, Nicholas Sammond shows that the concept of the child
has evolved vis-à-vis mass consumer culture (particularly
Walt Disney), through popular literature on child rearing,
American sociological writing, and arguments on the effects
of mass media on children. Therefore, the concept of the child
represents vital assumptions about personhood and citizenship beyond those of specific age limits. In the 1920s and
1930s, as the emerging generic child became the consuming

child, "the child became a focal point in the struggle to preserve those American ideals and enforce their inclusion in mass-mediated products," whose ability or failure to embody public values were linked to a broader progressive program of education.[32] Child study, pediatrics, and child guidance all emerged as scientific disciplines in early-twentieth-century America in conjunction with rapid immigration (the forgetting of old and learning of new languages), urbanization, and the development of new mass media within America's specific kind of democratic, capitalist society.

Critics of contemporary American liberalism from Alasdair McIntyre to E. D. Hirsch Jr. have argued that young people lack not only the shared information we often associate with the "liberal arts" tradition but also a common language with which to communicate effectively.[33] In *Cultural Literacy: What Every American Needs to Know*, Hirsch, whose father once instructed employees with lines from *Julius Caesar* (a curious managerial choice considering that story's outcome) and whose son teaches Latin to otherwise woefully undereducated teenagers, argues that "cultural conservatism is useful for purposes of national communication. It enables grandparents to communicate with grandchildren, southerners with midwesterners, whites with blacks, Asians with Hispanics, and Republicans with Democrats—no matter where they were educated."[34] I want to focus on Hirsch's assumption that the communication between grandparents and grandchildren is vital to the American public sphere, or analogous to the communication between people of different races, regions, or political parties. Of course, the fact that, among new Americans, children have rarely known their grandparents, let alone spoken the same language, has been taken by many as a sign of America's vitality. In this context, the invocation of "dead" languages as models for useful learning, assumes an especially troubling aspect.

Counter to Hirsch's assumptions about the value of shared *content,* others have claimed that if Latin lessons are useful at all, it is because teaching Latin instructs children in *forms* of thought and behavior. If ancient languages were to be learned, Jefferson remarked, they should be studied in childhood, when character is formed. "Their acquisition should be the occupation of our early years only, when the memory is susceptible of deep and lasting impressions, and reason and judgment not yet strong enough for abstract speculations."[35] In the 1970s and 1980s, the US government funded Latin classes in underperforming urban school districts with highly effective results. Latin enrollments have surged more recently. According to a December 2, 2000, article in *Time,* children who were given a full year of Latin performed five months to a year ahead of control groups in reading comprehension and vocabulary. Latin students also showed disproportionate gains in math, history, and geography. Scores of elementary schools in high-stakes testing states such as Texas, Virginia, and Massachusetts have added Latin programs. Allen Griffith, a member of the Fairfax City school board, reported to *Time:* "If we're trying to improve English skills, teaching Latin is an awfully effective, proved method." The notion that Latin instruction facilitates basic linguistic comprehension of modern languages, even of the student's native tongue, is a long-held belief. As one teacher told her students, "You're going to be able to figure out the meaning of words you've never seen before."[36]

Interest in Latin speaks to general concerns about the state of public discourse. In the view of one conservative journalist, it represents a "fresh breeze passing through . . . public conversation;" for Latin can "give us codes of clarity and fluency."[37] Current advocates argue that it "builds vocabulary and grammar for higher SAT scores, appeals to college admissions officers as a sign of critical-thinking skills, and fosters true intellectual passion."[38] Maureen Dowd, whose Catholic education, career, and writing style bear similarities to Mary McCarthy's (down to fond memories of translating Julius Caesar), comments: "The study of Latin and Greek . . . reached a nadir in the greedy '80s and '90s, when it seemed irrelevant for kids who yearned to be investment bankers and high-tech millionaires. But now we've learned the hard way that greed is bad—avaritia mala est—and the classics have staged a comeback."[39] Others trace the decline in contemporary political discourse to the fact that public figures are not sufficiently versed in Latin. But this argument often recapitulates a tendentious conservatism that dates back to the nineteenth century. Author Harry Mount complains that none of the leading presidential contenders of 2008 majored in Latin, unlike in the days of Jefferson. The rhetorically gifted and liberal Barack Obama has no Latin, Mount points out, whereas President George W. Bush "was lucky enough to catch the tail end of the American classical tradition."[40]

What Hellman would term the "children's hour" is the formative period of language acquisition that combines the learning of second and third languages (self-conscious language learning) with other kinds of learning in subjects ranging from literature to sewing, domestic economy to acting (onstage and in life), and ethics public and private. Hellman and McCarthy's distinctive yet richly interrelated ideas about language, education, and intergenerational relations serve as allegories for the challenge of forging a common moral language in a liberal culture. Hellman's plays, especially *The*

Children's Hour, and McCarthy's *Memories of a Catholic Girlhood* focus on both education and the disastrous relationships of girls with their grandparents, but the social philosophies that guide them differ significantly. Hellman and McCarthy both represent Latin lessons, and their writings can enhance our own thinking about the problem of constituting a well-functioning society from a diversity of tongues.

The Children's Hour: Plain Speaking and Something Else

From plays and memoirs to legal documents and conversations, the challenge Hellman presents is overtly pedagogical; it is the problem, literally, of how to teach a language of public morality in an age of mass media, economic upheaval, and war to a liberal, cosmopolitan society founded on individualism, rights of private property, and moral diversity. How, in this pluralistic context, does one forge a shared language? By a shared language I mean the kind of conceptual framework that is revealed most often in the breach, beyond simple disagreement, as when moral conversation breaks down, and one person says to another, "You and I just don't speak the same language!" A moral language involves a structure and vocabulary for making sense of the world. It reflects a particular set of interests and assumptions; most people tend to be unconscious of the way rhetoric structures their experience until a crisis reveals their conversational limitations and the possibility of expressing themselves otherwise. Fundamental social challenges arise when people lose confidence in the moral capacity of ordinary language. Hellman's texts literally teach us about their own language; they both present explicit language lessons and demonstrate the coercive power of words that, depending upon their context, can shape individual lives and the life of a society.

In spite of the polemics against her for being a liar and for adopting a literary style that is only quasi- or even faux hard-boiled, it is remarkable how little attention is paid, by friends and enemies alike, to the actual texture of Hellman's writings (especially in the plays), to specific tropes and figures and words. In the interview with Dick Cavett, McCarthy had called Hellman "tremendously overrated, a bad writer, and *dishonest writer*." When Cavett asked what was dishonest about Hellman, McCarthy replied, "*Everything*." Dishonesty certainly is one of Hellman's vital subjects. Yet Hellman knew better than most that to be dishonest in everything is to be a bad (that is, ineffective) liar. Great liars choose every word with care. (McCarthy knew this too, as she commented at the Watergate Hearings: "Clever lying always has large amounts of truth mixed into it, which both tend to support the fabrication and imperil it.")[41] Hellman was a great liar who was also obsessed with honesty. She continually explored how language shapes the world. As a sign of her self-awareness, language lessons pervade her plays in particular, as suits a genre that depicts interpersonal action, dialogue, and the spoken word.

Hellman's career as a celebrated writer began in 1934 with a striking scene of dual recitations in her first play, *The Children's Hour*. Guided by her lover Dashiell Hammett to a book by a Scottish law historian documenting interesting trials, Hellman found the history of a nineteenth-century lawsuit in which a fourteen-year-old girl at a genteel boarding school accused her two teachers of lesbianism. (In classes at Harvard and Yale, Hellman would later teach her writing students

"how to steal and yet make something your own.")[42] Hellman's play is set not in Edinburgh but in a Massachusetts
farmhouse. As the students go about their studies, one girl
reads Portia's famous monologue about the "quality of mercy"
from *The Merchant of Venice* as a second recites from her Latin
grammar: "Ferebamus, ferebatis, fere—fere—fere—." What is
remarkable about the opening scene is not its portrayal of a
historical event, the actual case from Scottish legal history, but
its representation of two forms of learning by recitation: the
meta-theatrical monologue (the quoted scene is also a play-
within-a-play: Portia, a rich heiress, plays a male lawyer) and
the study not only of a language but also of Latin in particular.
The artificiality or unnaturalness of these parallel activities
becomes a central concern of the play, whose crisis hinges on
the use and misappropriation of the word "unnatural."

In this opening dialogue the vital and versatile Latin
verb *ferō,* among whose many meanings are "to bear, to carry,
to endure, to make known, to report, to relate, to say, to tell,"
bears considerable weight.

PEGGY. " 'Tis mightiest in the mightiest; it becomes
the throned monarch better than his crown; his
sceptre—his sceptre shows the force of temporal
power, the attribute to awe and majesty, wherein—"

LOIS *(from the back of the room chants softly and
monotonously through the previous speech).* Ferebam,
ferebas, ferebat, ferebamus, ferebatis, fere—fere—

CATHERINE *(two seats away, the book propped in
front of her).* Fere*bant.*

LOIS. Ferebamus, ferebatis, fere—ferebant.

MRS. MORTAR. Who's doing that?

PEGGY (*the noise ceases. She hurries on*). "Wherein doth sit the dread and fear of kings, it is an attribute to God himself—"

MRS. MORTAR (*sadly*). Peggy, can't you imagine yourself as Portia? Can't you read the lines with some feeling, some pity? (*Dreamily*) Pity. Ah! As Sir Henry said to me many's the time, pity makes the actress. Now, why can't you feel pity?

PEGGY. I guess I feel pity.

LOIS. Ferebamus, ferebatis, fere—fere—fere—

CATHERINE. Fere*bant*, stupid.[43]

The scene dramatizes two modes of rote learning (memorizing a great speech and memorizing a great language), each of which is part of a "proper" education. But how else are the lines related? Each recitation aims to impart a certain kind of value, and each attests to the ineffectiveness of this pedagogical regime. The characters themselves assume that the lines are worse than unrelated, that the banality of the grammar lesson is a distraction from the lesson on pity, interrupting those who wish to concentrate on Shakespeare. One student reads, in "a singsong, tired voice," the highest form of the English language ("the immortal words of the immortal bard," as Mrs. Mortar puts it), the Shakespearean monologue and, in particular, a subtle speech about ethics and the nuances of law. The other struggles with a conjugation, trying to comprehend the third-person plural. Does ignorance of the particularity of that conjugation gain importance when juxtaposed to speeches about pity and the key word, "mercy," that is the subject of Portia's monologue, here deferred?

The irregular verb *ferō* is versatile not only because of its range of meanings but also because it is the root of many compounds, such as "to differ" (dis+ferre) and "to suffer" (sub+ferre), states of being that call for compassion or should evoke pity. In Latin, as in the English derivatives, *ferre* means "to bear" meaning (*ut ferre:* as people say) as a woman bears a child (*ventrem ferre:* to be pregnant), as well as the verb to cast a vote or pass judgment (*sententiam ferre*). To be ignorant of etymology may not be a symptom of immorality, but the scene plainly presents a moralistic woman and a girl with a limited capacity for pity. Hellman primes the audience to learn a lesson that the characters miss about both the paltriness of rote education and its surprising payoffs: it teaches us to see the conventionality of lofty values and the value-laden aspect of language.

A key problem for the students is not recitation itself but mechanical learning and the failure to recognize, more broadly, that the analogous activities of *making* they practice in the "sewing and elocution hour" are not distinct from the "nature" they experience but help to constitute its fabric. Learning by recitation was standard practice in the first half of the twentieth century, as it had been for generations before and was to remain, but there were different purposes to which recitation could be put, and it was precisely the stultifying process of learning by rote that leading Progressive Era pedagogical theorists set out to critique and correct. The fact that so many twentieth-century American educators, from Alexander James Inglis and Charles Baker (coauthors in 1909 of the *High School Course in Latin Composition*) to Neil Postman and Charles Weingartner (coauthors in 1969 of *Teaching as a Subversive Activity*) have focused on what Postman and Weingartner have called "languaging" indicates the importance of philosopher John Dewey and Columbia University, Teachers College, where he taught from 1904 until his death in 1952. It was Dewey's influence, Postman and Weingartner remark, that led them to recognize the essential role of meaning-making for the "new education," replacing a static conception of "the mind" (as a thing) with one of "minding" (as a process).

In Latin instruction, the practice still standard in the 1920s had been to employ recitation as an examination of knowledge acquired, a place where the child shows off to the teacher and other students the amount of information she or he has assimilated. But, as Dewey remarked in his ground-breaking book *The School and Society*, there is another more positive use to which recitation could be put, as "a social clearing house, where ideas and experiences are exchanged and subjected to criticism, where misconceptions are corrected, and new lines of inquiry are set up."[45] In the first scene of Hellman's play, one problem that the dual recitations present is that Latin seems divested of context. "It is not the mere syntactical structure or etymological content of the Latin language that has made it for centuries such an unrivaled educational instrument," Dewey notes. "It is the context of the Latin language, the wealth of associations and suggestion that belongs to it from its position in the history of human civilization that freight it with such meaning."[46] However, for the audience, the marring of the Latin grammar and its juxtaposition to *The Merchant of Venice* should be instructive, as the rest of the play will illustrate, when words wrenched from one context to another become libelous.

At the same time, learning the history of the civilizations in which Latin was employed does not guarantee a pragmatic response or understanding. On the contrary, to learn Latin

and history both as related but discrete and ultimately un-
useful forms of knowledge, a sort of code with strict reference
to a singular Truth, contributes nothing to a shared public
discourse. In *Memories of a Catholic Girlhood,* McCarthy, who
found herself "saved" by religion as an orphan in parochial
school, describes the sectarian approach to education and specifically to language as enabling a particular kind of personal
empowerment. She acknowledges that Catholicism simply
may not be a religion suited to "the American laity," and her
own attraction to it as a child had much to do with identifying
herself "passionately with a cause that became, politically speaking, a losing cause with the birth of the modern world." Of the
intellectual benefits but public uselessness of learning Latin,
she writes:

> I am not sorry to have been a Catholic, first of all
> for practical reasons. It gave me a certain knowl-
> edge of the Latin language and of the saints and
> their stories which not everyone is lucky enough to
> have. Latin, when I came to study it, was easy for
> me and attractive too, like an old friend, as for the
> saints, it is extremely useful to know them and the
> manner of their martyrdom when you are looking
> at an Italian painting, to know, for instance that a
> tooth is the emblem of Saint Apollonia, patron of
> dentistry. . . . If you are born and brought up a
> Catholic, you have absorbed a good deal of world
> history and the history of ideas before you are
> twelve, and it is like learning a language early, the
> effect is indelible. Nobody else in America, no
> other group, is in this fortunate position. Granted
> that Catholic history is biased, it is not dry or dead,

>its virtue for the student, indeed, is that it has been
>made to come alive by the violent partisanship
>which inflames it. . . . To me it does not matter that
>this history was one-sided (this can always be rem-
>edied later), the important thing is to have learned
>the battles and the sovereigns. . . . To an American
>educator, my Catholic training would appear to
>have no utility whatever.[47]

The utility that McCarthy finds in the study of Latin is idiosyncratic and parochial, not public in the sense that it would
enable communication among diverse language groups, draw
unlike people together, or facilitate the dynamics of the marketplace. American educators in the 1920s and 1930s were obsessed with efficiency, as industrial organization, repetition,
and mechanization were increasingly applied to schools and
the home, but McCarthy's schooling both in Minneapolis and
in Washington State was largely untouched by this ideology, a
background that tended to place her in productive tension
with another side of herself as well as with the New York
intellectuals whose crowd she joined and whose political
outlook she generally shared a decade later. "With secondary
education become a mass experience, the feeling has grown
that education must not only be good but must be good for
something—to the individual and society."[48] Learning Latin,
like the "language" of Catholicism, in McCarthy's description, runs directly counter to the ideology of formal training
that educators and that McCarthy herself continued to employ to justify and explain the importance of Latin in the curriculum. In this part of her book, she assumes the mantle of
Catiline, the rebel without a cause, or the loser in a noble cause.
McCarthy, as one critic astutely observed, was a "neoclassicist

in a country of romantics."[49] Hellman's depiction of Latin's inutility is, in fact, more consistent (which is not to say better) than McCarthy's multiple justifications for learning Latin. It is also less sentimental. For Hellman, the rote learning of Latin, like Catholicism, represents a retreat from reality, or at least from one's obligations to the public sphere.

In *The Children's Hour* as in several other plays, Hellman evokes a Protestant tradition of "plain speaking." That is a tradition often traced to Martin Luther that sets up an opposition between the Word in its "vulgar" or democratic form, available to any individual who trusts his or her own experience, and the supposedly higher tradition (whether ecclesiastical or secular) in which authority is derived not from what your conscience tells you (internally) but only through an institutional or linguistic hierarchy. Kurt Müller, the antifascist hero of Hellman's 1941 play *Watch on the Rhine,* cites Martin Luther: "I remember Luther, 'Here I stand. I can do nothing else. God help me. Amen.'"[50] Luther's famous defense at the Diet of Worms serves as a vital touchstone and model of plain speech and self-reliance in Hellman's work and career, however dubious her own theology (her father described her as a Jewish nun).[51] Grammar may be fundamental, but Latin is a language freighted with institutional authority. Learning or ignorance of Latin (classical languages) is a moral signifier in numerous Hellman plays, from *The Children's Hour* to *Another Part of the Forest* to *The Lark.* In the last, the heroic Joan of Arc does not know any Latin, as she tells one of her inquisitors when asked why she did not speak to the archangels in the tongue of the Church. In more ways than one, the men of the Church "do not like the way [she] speak[s]."[52]

The young, those just learning and as yet barely constrained by a grammar, or by conformity, are best able to change the status quo. In the "Julia" chapter of *Pentimento*, Hellman recalls, "I was back in Paris before I remembered that when we were kids, doing our Latin together, we would take turns translating and then correcting. Often one of us would say to the other, 'Something else is needed'; we said it so often that it got to be a joke." Language study, confined to the classroom or to learning by rote, quickly becomes insufficient because it restricts appreciation for the language to units of language, words or syllables, isolated from richer contexts. In Hellman's case, this is not necessarily a bad thing, because, without that sense of insufficiency, there would be no joke, no opening for creativity. Recognizing the limitations of studying language in the abstract led increasingly in the mid-twentieth century to a more functional approach to the act of communication. New ways of thinking about languages discouraged the isolation of particular words or utterances from what Russian linguist Roman Jakobson called a larger "speech event." "The question of relations between the word and the world," he added, "concerns not only verbal art but actually all kinds of discourse."[53] Hellman's anecdote anticipates this functional and more playful approach.

The sense that "something else is needed" does not leave the kids pining for wholeness but enjoying the lack of it. After remembering this experience, Hellman notes, "And so I went back to New York, finished *The Children's Hour*."[54] In the play, a paradoxical "something else" does ultimately interrupt the boredom of the language lesson; it is the arrival in the opening scene of the student Mary Tilford with first a small lie (that she is late for class because she went to pick flowers for Mrs. Mortar) which initiates the conflict that leads to the larger lie (that her teachers, Martha and Karen, have an "unnatural" relationship) radically altering the reality of everyone in the school. Lies, too, may be taken as jokes at the expense of those who think that "word-forms" are "significant in themselves," as the editors of *Allen and Greenough's New Latin Grammar* did. Those scholars imagined little space for the creativity of children, commenting that a child's naming "of some familiar object will stand for all he can say about it."[55] However, the lie that Mary introduces to *The Children's Hour* also subverts the notion that the "something else" to which language lessons refer might be some moral or metaphysical truth entirely outside the playing field of language games. The moral crisis that erupts in the community comes not from outside but from within the domain of language.

Grown-ups in Hellman's work become lazy in their speech and rigid in their thinking. In failing to study their own language, they abdicate their responsibility to themselves and to their children. The third of her memoirs, *Scoundrel Time*, evidences the persistence of this concern with studying the internal workings, the self-referentiality of language and the public importance of the topic, when Hellman comments: "We, as a people, agreed in the Fifties to swallow any nonsense that was repeated often enough, without examination of its meaning or investigation into its roots."[56] But linguistic laziness is already the crucial factor in the catastrophe that will befall the innocent schoolteachers in *The Children's Hour*. Feeling persecuted at school, Mary runs home to her grandmother, Amelia Tilford, to whom she will utter the defamation that will destroy her teachers. Before learning of anything amiss, however, the enabling Mrs. Tilford confesses that while she loves Mary "as much as all the words in all the books in the world," her granddaughter must return to school because "I'm afraid my Latin is too rusty—you'll learn it better in school."[57] To claim that one loves as much as all of the

words in all of the books in the world, that one's love is infi-
nite or incommensurable, in this play is more than hyperbole. It shows Mrs. Tilford's lack of rigor in choosing her own
words, a complacency akin to accepting the fact that her own
Latin is rusty. Preferring quantity to quality, she is content to
let any and all words speak for her, so long as they are in
books, an unreflectively bookish morality. She abdicates responsibility in Mary's moral education. Given that Mary and
Mrs. Tilford are about to ruin two people and corrupt many
others, it may seem that in spite of having many languages
available to them ("all the books in the world"), none is sufficiently meaningful to serve as a mode of moral discourse. The
moral premises of Mrs. Tilford, a pillar of the society, are, as
Jeffrey Stout suggests in *Ethics after Babel,* "like so many incommensurable fragments of lost languages."[58]

Opposite to Mrs. Tilford, the refined yet self-righteous
pillar of the community, but also mirroring her, Lily Mortar,
the instructor in elocution, is a second-rate actress, and the
author's namesake. She has dyed hair, and her dress is "too
fancy for the classroom."[59] Like Portia, whose speech she takes
up for the purpose of instructing Peggy, Lily Mortar raises
questions about relations between words and justice and about
the construction of community. But she is a negative example. In spite of her exhortation to pity, she forgets three lines
that refer to Shylock and the limits of a formalistic justice
("Therefore, Jew, / Though justice be thy plea, consider this, /
That in the course of justice, none of us / Should see salva-
tion"). The Jew and the idea of moral difference are erased,
but so too is the warning against a rigid and putatively inhu-
man justice. After the verdict, Shylock's claim to "stand here
for the law," his demand for justice, that his bond (words
made flesh) be honored, may come to seem as quixotic as

Hellman's case against McCarthy. It is a case lost from the start. Or is it?

Shylock, who asserts the rights of personal property against the state, haunts Hellman's play. It is not necessary to notice that Hellman herself is the child of Jewish merchants and financiers, or that in 1934 the position of Jews in both America and Europe raised issues of social and political status, to observe that what Portia and Lily Mortar fail to acknowledge is the language (in Mrs. Mortar's case the actual words) that constitutes the humanity of the other. That failure is a result not only of being an insufficiently rigorous talker but also of being a poor or complacent listener. The lack of real *conversation* indicates an ethical inadequacy, leading in Shakespeare and in Hellman to violence. In Shakespeare, forced *conversion* is the brutal stand-in for conversation. In Hellman, one kind of talk ends with the suicide of Martha Dobie, one of the cofounders and teachers of the school, but a new form of conversation seems, finally, likely to begin.

A similar tension between conversion and conversation characterizes Hellman's ethically challenging postwar drama *Another Part of the Forest*. In it, the cruel but charismatic domestic tyrant Marcus Hubbard manifests extraordinary linguistic sensitivity but refuses to listen to his own wife, Lavinia, to whom he makes an annual promise to have a conversation on her birthday but perpetually reneges, preferring on the day of the play to read classics with his daughter Regina. As a literary figure, the pathetic Lavinia evokes her abused and tongueless namesake in Shakespeare's *Titus Andronicus* and, even more directly, the vengeful heroine of Eugene O'Neill's *Mourning Becomes Electra*, yet as Hellman's extensive research and concern with character names suggest, her literary heritage stretches back to Roman mythology. Lavinia (*purity* in Latin), the wife of Aeneas, was the daughter of Latinus, king of the Latins, the first Latin speakers, who were later incorporated into Rome. The allusion would be a mere curiosity but for the richly embedded themes of Latin study, lies, and liberal education in so much of Hellman's work, not least in this play, in which Lavinia aspires to be a teacher to poor black children in backwoods Alabama and exposes the lies upon which Marcus's racist edifice and business empire rest: "One lie, two lies, that's for all of us: but to pile lie upon lie and sin upon sin, and in the sight of God." Marcus's refusal not only to listen to her but also to allow her to establish her school leads her to expose the lies within lies that result in the crisis: "For ten years he swore a lie to me. I told God about that last night, and God's message said, 'Go, Lavinia, even if you have to tell the awful truth. If there is no other way, tell the truth.'" The God-crazed Lavinia is not a liberal figure, but like their mythological forebears she and Marcus are the progenitors of a new kind of society, one that is dynamic, materialistic, and intensely competitive.[60]

In *The Children's Hour*, Mrs. Mortar's complacency (she is *hardened*), her moral shortcomings, her lack of pity for her own niece, are ironically foreshadowed in the elision of Shylock. The cramming student, Lois, says admiringly, "I bet you were good at Latin, Mrs. Mortar." "Long ago, my dear, long ago," she replies, like Mrs. Tilford. "Now take your book over by the window and don't disturb our enjoyment of Shakespeare."[61] We ought not to accept her hierarchy of value (Shakespeare over Latin grammar in the opening scene). That there is a kinship between acting and lying is an ancient charge. Mrs. Mortar and the drama's central character, Mary, are connected by a particular way of acting that is both "bad" and "unnatural," but it is not bad because it is unnatural.

Shakespeare too is a tissue of artifice, but, as Portia says, "Nothing is good . . . without respect."[62]

The word "bad" permeates the play, as Carl Rollyson notes, but it is not, as he goes on to suggest, applied with "consistency."[63] On the contrary, the statements that Mary is "bad for the other girls," that it is "bad having [Mrs. Mortar] around children," that when Joe Cardin is in the house it "is a bad day," that running away from school is "a very bad thing to do," that Mary has a "bad temper," and that Karen and Martha, themselves, are "bad people" are wildly divergent usages if judged from a single vantage point; they are remarkable instead as instances of the contingency of value.[64] The bad is neither an objective property of things nor a subjective response to them but the product of numerous changing and interacting factors And in Hellman, terms of value are explicitly economic. The economic precariousness of the Wright-Dobie School for Girls both informs the personal relationships of those within the world of the private school and indicates external pressures that can alter those relationships. It also offers tacit commentary on what many in the 1930s perceived as a crisis for the nation, as public schools, weakened both by economic crisis and by a variety of hostile social and political forces, appeared unable to fulfill the promise that Horace Mann had envisioned of free universal public education as the basis of a just democracy.[65] As in all of Hellman's plays, every action in this play derives its value from interacting economies: Mrs. Tilford is a philanthropist who funds the school and "spoils" Mary. Martha and Karen struggle and fail to keep the school afloat. Mrs. Mortar is a charity case. Each evaluation depends on who is doing the evaluating, her temperament and situation. What "bad" means depends on how it applies to specific rules for action and concrete consequences.

Mary is the villain, though she is also from another angle the protagonist and was, for most audience members and for Hellman herself, the most compelling character in the play. She sets the plot in motion when she discovers a conversation that two classmates have overheard between Martha Dobie (one of the teachers and cofounder of the school) and her aunt, the failed actress who has been hired in an act of charity. Aunt Lily Mortar accuses her niece of being jealous of the other owner of the school, Karen Wright, on account of Karen's impending marriage. The student, with minor grudges from having been exposed in numerous lies and much motiveless malignity, runs home to her grandmother and launches the accusation that Martha's jealousy is "*unnatural.*" Mrs. Tilford, unsure at first just what to believe, reprimands her: "Stop using that silly word, Mary." "But," Mary replies, "that was the word *she* [Lily Mortar] kept using." Mary has "picked up some fine words."[66] In an uncanny foreshadowing of the disputes regarding justice, language, and personal history at the end of Hellman's life, the sensationalism of the lie is the drama's subject.

As Miss Wright tells Mary: "This kind of lying you do, makes everything wrong."[67] What, then, distinguishes one kind of lying from another? "All writing is contrived," Hellman remarked in an article for the *New York Times;* "some of it is contrived badly, some of it is contrived wonderfully."[68] Mrs. Mortar—the bad actress that, as her surname suggests, holds the play together—is the "source" of what is "unnatural" in the play. The indictment of Martha and Karen both is and is not a lie. Examining how it can be *both . . . and . . .* is vital to the moral work of the play, concerned, as it is, with the constitution of both sources and lies. "This is not really a play about lesbianism, but about a lie," Hellman told a reporter, before saying, in terms exactly contrary to those of Miss Wright: "The bigger the lie, the better, as always."[69] Unlike the upright teacher, Hellman the playwright, though referring to the economy of the play, seems glibly to collapse justification and truth, and to propose a relativistic or even nihilistic conception of moral truth, and she continually provokes readers by implying that "fiction" and "reality" are not separate categories: bigger lies are "always" better.

Yet rather than being provoked or letting the line drop as if it were a joke, we may hear in it a warning to resist a single definition of moral truth or, as Karen Wright's name suggests, what's "right." To imagine the magnitude of the lie is to imply both that the utterance and reception are part of the same verbal action and that the lie is commensurable, that its impact can be measured. The statement assumes a "pragmatic method," as William James described it: "You must bring out of each word its practical cash-value, set it at work within the stream of your experience. It appears less as a solution, then, than as a program for more work, and more particularly as an indication of the ways in which existing realities may be *changed*."[70] Whether Hellman, or Mary, would advocate a language of cost-benefit calculation is less important than the way of imagining the work of language in terms of a lived reality that collapses any difference between facts and values (though such cost-benefit calculation in language use is explicit in *Autumn Garden*, when the multilingual teenager Sophie Tuckerman demands that the word "blackmail" rather than "loan" be used in order to enable her to get out of town after she is compromised by a man in her bed).

Mary is not simply an antagonist or villain but also a figure for a positive, if dangerous and provocative, kind of creativity (as her symbolic name also suggests, an immaculate conception). Oscar Wilde is never far from this play, not only as a figure for the "love that dare not speak its name" and a failed libel suit but also as a model of both artistic and moral (antimoralistic) work. America's crude materialism, Wilde joked in his dialogue "The Decay of Lying," is "entirely due to that country having adopted for its national hero a man who, according to his own confession, was incapable of telling a lie, and it is not too much to say that the story of George Washington and the cherry-tree has done more harm, and in a shorter space of time, than any other moral tale in the whole of literature." He pleads, on the contrary, for characters like Mary, "the true liar, with his frank, fearless statements, his superb irresponsibility, his healthy, natural disdain of proof of any kind." What distinguishes one kind of lying from another? Wilde suggests that people without imagination "never rise beyond the level of misrepresentation," whereas a fine lie is "that which is its own evidence."[71] In spite of Mary's many limitations, she is a creative liar; her lie reveals Martha to herself. "There's something in you," Martha finally observes, "and you don't know it and you don't do anything about it. Suddenly a child gets bored and lies—and there you are, seeing it for the first time."[72] Mary, for reasons of her own, demanded change and was willing to say what no one else would. As Hellman remarked in an interview, "The charge made against [Martha] had some moral truth, although no actual truth."[73]

Destructive and irresponsible as it is, the lie establishes a new reality. It is an act of creative destruction. In the third act, after the school has been ruined, Karen and Joe attempt to imagine a future together and discover that their reality has been irrevocably altered on the level of ordinary language itself.

CARDIN. My God, we *can't* go on like this. Everything I say to you is made to mean something else. We don't talk like people anymore. Oh, let's get out of here as fast as we can.

KAREN *(as though she is finishing the sentence for him)*. And every word will have a new meaning. You think we'll be able to run away from that? Woman, child, love, lawyer—no words that we can use in safety anymore.[74]

That no words that can be used in safety is a way of saying that one does not have sole property in one's language, that the words one utters are never fully one's own, and that they are always susceptible to appropriation. However, the specific words Karen gives as examples of ordinary language are not just random. Ordinary as they are, "woman," "child," "love," and "lawyer" are ideologically loaded. They constitute a reality, and are constituted themselves, in different ways depending on their context. The crisis in language that Joe and Karen identify is not that, all of a sudden, there is a failure in the correspondence between words and their significance but that the enabling conventions, the grammar, or the language game has changed. If Joe and Karen are bewildered, their mistake was ever to have expected language to relate directly to objects and ideas.

In a 1968 interview, Hellman describes an evolution in her approach to teaching (at that point she was teaching writing at MIT) in linguistic terms: "Having started out in the belief in strict definitions, I've come to believe that I don't really think any of them are any good. I don't believe in sharp definitions any more."[75] Hellman is a provocative moral thinker, and her thinking about ordinary language has significant elements in common with contemporary developments in the philosophy of language and with some aspects of poststructuralist critiques of rationalism, the politics of supposedly objective description, and the notion that the world can ever be comprehended by a single order of meaning, like a single language or semantic code. Hellman, though considered to be finished as a playwright by 1960, when her last play, *Toys in the Attic,* was produced, and as a throwback in any case to the social realism of the 1930s and beyond, is deeply in touch with a central concern for the future of liberalism that is vital to the thought of American pragmatists, such as James and Dewey, who themselves went out of fashion in the postwar years only to be revived by a later generation. She expresses profound disillusionment with "liberalism" around 1952 (the year of Dewey's death and of her appearance before the House Un-American Activities Committee), but her engagement with the way in which the language of liberalism is related to its ends remained a central topic in her writing.[76] For Dewey, in a short essay titled "The Future of Liberalism" (1935), the central problem of the mid-twentieth century is dogmatism and the use of force to effect change, against which "the liberal is bound to emphasize the crucial importance of the means and methods by which change is brought about." The means cannot be separated from the ends, which are "ends" only in the sense in which the word does not signify abstractions.[77]

Lies and Latin from Hellman to Harry Potter

In J. K. Rowling's Harry Potter books, a word of Latin literally transforms the world. The word *accio* (to call or send for) brings any item to hand, even from miles away. Say, "*Expecto patronum*" (I need or await my protector), and the protector appears and not only saves the imperiled but also warms the atmosphere. One word of Latin can wipe your memory clean or bring back memories you never knew you had. On October 19, 2007, during an event featuring Rowling at Carnegie Hall, a young fan asked if the headmaster of Hogwarts School of Witchcraft and Wizardry would ever find true love, and she said, "I always saw Dumbledore as gay." Global reaction was instantaneous. On the one hand, some claimed, this news changed everything, some readers going so far as to say that this news ruined the books for them. On the other hand, many said it changed nothing. Readers can find suggestions specifically in the fictional Rita Skeeter's libelous biography "The Life and Lies of Albus Dumbledore."[78] In real-life newspapers, Dumbledore's private life trumped news of war in Iraq, forest fires in California, and the decline of the dollar. Most of all, it has been noted that the question of the headmaster's sexual orientation is especially important, harmful, or scandalous because it changes or corrupts a book for children.[79]

Maybe Latin and the classics can teach us something about Dumbledore's love life. Latin, after all, is the esoteric but immensely practical language of wizardry. It is the language of spells. Its abstruse appeal and weird power ironically evoke what troubles many contemporary American Catholics most about Pope Benedict's proposal to bring back the Latin Mass—it's ironic because many of the same people find risible the pope's opposition, when still Cardinal Ratzinger, to what he called the "subtle seductions" of the Harry Potter novels.[80] Curiously, Rowling's spells do not use the imperative form of the verbs but the first-person present form, eliding the differ-ence between demanding and describing. Spells are words that make things happen. But for most readers they are words that have totally lost both the denotations and the connotations that they had in a fully formed, syntactical language. They have been desemanticized; so these individual words func-tion as a kind of code, and in this respect anyway, the parallel world of the magical and muggle communities does not seem far different from the "straight" and the "gay."

These parallel realities also, of course, suggest those most politically loaded during Hellman and McCarthy's life-times, the communist and anticommunist. From the 1920s through the 1950s, when homosexual experience happened much more deeply underground than it does today, another intricately related parallel universe was that of spying, as well as a parallel, so-called Aesopian language. In recounting his childhood, the Soviet spy, closeted homosexual, editor, and translator Whittaker Chambers writes of a new stage of self-consciousness marked by a turn from parlor theatricals he loathed for the "indignity of this public exposure," to the study of language, which followed when "nature" set him "on the way to manhood" and "organic turmoil" in high school:

> I had always been docile and obedient. I became
> impudent and rebellious, and one of the school
> mischief-makers. . . . I had never cursed, but, with
> an effort, I acquired the knack and found that
> there was nothing easier. I loathed foul language,
> but I forced myself to use it. It was almost harder
> for me not to learn than to learn, but I made a
> brave effort and soon my marks tumbled to just

above failing. Only in English and Latin, when the
spell of Vergil overtook me, did my marks hold up
despite myself.[81]

For Chambers, the literary forms of Latin and English are the
replacement or supplement for "foul," unsanctioned language. He turns tellingly not to the rhetorician Cicero or the
general and politician Caesar but to the poet and, most significant, Dante's guide out of the dark wood, Virgil. Chambers too, like Dumbledore and Virgil, is a character in a book,
Witness, which has been and can be read without imagining
the most intimate details of a non-straight private life. He too
had a closeted sexual identity that contributed directly to his
major intervention into the public sphere of Cold War America, as his biographer Sam Tanenhaus has shown. However,
unlike Dumbledore, Chambers is also the author of the book
in which he appears as a character (his autobiography), and
his book manifests the self-consciousness about (bad) language, about language learning, and about childhood development characteristic of Americans of his, Hellman's, and
McCarthy's generation. As a boy, Chambers was highly alert
to the multiplicity of languages, foul and clean, circulating in
Progressive Era America; the study of English and Latin
grammars together, therefore, appears as a way of rooting at
the very foundations of reality that, he clearly believes, helps
to explain his own importance as an interpreter and repre-
senter of his historical reality. Knowing whether Chambers
told the truth or not in the case of Alger Hiss in 1949 (and now
whether he was gay or straight) remains a hot-button issue in
the conflict between liberal and conservative America.

The immensely appealing Dumbledore, wise, bearded,
ugly yet seductive, most resembles in body and spirit—and in

his teasing pedagogical practice—the greatest teacher of the ancient world, the brave and ironic idealist Socrates. Dumbledore and Socrates both teach and demonstrate a relationship between love and knowledge, but as the deaths to which both willfully submit also suggest, they do not have a place in a liberal society. At the end of the *Symposium,* the satyr-like Socrates wraps up his eloquent treatment of love and beauty by asking: "What if men had the eyes to see the true beauty— the divine beauty I mean, pure and clear and unalloyed, not clogged with the pollutions of mortality, and all the colors and vanities of human life . . . bringing into being and educating true creations of virtue and not idols only?"[82] Two minutes later, there is a great knocking at the door, and into the lounging group of thinkers and lovers barges the intoxicated general Alcibiades, who proceeds to press his sexual attraction to Socrates. Why disrupt, Rita Skeeter–like, the gathering of Greek idealists with such a depraved and self-interested intrusion?

The value of injecting the word that changes one reality for another or, to be more accurate, exposes one reality for being what it is—*one* reality—democratizes the space, upsetting the hierarchy. This structure characterizes every teacher-student relationship, turning it into a competitive arena in which the "will to power" is not a corrupt desire to dominate others (though that may be part of it), or an impulse to dethrone the real Truth and set up one's own personal version. Rather, it is an acknowledgment of multiplicity and conflict in the arena where truth is constituted, a confrontation that evokes a contrast not only between the modern Nietzsche and the ancient Socrates but also between Lillian Hellman and Mary McCarthy, an age-old debate that has had highly particular historical resonance (and practical effects), which

Richard Lanham has described as a quarrel between "rhetorical man" and "serious man."[83] The former manipulates reality; the latter describes it. The former is an actor without a stable identity; the latter possesses an authentic central self. This pair of characters may have been around for a long time, but in the first third of the twentieth century, their opposition spoke directly to the character of a society under the pressure of massive change, in demographic and technological terms, a world of social, economic, and geographic mobility that both Hellman and McCarthy experienced firsthand to jarring and instructive effect.

But we can find Latin invoked to indicate the awakening of race consciousness even into the civil rights period in as unlikely a place as *The Autobiography of Malcolm X*. There the author speaks of his self-rehabilitation and rebirth in prison where he studied Latin in a correspondence course. Then, most surprisingly, he describes his relationship to his teacher and mentor, the minister Elijah Muhammad, as one of adoration, "from the Latin word for adore, *adorare*." With his Latin etymology Malcolm X explains that he wants to convey an intensity of meaning, "much more than our 'adore.'" The Latin word, he says, evokes "worship." But his narrative has already signaled a crisis to come later in the book, and this use of Latin both hints at disillusionment and indicates the corruption that arises from the failure to look closely at language. As he writes later, "I love language. I wish I were an accomplished linguist." Latin etymology conveys the seriousness of the student and expresses what proves to be an ironic homage to the teacher. In this narrative of self-discovery, the reference to Latin in the context of Malcolm X's key pedagogical relationship signals his awakened self-consciousness, but it is only a provisional, not a final, self. At the time of composing the autobiography, he had long since broken with Elijah Muhammad, having discovered his teacher to be neither "sincere" nor "true" but sexually promiscuous, a "faker," and a spreader of lies that, as he anticipated, would lead to his own death.[84]

When William Wyler directed and Lillian Hellman rewrote the script of *The Children's Hour* for the 1960 film version, which had taken on a new allegorical significance in a 1953 revival on Broadway during the anticommunist witchhunts, a French lesson replaces the Latin lesson of the play. This seemingly minor change made sense in 1960 because at that point few spectators studied Latin in school. However, to have changed this detail, so insignificant in terms of the plot, is to have lost a sense that what was at stake in the 1934 play is not sexual freedom, dishonesty, or puritanical social mores but questions about the formation of the liberal subject. In this respect, the play still has an important currency. The word "private" is itself a Latin word, *privat-us,* and its ancient historical connotations are largely negative; to be private is to be withdrawn from public life or deprived of office. *The Children's Hour,* a drama about a libel suit, anticipates a continuing constitutional debate over privacy in the sexual realm that intensified in the 1970s and 1980s. High-profile cases during this period include *Eisenstadt v. Baird* (1972), about the right of unmarried people to possess contraception, *Roe v. Wade* (1973), which applied the right to privacy to abortion, the Supreme Court's affirmation of a Virginia sodomy statute in *John Doe v. Commonwealth's Attorney* (1976), and *Bowers v. Hardwick* (1986), in which the Supreme Court upheld a Georgia law that criminalized oral and anal sex between consenting adults in private. As Daniel Kornstein has convincingly argued, "The specific subject matter of the libel [in *The*

Children's Hour] forces us to examine the Constitution's as well as our own attitudes . . . toward all forms of private sexual conduct, and, more generally, toward privacy and tolerance of individual differences in society. Tolerance of different sexual needs breeds tolerance of different political creeds, an issue at the heart of the individual's relationship to society."[85] However, although it is true that *The Children's Hour* can enable a reexamination of the Constitution's as well as our own attitudes toward privacy, an ideology of "tolerance of different sexual needs" is not in the play itself; it is a projection of the reader. Instead, *The Children's Hour* illustrates the failure, because of the law, of a dynamic of competing privacies that is essential to a healthy liberal culture.

III
Words of Love

I was so desperate to find an abortionist that, foolishly, I
asked if he knew such a doctor. He found one immediately,
swore himself to secrecy, and I made an appointment with
the doctor for the following week. The morning following
Donald's vow of secrecy, every member of the firm called me
into his office to offer money, to ask the name of the father,
to guess that it was one of them, to make plans and plots for
help I didn't want. I was angry about that and so, throughout
the good-natured questioning, I sat sullen, staring into space,
refusing answers, trying not to think about the vicarious,
excited snoopiness I knew was mixed with the kindness.
—Lillian Hellman, *An Unfinished Woman*, 1969

Abortionists, she had always heard, did their task much more
proficiently than licensed doctors, and why shouldn't they—
they had more practice at it. In two days, it would be over.
After it was over, she might possibly tell John. Perhaps she
owed him the truth, so that he could hate her if he chose
to. . . . Yet it would be good to have truth between them again.
—Mary McCarthy, *A Charmed Life*, 1955

On a steamy Monday evening in June 1925, after a day of work as a manuscript reader at Horace Live-right's publishing firm in New York and six months before she married Arthur Kober, the nineteen-year-old Lillian Hellman visited a Coney Island "half-house" and, with the doctor's mother serving as assistant and no anesthetic, had the first of seven abortions. All month she had expected to be fired for misplacing a manuscript, but the abortion seemed to improve her position; the editors took a new interest in her. On Tuesday, she returned to work at the five-story brownstone, located in the speakeasy district of midtown Manhattan. Horace, a hard-drinking playboy, gave her a glass of midmorning champagne; his partners, Donald Friede and Julian Messner, were solicitous but puzzled. "I don't understand what you're about," said Julian. Friede pressed Hellman to reveal the name of the father, but she refused. "What are you made of, Lilly?" asked Liveright's head editor, T. R. Smith. "Pickling spice," she said, "and nothing nice." Smith's patronizing question and Hellman's sarcastic, angry answer indicate a contest of assumptions about women's autonomy in the male-dominated workplace, about "respectable girls," and about protecting prospective mothers from their own moral weaknesses. The form of Hellman's language, a nursery rhyme, makes her as difficult to pin down as a constitutional right to privacy. "That kind of talk," said Smith. "I don't understand you kids."[1] In 1969, when Hellman won the National Book Award for *An Unfinished Woman,* which includes this anecdote, abortions were illegal in New York, which had one of the strictest laws in the nation.

Hellman's "kind of talk" points to one of the frameworks, or models, of moral language that provoked Mary McCarthy and prompted the 1980 libel suit. She and Smith do not speak the same language. Her oblique reference to privacy (refusing to say what she's "made of") suggests a way of thinking about how language shapes and is shaped by particular interests and assumptions. The meaning of privacy depends on its context and usage. In legal terms, a "right to privacy" might refer to the right to control information about oneself or to the right to make personal decisions. These privacy rights are closely related—perhaps, since the 1960s, two parts of a broader concept of privacy—but they are not equivalent. Hellman and McCarthy often seem to be speaking conflicting languages of privacy, particularly when expressing what they both regard ironically as "words of love." In legal terms, Hellman tends to speak a language of informational privacy; McCarthy emphasizes the right to make personal decisions. But this legal schema also breaks down. For female authors of their generation, privacy concerns spoke to relations between freedom of expression (publication), on the one hand, and freedom to control one's procreation, on the other. Far from avoiding ambiguities that arise from conflicting vocabularies of privacy in America, I want to examine strategic points where ambiguities arise in Hellman's and McCarthy's divergent attitudes. In this chapter, I focus on the language of sex and reproduction, birth control and abortion, as it was published, censored, and otherwise constrained for women who came of age between first- and second-wave feminism.

Hellman explicitly positions herself between these movements in women's history. At the beginning of the publishing and abortion chapter of *An Unfinished Woman*, in a style that would make her an equivocal feminist icon in the 1970s, she remarks:

> By the time I grew up the fight for the emancipation of women, their rights under the law, in the

office, in bed, was stale stuff. My generation didn't
think much about the place or the problems of
women, were not conscious that the designs we
saw around us had so recently been formed that
we were still part of the formation. . . . By the
time we were nineteen or twenty we had either
slept with a man or pretended that we had. And we
were suspicious of the words of love.[2]

In contrast to activists such as Margaret Sanger, who
were reared in the nineteenth century on notions of scientific
progress and positive knowledge, Hellman speaks for a generation that is as conscious of being shaped by as shaping
history. Emancipation is bound up with inescapable entanglements both in the office and in the bedroom. Hellman
conflates them "under the law," as if to insist on the breakdown of public-private distinctions and the impossibility of
defining these zones against one another. She indicates the extent to which the language of legal rights—specifically, by 1969,
the constitutional argument regarding the "right to privacy"—
has come to define the contours of intimate experience; and,
more important, she suggests its limits. Self-expression is
constrained by the available language, but like the nursery
rhyme, it can evade constraint in being elliptical. Throughout
her work, Hellman depicts individuals who are part of the
formation that they themselves aim to form. They are suspicious not only of "words of love" but also of idealistic language in general.[3] Their independence often takes the form of
experience that is unspoken or unspeakable. As a result, they
dramatize a particular tension built into the eclectic justification of a constitutional "right to privacy" between, among

others, the First Amendment protection of free speech and the Fifth Amendment protection against self-incrimination.

Mary McCarthy was a lapsed Catholic, a product of the radical 1930s, and an author who seemed bent on shocking her readers. Her son, Reuel Wilson, says, "Overall, she had a possibly exhibitionistic tendency (sometimes self-destructive) to provoke controversy. She saw this as truth-telling."[4] She also had multiple abortions and little sympathy for feminists. She hated Lillian Hellman, partly due to her perception that Hellman's repeated invocations of privacy, in her 1952 appearance before the House Un-American Activities Committee, in her extremely selective personal histories, and as a protection in the 1980 libel suit, shielded hypocrisy and lies. She tried and failed to have Hellman's libel suit dismissed on the grounds that Hellman was not a private but a public figure. Hellman and McCarthy's dispute about "every word" reflects their respective attitudes toward and struggles for reproductive freedom, by which I mean both the ability to reproduce themselves in words and the freedom to choose to prevent or terminate a pregnancy. Female authors of their generation often made this connection explicitly. The conclusion of Tess Slesinger's autobiographical novel, *The Unpossessed* (1934), for instance, centers on the "little illegality" of Margaret Flinders, who has an abortion in order to "bear a Magazine."[5] These forms of reproduction are deeply interrelated not only in women's experience throughout the twentieth century but also in law. Legal theorist Roy Lucas, who in 1969 filed the first abortion rights lawsuit in New York, argued that a woman's right to decide not to remain pregnant was a fundamental constitutional right like the freedom of speech.[6] Focusing on how women of their generation wrote about birth control and abortion in conjunction with publishing and censorship can help us to understand how their lives, like laws, are embedded in the writing and vice versa.

The subjects of sex and reproductive rights were vital not only to these women's lives but also to how they represented them—the lives and the language are inseparable. Hellman's account of her abortion in chapter 4 of *An Unfinished Woman* is an autonomous episode within the larger story. Focusing on conception in a literary sense, it both advances the narrative of her necessarily unfinished life (a condition of autobiography) and stands, in itself, for the whole work. Placing the abortion in the context of Liveright's, where she had to sprint up and down the long staircases to keep from being pinched or thrown by a clutching hand on a leg, is a way of reflecting on the project of life-writing, respecting yet evading literary and personal constraints. Conflating literary and biological reproduction, Hellman's chapter is fully alive to the irony of situating the intimacy of her sexual experience, her struggle to make choices about her own body and her capacity to control her own reproductive "rights," in America's premier publishing house, felicitously named Live-rights (Hellman never uses the firm's full name: Boni and Liveright).

The primary right that preoccupied the publisher was freedom of expression. Boni and Liveright published William Faulkner, Sigmund Freud, Ernest Hemingway, and Hart Crane, as well as anarchist Alexander Berkman. They continually pushed the boundaries of existing censorship laws. Theodore Dreiser moved to their publishing house in 1925, when Hellman was there, after his previous American publisher failed to stand up to the New York Society for the Suppression of Vice. His novel *An American Tragedy* centers on the murder of a pregnant woman who cannot procure an abortion.

Though threatened with legal action by the Boston district attorney for endangering the "morals of youth," Liveright sent Donald Friede (who couldn't keep Hellman's abortion secret) to Boston, where on April 15 he sold a copy of *An American Tragedy* to Lieutenant Daniel J. Hines of the vice squad. Friede was arrested, booked, found guilty, and fined.[7] In 1921 T. R. Smith, Liveright's head editor (the one who asked what Hellman was made of), had published the most comprehensive collection of erotic verse ever compiled in the United States. His three-volume anthology *Poetica Erotica* also was censored, and large amounts of material deleted from subsequent editions.

In 1926 Liveright published E. E. Cummings's collection of poems *Is 5*, which ridiculed John S. Sumner, executive secretary for the New York Society for the Suppression of Vice. Sumner had raided Liveright's in the early 1920s and targeted Cummings's 1921 war novel *The Enormous Room*.[8] In 1927 Liveright published Cummings's play *Him*, which opens with a doctor anaesthetizing a pregnant woman, Me. The doctor later becomes a censor, John Rutter, "of the Society for the Contraception of Vice," who emerges from the theater to stifle profanity in a play-within-the-play. The work concludes with the performance of a pregnant exotic dancer, who, on unveiling, turns out to be Me, holding a newborn babe, which fills Him, the playwright and father, with terror.[9] The recurrent figure of the pregnant woman in the work of male authors of the 1920s suggests a fraught combination of masculine wish fulfillment, the image of male potency, and, insofar as the pregnant woman causes terror or leads to murder, anxiety at feminine expressiveness.

In 1929, in *People v. Friede*, Donald Friede was prosecuted for publishing Radclyffe Hall's *Well of Loneliness*. In

1928 Friede had left Liveright and founded Covici Friede, where Mary McCarthy later worked. The judge found against Friede because the novel dealt shamelessly with the theme of lesbian lovemaking and therefore was morally "depraved" and "obscene."[10] The decision was overturned on appeal. The ongoing lawsuits and the numerous raids of the vice squad indicate the oppressive conditions of censorship in the 1920s. But they also illustrate the mutually reinforcing relationship between censorship and a particular (liberal and Freudian) model of self-expression that Hellman treats with irony as the "excited snoopiness" of the courageous male publishers. In subverting the social-welfare model of the law, Liveright's editors and authors also help to legitimize it. After all, a nominal aim of the vice squad is to protect individuals (like Lilly) from inequalities of status and power in the liberal workplace.[11] When liberty trumps equality, a central paradox emerges: to promote Lilly's sexual freedom (but really their own), the publishers insist on violating her privacy. What is a girl to do? In a word, she lies. In *An Unfinished Woman,* Horace, Donald, Julian, and Tom themselves embody a form of literary and social constraint that leads to a central instance of her literary lying, a self-reflexive form of storytelling that suggests a way out of the double trap of the invasive liberal workplace and the oppressive protections of the New York Society for the Suppression of Vice.

After failing to understand Hellman's behavior, Tom Smith turns back to a manuscript, but then he resumes the interrogation, linking her to the text or texts in general. "What's your generation about?" he asks. Lillian doesn't know. "How many men have you slept with?" he pursues. "Three hundred and thirty-three, Tom, not counting my brothers and uncles who don't much like to be counted. . . . And it's none of your business." The editor decides that she belongs to a new generation, that Liveright needs "to publish it," and that she "better start telling us about it."[12] So at the next wild party at Horace's duplex apartment, Smith invites Samuel Hopkins Adams, author of the popular 1923 pulp romance and movie *Flaming Youth*. (Announcing his anticensorious intentions in an opening letter to the novel, the pseudonymous Dr. Warner Fabian contrasts himself to women writers, who, "when they write of women, evade and conceal and palliate.")[13] At the party, Smith shuts Hellman and two of her friends in a small library–guest room with Adams, who begins by asking, "How old were you when you had your first sexual encounter?" The young women become angry and resentful and drunk. So they start to tell stories. They lie. Hellman says, "I had my first encounter in a chicken coop in New Orleans when I was four years old." As the interrogation draws to a close, they discover that the editor has locked them in. The middle-aged (male) author finds it difficult to escape through the bathroom window and down the fire escape, but not the young women. He angrily tries to grab the leg of Hellman's athletic friend Marie-Louise, who manages to reach the sidewalk and then to release her friends, bringing the anecdote to a close.[14]

This episode can help us not only to take another look at Hellman's reputation as a liar but also to understand how the difficulty of defining a right to privacy, epitomized by the Supreme Court's notoriously nebulous *Griswold v. Connecticut* decision that established its constitutionality in 1965, challenges conventions of reading and writing. As Hellman showed in her first play, *The Children's Hour* (1934), the right to privacy applies both to invasions of the bedroom and to the harms caused by defamation. Like the law regulating birth control, libel law pertinent to the Hellman-McCarthy case underwent a significant change in the mid-1960s as privacy became both more important and harder to define. Both areas of law were shaped by evolving standards of privacy in landmark cases, and both placed restrictions on free expression. As libel is about the legal consequences of telling stories, so is the law regulating abortion, which controls a medical practice by compelling, allowing, restricting, or forbidding women to tell stories about their lives, whether to doctors, healthcare workers, parents, spouses, politicians, each other, or the public at large.

The history of birth control and abortion is a history of a particular form of intimate storytelling. In her autobiography, Margaret Sanger (1879–1966) recounts the affecting tales of poverty and sickly children of the poor women who visited her first clinic in Brooklyn. "Jews and Christians, Protestants and Roman Catholics alike made their confessions to us, whatever they may have professed at home or in church. Some did not dare talk this over with their husbands; some came urged on by their husbands.... [To] the nurse, and myself, these women told the constantly reiterated but ever varying story of low wages and high rent.... Fine, hopeful men came to us with stories of wives broken in health and husbands broken in spirit."[15] As Sanger repeatedly emphasizes, this storytelling is both socially and legally proscribed. Justice Harry Blackmun's 1973 *Roe v. Wade* decision maintains the importance of sharing information in procuring an abortion. According to Blackmun, the right to privacy "is broad enough to encompass a woman's decision whether or not to terminate her pregnancy," but a pregnant woman does not have an absolute constitutional right to "abortion on demand." The state has an interest in "safeguarding health, in maintaining medical standards, and in protecting potential life" after the first trimester. In a related abortion case, *Doe v. Bolton,* Blackmun conceded that it was the woman's prerogative to make "the fundamental personal decision whether or not to bear an unwanted child" but added that "the pregnant woman cannot be isolated in her privacy." Ultimately, it is on the "best medical judgment" of the attending physician that the abortion decision rests. Despite asserting the woman's autonomy, Blackmun notes that the woman and her responsible physician will consider all factors in consultation. Faced with a reluctant physician, a woman seeking an abortion needs to be a compelling storyteller. Norma McCorvey was a tiny, twenty-three-year-old single mother when she became pregnant for the third time in 1969. Having difficulty aborting the pregnancy in Dallas, where abortion was a crime, she lied that she had been raped. The doctor still refused. McCorvey became "Jane Roe" of *Roe v. Wade.* In his decision, Blackmun was vague about balancing the interests of women, doctors, and the state or specifying what those interests are. Instead he fostered a structure of constraints that continue to be revised as partisan agendas ebb and flow.[16]

Between the 1920s and the 1970s, models of storytelling changed along with the identities of the storytellers. At the same time, abortion came to be seen as the quintessential women's issue—"the right of a woman to control her own body and life"—for which women lawyers were uniquely qualified to speak.[17] The historical experiences behind Hellman's abortion/publishing chapter, read in light of the late 1960s when they were written, reflect a transformation of what lawyers call the "domain of intimacy" in the middle decades of the twentieth century. During those years, Americans seriously debated the importance of marriage and reproductive sex, gender hierarchies, and sexual harassment in the workplace.

The erosion of a rigid dichotomy of the public and the private and the questioning of assumptions about the law's neutrality led to more self-reflexive, nuanced, and, some would say, female models of self-expression.[18] As a woman who manipulated legal, social, and literary distinctions between public and private life, Hellman epitomizes these developments. She challenges us to rethink our assumptions about representation and regulation, publication and interpretation, relations between language, which people share, and more discrete features of their personhood: their property, their bodies, their memories.

Like America's first official censor, Anthony Comstock, Hellman and McCarthy approach reproduction and sex in terms of literature, and literature in terms of sexual reproduction. As literary themes, abortion, contraception, and the hazards of childbearing pervade their autobiographical works, suggesting that they have particular explanatory power. In *Pentimento,* Hellman pulls a prank that involves inscribing, rolling, and distributing condoms at a cocktail party (condoms were exempted from certain birth-control restrictions because they protected men from venereal disease). The elaborate prank takes many days (and pages) to pull off, though it seems incidental to the bigger project of Hellman's life-writing. She notes that the joke involving the condoms went on during "bad days, growing dangerous," as Samuel Goldwyn's legal department asked to see her about something or other and she skipped work at the studio. After evading Sam Goldwyn himself, who demanded that she come to see him, her writing and condom-rolling partner George Haight calls her "a dope and a liar." Hellman wittily and salaciously objects, "I was not meant to spend my life on condoms."[19] She concludes the episode by noting that she and George never spoke about condoms again.

An *Unfinished Woman* opens with Hellman's own problematic birth and her mother's "dangerously botched childbearing." Julia Hellman (whose name goes to the mother of
the lost child in "Julia") never had another pregnancy; twenty-
one years later her anxiety for then-pregnant Lilly gives way to
relief when her daughter loses the child, too. In another early
episode, an Italian housepainter whose bride died in childbirth eyes the teenage Lilly as a possible replacement. In chapter 2, she talks about sex with her virgin aunts, consultants to
many neighborhood girls before their first intercourse. They
advise a glass of ice water before the sacred act and three sips
during it. When Lillian marries, they telegram: "FORGET
ABOUT THE GLASS OF ICE WATER TIMES HAVE CHANGED." The
humorous tone and apparent openness contrast with an ambi-
ence of secrecy and euphemism associated with sex. The Comstock Laws ensured that virtually no information on birth
control was available to young women in America. (Sanger,
America's leading birth-control advocate, had to go to Europe
to study the subject effectively in 1915.) Hellman uses the language of secrecy to tell her father about her first menstruation.
She describes her sexual coming of age, after running away
from home and lying about her origins, when her father picks
her up: "Papa, I'll tell you a secret. I've had very bad cramps
and I'm beginning to bleed. I'm changing life."[20]

Autobiography, memoir, and confession make personal
information public, but in doing so they challenge assumptions about the value of personal autonomy and the possibility of creating a complete and independent life. To define and
thereby create a notion of private life depends paradoxically on publishing it, on resituating the living person in
shared words. In publishing seemingly intimate details of
life, these genres also raise questions about how selective the

self-disclosure may be. Who determines what is worth saying? How does a female employee of a masculine publishing house establish norms of nonintrusion? In understanding privacy as the ability of an individual to control what can be known about him or her, we need to examine our assumptions about what an individual is, where she or he begins and ends, or what it means to say that someone remains "unfinished." In the second half of this chapter, I focus on Mary McCarthy's extreme ambivalence about personal autonomy and independence and show how her severe critique of aspects of privacy, such as privacy's protection of wrongdoing, is interwoven with her hatred of Lillian Hellman. The libel case against McCarthy with which Hellman ended her life speaks directly to debates about abortion, birth control, and free speech (and their interrelatedness), subjects both writers addressed in various literary forms. Both Hellman and McCarthy had numerous abortions, gaining intimate experience of the issue that, perhaps more than any other, has charged American public discourse with moralistic and partisan rancor in the past few decades.[21] Yet their similar experiences also illuminate their differences. In the following pages I ask why they made those decisions and why they wrote about birth control and abortion as they did. Answering these questions sheds new light on what McCarthy meant in saying that every word Hellman wrote was a lie and what was at stake in Hellman's suing her for libel.

The Right to Remain Silent

From a legal standpoint, birth control, abortion, and publishing were lumped together for nearly a hundred years in the United States under the Comstock Laws, an umbrella term derived from a bill pushed through Congress in 1873 by Anthony Comstock, the first official censor of the United States. In addition to banning contraceptives, the Comstock Act (and the state restrictions that it inspired) banned the distribution of information on abortion: "Every written or printed card, letter, circular, book, pamphlet, advertisement, or notice of any kind giving information, directly or indirectly . . . for the procuring or producing of abortion . . . or how or by what means conception may be prevented or abortion produced."[22] Comstock meant the prevention of conception in the broadest possible sense. Twenty-four states passed such prohibitions. The Comstock Laws defined contraceptive *information* as "obscene," placing birth control and abortion under the same interdiction as pornographic, medical, sociological, and indeed all forms of literature.[23] Although the federal legislation dealt only with the mails and public carriers, state laws were more restrictive. Section 1142 of the New York Penal Code stated that no one could give information to prevent conception to anyone for any reason.

Birth control activist Margaret Sanger saw her fight for women's rights in terms of the First Amendment to the Constitution: as freedom of speech. At the time, however, the courts did not see it that way. In founding her journal, the *Woman Rebel,* in 1914 and aiming to challenge Postmaster General Anthony Comstock, Sanger included articles not only on women's health, child labor, and the unhappy results of having too many children but also on anarchism and political assassination: "People of whom no one had ever heard turned up to offer advice on every possible subject," she wrote. "They challenged, defied me to publish them in the name of free speech! It got to be something of a riot, but a lark nevertheless. I accepted all challenges and printed everything."[24] Though she disparaged the anarchist writings as silly stuff, the latter, not the former, would prompt the Supreme Court's first major twentieth-century opinion on free speech, when Justices Oliver Wendell Holmes and Louis Brandeis dissented in the 1919 espionage case *Abrams v. United States*. Unlike the Comstock Act, which seemed to be about "private" life, the Espionage and Sedition Acts, passed by Congress in 1917 and 1918, made it a crime to "utter, print, write or publish any disloyal, profane, scurrilous, or abusive language" about the form of government of the United States, the Constitution, the armed forces or the flag.[25] In his opinion, Justice Holmes articulated his famous rule "that the best test of truth is the power of the thought to get itself accepted in the competition of the market."[26] This test applied to nominally political topics but not to sex. Until the 1960s, the protection of sexual privacy, like libel, was considered to be outside the scope of the First Amendment.[27]

The *Woman Rebel* was banned, and in August 1914 the US attorney's office in New York charged Sanger with four counts of violating the Comstock statutes. Rather than prepare a defense, she composed a sixteen-page statement entitled "Family Limitation," arranged for the printing of a hundred thousand copies, and fled to England, where she studied in the British Museum under the tutelage of sexologist and social reformer Havelock Ellis. In her article "Comstockery in America," she writes that "American woman, born on American soil, must leave the 'land of the free and home of the brave' to escape imprisonment for discussing the subject of Family Limitation."[28] But Sanger continued to challenge censorship at home. With her case pending, she returned to the United States when her husband was convicted in New York for giving the pamphlet "Family Limitation" to a decoy sent by Comstock. Though the nation's first birth control advocacy group, the National Birth Control League, refused to support her case, the press took up the issue, and polls showed Americans increasingly receptive to "birth control," the phrase she coined.[29] On September 21, 1915, Comstock died. The prominent lawyer Samuel Untermeyer urged Sanger to sign a statement that she would not break the law again. With that, he believed, he could convince the court not to send her to jail. But Sanger replied, "It's the principle involved. This information is not obscene."[30] She insisted on forcing the trial and on defending herself, prompting the *New York Sun* to comment on "the anomaly of a prosecution loath to prosecute and a defendant anxious to be tried." In the face of public opinion stoked by American journalists such as John Reed and Walter Lippmann—"the 'story' was played up by the newspapers from coast to coast"—and an open letter to President Woodrow Wilson signed by notable English authors William Archer, Gilbert Murray, and H. G. Wells, the government dropped all charges in February 1916.[31] That October Sanger opened America's first public birth control clinic at 46 Amboy Street in the Brownsville section of Brooklyn, New York, only to be arrested when an undercover agent of the vice squad purchased a copy of her tract *What Every Girl Should Know.* For another fifty years, her battle with Comstock and his legacy, taken up by the Catholic Church, would be carried on by birth control advocates.

Connecticut, Comstock's home state, would become a key testing ground. In 1940, in a nationally heralded case, the Connecticut Supreme Court handed down a decision against the dissemination of birth control information in *State of Connecticut v. Roger B. Nelson et al.,* based on a statute that Comstock and circus man P. T. Barnum had pushed through the Connecticut legislature in 1879. The 1940 ruling effectively closed down birth control clinics in the state for the next twenty-five years, but it also focused national attention on Connecticut's struggle to legalize birth control. This historic campaign culminated in 1965 when the Supreme Court first established a constitutional "right to privacy" in the landmark *Griswold v. Connecticut* decision. That decision referred to no less than six amendments to the Constitution. Throughout the 1950s challenges to Connecticut's anticontraception statute had been largely based on First and Fourteenth Amendment grounds, and initially these were the basis of the defense of Estelle Griswold (executive director of the Planned Parenthood League of Connecticut). The Fourteenth Amendment protects persons from invasions of their privacy by the states. But increasingly other guarantees of the Bill of Rights were seen as pivotal to a right to privacy, including the Fourth, which guarantees the right of people to be secure in their persons, houses, papers, and effects against unreasonable searches and seizures, and the Fifth, which protects people from self-incrimination. Following a groundbreaking 1962 law review article by New York University law professor Norman Redlich, constitutional experts also turned to the Ninth Amendment: "The enumeration in the Constitution, of certain rights, shall not be construed to deny or disparage others retained by the people." The Constitution guarantees rights that it does not explicitly articulate. As Redlich put it, "Words were considered inadequate to define all of the rights which man should possess in a free society."[32] Three years later, writing in extraordinarily metaphorical language for the majority in *Griswold,* Justice William O. Douglas claimed that although the Constitution does not specifically name a right to privacy, "specific guarantees in the Bill of Rights have penumbras, formed by emanations from those guarantees that help give them life and substance."[33]

Critics complain not only that language used to justify the "right to privacy" is vague, which is not particularly unusual, but, more important, that it does not refer to the words of the Constitution at all. This is the core of legal scholar John Hart Ely's famous critique that the *Roe* decision fails to specify whether the right involved arises from the Ninth or the Fourteenth Amendment.[34] Of course, the Ninth Amendment's protections are essentially negative anyway, in that they refer to rights not otherwise explicitly named, but Ely's point is that the Ninth and Fourteenth Amendments are procedural or formal rather than substantive. To this, some critics such as Stanley Fish reply, the form of the law is always also substantive, already shaped by the perspectives and morals of those who wrote and interpreted it.[35] But the point I wish to emphasize here is the importance not of formal aspects of the law but of lacunae, of the real value of absence, silence, and evasion that are built into our constitutional and, by extension, our imperfect public discourse. Not all is transparent. Nor, according to Hellman, should it be. In particular, to understand the fight for reproductive rights in America in the 1960s, it is vital to recognize a shift in attention from what people could say or write to what they did *not,* could not, or should not say.

The key to the development of sexual freedoms, such as the freedom to choose to use birth control or procure an abortion, the so-called right to privacy, is inseparable from hostility to free expression of the press. The "right to privacy" was first articulated as a doctrine of tort law by two Boston lawyers, Samuel Warren and Louis Brandeis, in an 1890

Harvard Law Review article. In using the phrase Brandeis
and Warren were concerned principally with the law of slander and libel, because reputations and the "right to be let
alone" had seemed increasingly endangered by the invention
of the instantaneous photograph and, as they put it, newspaper enterprise.[36] Far from intending to apply this right to
female sexual autonomy and decision-making, their forth-
rightly patriarchal conception drew on the law's protection of
a man from physical interference to recognize the privacy of
his "spiritual nature, of his feelings and his intellect" and, by
extension, the need to protect the honor of his family, including his children and his wife. This right to privacy gained
widespread recognition in the civil law of most states by the
1930s.[37] Although this vision of privacy did not clear up (in fact,
it complicated) important questions about how much autonomy or decision-making freedom individuals might have,
Warren and Brandeis's extension of a right to privacy "beyond
the body of the individual" paved the way for a new "zone of
privacy" in the sexual relations of married couples seventy-
five years later.

This understanding of privacy highlights the fact that
persons are not limited to their bodies or to the words with
which they express themselves. We are all always "unfinished," not only because our lives are unfinished until we are
dead but also because every account of our lives will be selective and incomplete. The right to privacy protects this unde-
fined part of ourselves, to a degree. The legal shift of the
mid-1960s evokes a related feminist concern in literature for
what author Tillie Olsen calls "*hidden* silences; work aborted,
deferred, denied."[38] In her book *Silences* Olsen describes literary silences of her own life and those of women throughout
history forced to choose between literary production and bio-

logical reproduction. Censorship silences, she writes, but so does self-censorship. In speaking of "the lives that never came to writing," Olsen equates silences with abortions. But, as the title of her book implies, she believes too that silences are important. In this way, silence assumes a paradoxical value. Although the right to remain silent (a phrase applied to police interrogations in 1966 by *Miranda v. Arizona*) may seem a mirror image of the right to speak freely, the two rights are not symmetrical. In fact, they often conflict.

Like Louis Brandeis, Justice Abe Fortas, who joined the Supreme Court two years after *Griswold*, privileged privacy over the freedom of speech. Hellman had called Fortas for advice in 1952 when she was subpoenaed by the House Un-American Activities Committee. Fortas, then in private practice in Washington, came up to Hellman's Manhattan apartment the next day, admired the china birds on the fireplace, played a few notes on the piano, and told her he had a hunch. The committee had subverted the constitutional protection of the Fifth, making silence—the refusal to testify so as not to incriminate oneself—appear as proof positive of membership in the Communist Party. Hellman recalls Fortas saying, "The time had come, the perfect time, for someone to take a moral position before these disgraceful congressional committees and not depend on the legalities of the Fifth Amendment. To Fortas the moral position would be to say, in essence, I will testify about myself, answer all your questions about my own life, but I will not tell you about anybody else."[39] To preserve the privacy of others, Hellman would have to give up her own privacy, though, as she recognized, the distinction was a false one because personal autonomy is inevitably defined in relation to others. It was a risky gambit that could send her to jail, and Fortas acknowledged that it was "legal shit."[40] Moreover, although he represented other victims of the communist witch hunts, Fortas declined to represent Hellman. Instead he guided her to noted civil liberties lawyer and leader of Americans for Democratic Action Joseph Rauh. An enormous man with a penchant for bow ties, the kind and crinkly faced Rauh coached Hellman for months. He helped her to compose a letter specifying the type of questions she would and, more important, would not answer (the letter was rejected), and he then directed her in a cat-and-mouse game with the House committee on May 21, 1952. Her partner, Dashiell Hammett, had been sent to jail in 1951 for refusing to give the names of contributors to a bail fund of the Civil Rights Congress. Feeling extremely nervous, Hellman went to Washington nearly a week before the hearing and tried to distract herself by visiting the zoo and shopping.

It was eleven o'clock on a cloudy morning when, in a close-fitting black hat and an elegant brown-and-black silk dress, Hellman entered the House Caucus Room. Seated at a table next to Rauh about twenty feet from the raised platform from which the committee gazed down at her, she pled the Fifth. When committee counsel Frank Tavenner pressed her by asking if her response implied that she simply did not want to be interrogated about communist activities, she replied that he should attend to her exact words. Then she referred the committee to the letter she had earlier submitted to Chairman John S. Wood. This was the coup de grâce, for Rauh instructed his assistant Daniel Pollitt to pass it out to the assembled members of the press. This famous letter, which is reprinted verbatim in *Scoundrel Time*, presented her wish to talk about herself but not about others: "I am most willing to answer all questions about myself. I have nothing to hide from your Committee and there is nothing in my life of which I am ashamed." It was an untenable legal position, but the letter explains that she doesn't really understand the Fifth Amendment: "My counsel tells me that if I answer questions about myself, I will have waived my rights under the Fifth Amendment and could be forced legally to answer questions about others. This is very difficult for a layman to understand."[41] Hellman's clever use of the vague word "this" makes it hard to tell if she is speaking about the form or substance of the law. She insists only that she won't bring "bad trouble" on people who were innocent of any talk that was disloyal or subversive. Claiming the rhetorical high ground, Hellman overtly infuses the law with moral content, showing in effect that the Fifth Amendment, like the First, is never neutral. It always involves choices between competing value judgments. The publishing of Hellman's letter was a public relations triumph, and it expressed a lie (she frequently writes about things of which she is ashamed and hides much). In *Scoundrel Time*, Hellman describes her anxiety at taking the Fifth, though it is "a wise section of the Constitution," because it too "has catches" for someone like her whose private life is not clearly distinguishable from her public.[42] Rather than noticing that she had taken the Fifth, most people praised her courageous stand against the unscrupulous intrusions of the state. She had escaped where many had been trapped.

For Mary McCarthy, Hellman's manipulation of the Fifth Amendment's right to remain silent for her own purposes and the ennobling of her actions in *Scoundrel Time* are among the most infuriating instances of Hellman's lies.[43] In letters to her lawyer Ben O'Sullivan, to her friend Dwight Macdonald, and in her deposition in the libel suit, McCarthy contrasted Hellman's behavior to that of Arthur Miller in

1956, when Miller (who was also represented by Joseph Rauh) refused to name names but did not invoke the privilege of the Fifth. It was not a fair comparison. Even in invoking her constitutional protection against self-incrimination, Hellman behaved courageously. She was subsequently blacklisted in Hollywood. Furthermore, as many noticed, Miller, too, pulled evasive maneuvers.[44] One of the most interesting aspects of Miller's account of his experience with HUAC in his autobiography, *Timebends,* is how he interweaves that narrative with his upcoming marriage to Marilyn Monroe and the American press's obsession with sex and implies that evasion may be a necessary if feminine ploy. Interspersed with descriptions of his preparation for the committee is a seemingly unrelated anecdote about Marilyn fleeing in disguise down a back alley to avoid the media, only to be trapped by the trash cans; or of a press conference where her shoulder strap snaps, eliciting "excited gasps at the prospect of further revelations."[45]

More to the point, times had changed between 1952 and 1956. As Miller acknowledges, "The Committee had been on the wane for some time." Senator Joseph McCarthy, who, though not on HUAC, epitomized the communist witch hunts, was censured in 1954. Equally important, confessing in public had new meaning. In 1953 the courts explicitly recognized, as corollary to the right to privacy, a "right to publicity," the right of each individual to control and profit from the value of his or her name, image, likeness, and other indicia of identity.[46] Celebrities launched tell-all books that often seemed like preemptive strikes to assert property in their own image, since public exposure was crucial to their livelihood. In her 1952 autobiography, Tallulah Bankhead (star of Hellman's *Little Foxes* in 1939) acidly declared, "Tallulah has connotations which soothe or shrivel half the population. Its cachet is the product of too much suffering, too many revolts and accusations, too many attacks and counterattacks, to be bandied about by clods."[47] But taking control of one's personal history obviously raised First Amendment concerns, because it limited what could be published about the "private" lives of "public" figures.

So it was with Hellman, who demanded freedom to express herself but would curtail the freedoms of others, such as McCarthy, who represented her in ways she disliked. Hellman's selective self-disclosure in *Scoundrel Time*, her distortions and "lies" about history, provoked outrage, not, by then, in the halls of government but among former friends and acquaintances. Diana and Lionel Trilling, Irving Howe, Philip Rahv, and others with competing historical narratives spoke out against her. In a review of *Scoundrel Time* the sociologist Nathan Glazer denounced "the *obscenity* of speaking of world peace under the auspices of a movement [Soviet communism] whose leaders ran a huge system of slave camps for dissenters."[48] Diana Trilling debunked Hellman's history in *We Must March My Darlings* and then accused Hellman of instructing Little, Brown (Hellman's publisher) not to publish Trilling's book (published by Harcourt) and of blackballing her on Martha's Vineyard. It was hardly a case of censorship, but the dispute reached the front page of the *New York Times* in 1977, and Trilling later thought it would bolster Mary McCarthy's defense. The publication of *Scoundrel Time* in 1976 both eroded the distinction between Hellman's public and private life and raised her to legendary status. She posed, cigarette in hand, in a well-known Blackglama mink-coat ad beneath the caption: "What becomes a Legend most?" It also led the fact-checkers to sharpen their quills. By the 1970s American legends had come under intensive scrutiny, or else they went the way of George Washington and the cherry tree into the misty fields of mythology.

Hellman's HUAC strategy was central to the development of the configuration of privacy in the Cold War. It paved the way for Miller, as the language of his autobiography makes clear.[49] Five years after Hellman's HUAC appearance, and one after Miller's, Chief Justice Earl Warren, writing for a unanimous Court in *Watkins v. U.S.*, struck down the conviction for contempt of Congress delivered upon John Watkins, who, like Miller, had acknowledged involvement with the Communist Party but, forgoing the protection of the Fifth, refused to answer HUAC's questions relating to others who may have been communists. Watkins insisted that the question went beyond the legitimate purposes of the committee, and the language of harmful exposure permeates both his argument and the Court's decision. In ruling for Watkins, the Court noted his complaint that "the Subcommittee was engaged in a program of exposure for the sake of exposure."[50] As literary historian Deborah Nelson has shown, the *Watkins* case was crucial in establishing the right to remain silent as a key element of the right to privacy.[51] Justice William O. Douglas makes this connection explicit in his lecture *The Right of the People* (1958), where he argues that the right to be let alone becomes obviously necessary in the face of the unrestricted activities of legislative committees out on fishing expeditions: "The idea of exposure by an investigating committee merely for exposure's sake . . . is foreign to our system." Commenting on *Watkins*, Justice Douglas bases his evolving sense of a right to privacy on both the First and the Fifth Amendments, freedom of expression and the right to remain silent, which, with others, form "congeries of . . . rights that may be conveniently called the right to be let alone." Here he first refers to the "vague penumbra of the law."[52]

Hellman's inconsistencies, contradictions, and lies help us to consider what happens when free speech conflicts with privacy rights. She was a strong advocate of free speech, an active member and honoree of the American Civil Liberties Union (which had defended her play *The Children's Hour* in 1940 against attempts to ban it because of "lesbian content"),[53] and, in 1970, founder of the Committee for Public Justice, which focused on free speech and privacy rights. Yet her plays and her memoirs repeatedly dramatize the need for silence, evasion, and lying, often by threat of libel and blackmail. "Please don't let's talk this way," a wife pleads with her husband, who demands that she "tell me what you mean," in *The Autumn Garden,* which was produced in 1951, the year Hammett went to prison for contempt of Congress. This sort of exchange recurs constantly in her plays. Facing her judges in Hellman's 1955 HUAC allegory, *The Lark,* Joan of Arc says, "What do you want me to say? Please tell me in simple words," only to find that she is unable to answer them in any case. In her last play, *Toys in the Attic,* one character just says, "Everybody talks too much, too many words, and gets them out of order. . . . Please, Lily, let us cease this talking about talking."[54] The tension between censorship and freedom of speech was central to Hellman's plays, her memoirs, and the most famous moments of her life: her appearance before the House Un-American Activities Committee and her libel suit against McCarthy.

By the time Hellman wrote *Scoundrel Time,* Abe Fortas had been driven from the bench by negative press and Republican enemies, following Earl Warren's resignation and his own nomination as chief justice. The revelation of questionable financial transactions added fuel to the fire. As Fortas's biographer Laura Kalman observes, his belief in the right to privacy ran through his Fourth and Fifth Amendment decisions and in the limitations he put upon the First. Like Brandeis, who popularized the phrase "the right to be let alone," Fortas was deeply suspicious if not hostile to the intrusiveness of the press.[55] Indeed, he hoped to narrow the scope of the landmark libel case *New York Times v. Sullivan,* which raised the burden of proof for public officials in libel suits against the press. It is possible that Justice Harold Baer, who presided over Hellman's libel suit, had a similar objective in denying McCarthy's petition for summary judgment and allowing Hellman's case to go forward. The conflict between the newly established right to privacy and free speech came to a head in 1967 when the Supreme Court heard *Time, Inc. v. Hill,* the first case to examine the competing claims of privacy and freedom of expression.

Time, Inc. v. Hill centered on the reluctance of the family of James Hill to tell the story of being held hostage in their own home by escaped convicts. After intense press coverage, the family moved to Connecticut to avoid publicity. In 1953 Joseph Hayes wrote *The Desperate Hours,* a novel about a family held hostage by fugitives, which distorted the history of the Hills and made the convicts more brutal and sexual than they were; the book was then adapted as a Broadway play starring Paul Newman. *Life* magazine discovered that the story was loosely based on the Hills' experience and arranged for actors in the play to be photographed in the house where the event took place. The family (particularly Mrs. Hill) was devastated by this invasion of their privacy. Hill sued successfully, but *Life* pressed its First Amendment claim to the Supreme Court, where Hill was ably represented by a great hater of the press, Richard M. Nixon, then in private practice in New York. What followed is a curious tale of conflict between the right to privacy and freedom of speech. The majority of justices voted to affirm Hill's judgment, and Chief Justice Warren assigned the opinion to Fortas. But Fortas wrote such an intemperate condemnation of *Life*'s behavior, which he called a "deliberate, callous invasion of the Hills' right to be let alone," that he spurred Justice Hugo Black, the member of the Court most devoted to freedom of speech, to denounce his draft. In a memo Black urged his colleagues not to "punish the press so much that publishers will cease trying to report news in a lively and readable fashion as long as there is—and there always will be—doubt as to the complete accuracy of newsworthy facts." When the Court decided the case in January 1967, Fortas lost his majority and Hill lost his judgment.[56]

Hellman's representations of personal experience rely not on the First Amendment but on the Fifth: that no person shall be compelled to be a witness against him- or herself. It may seem ironic that Hellman, who chose to publish her own intimate experiences, is exercising a right to remain silent or that this right is even necessary to her privacy. Yet many readers have regarded her work as a central instance of the problem of figuring out where evasions turn into lies. For McCarthy, Hellman was a liar for this reason: "Omission and concealment in various guises contribute throughout [Hellman's work] to the eerie atmosphere of untruthfulness that pervades these supposed memoirs, to the point where the effect is positively uncanny. Not to name, not to identify, a crucial place or person or date—an odd procedure for an autobiographer—seems almost standard here."[57] The right to privacy, which is intended to protect against the defamatory harms of humiliation, embarrassment, and outrage, as well as against invasions of the bedroom, brings together incompatible elements that are both central to and newly illuminated by the Hellman-McCarthy dispute.

Hellman's stories return continually to the difficulty of remaining silent and the impossibility of telling the whole truth, in Congress, in a police station, in writing, or in a publishing house. The most brilliant of these is "Bethe," the first chapter of *Pentimento.* "Bethe" is the story of a relationship between young Lillian and Bethe, a poor German immigrant to New Orleans and a distant relative. In what must seem to liberal Americans the epitome of violated privacy and sexual constraint, Bethe's marriage to Styrie Bowman, a prodigal son living in New Orleans, is arranged by wealthy cousins. After Bethe arrives in America, Styrie abandons her to pursue his life as a gambler and a forger, which leads to his becoming the target of the Mafia. When he finally disappears, Bethe runs away and takes up with an Italian named Arneggio. Lilly pursues her and learns that Bethe and Arneggio share a passionate, sexual love. But Arneggio is also a gangster who ends up in pieces. A cop finds Lilly, looking again for Bethe, at the crime scene. He grabs her with such "a very firm hold . . . that I couldn't move." She asks that he remove his hand: "I don't like to be held down." But he picks up a letter she has dropped and, representing one kind of reader, demands, "What's this mean?" then releases her. She arrives home to find that the police have been there. "Why don't you mind your Goddamned business?" Aunt Jenny asks behind the chicken coops (where Lilly told Sam Hopkins she lost her virginity). Her aunts take her downtown for a traumatic interrogation. When asked again why she went to Arneggio's corner store, she can answer nothing but the word "Love" and is released. Then Bethe disappears for ten years. Hellman thinks of her as she prepares for her wedding to Arthur Kober and then again the first time she sleeps with Hammett. Finally, she returns to New Orleans and accuses her aunts Jenny and Hannah of abandoning Bethe because of her unconventional sex life (which resembles Lillian's with Hammett), only for the aunts to prove their generosity and lead her to where Bethe now lives on the margins of the city in a dilapidated shack with a plumber.

Hellman scholar Doris Falk gives an elegant and straightforward reading of "Bethe" in which she describes the neat dichotomies of the story: it is about Bethe and Hellman, past and present, eros (sexual love) and agape (charitable Christian love), beauty and ugliness, good and bad. But what interests me is the way "Bethe"—the story and the character— intentionally evades straightforward readings and dualistic models. It is a story, like many others in Hellman's oeuvre, about running away, avoidance of constraint, privacy in public, about writing itself. As Falk says, it evokes Nathaniel Hawthorne's *Scarlet Letter* (Bethe bears a slight resemblance to Hester Prynne), but more than that, it recalls Edgar Allan Poe's "Purloined Letter." Like Poe, an important precursor for detective-writer Hammett, Hellman plays upon the tension between revelation and concealment, locating power in the latter. Her tale's first words—"The letter"—refer to a letter from Germany notifying Hellman's family of Bethe's arrival, but "the letter" also stands for letters, or writing, in general. Readers learn that the letter from Germany has been stolen along with a valise of Hellman's grandfather's letters and notebooks and a letter from Bethe herself. At the age of sixteen, Hellman had discovered this trove of documents. Her aunts allowed her to take some to New York but then asked for them to be returned. Hellman writes, "That seemed to me odd, but I put it down to some kind of legality that grown people fussed with, and carried them back." After the aunts die, Hellman searches in vain for the valise. She assumes that Hannah gave instructions to somebody to remove it. "And why?" she asks. "Perhaps, I told myself, the last act of a private life."[58]

Like the early chapters of *An Unfinished Woman,* "Bethe" depicts an education in the relationship between privacy and interpretation. Bethe, a figure in a book, stands for figures in a book. Hellman comments that Bethe entered a journalist's book about the period, for reasons she did not know, on the day she met Styrie. After the murder of Arneggio, Bethe's name is mentioned in every press story. But she also frequently disappears. She demands to be left alone with her husband and lovers. She hangs a curtain between herself and the public with words. Her rich mix of English and German is opaque and, like Hellman's writing, draws attention to itself rather than any external meaning to which it might refer. In a childish "writer's book," Lilly practices a code based on Bethe's name. She wants to trade language lessons; she brings her English grammar to Bethe and tries to explain the pluperfect as Bethe stares solemnly back at her. As a girl, Hellman is convinced that Bethe has not only secrets but answers, yet Bethe does not provide them. "I said to Bethe before I began to cry, 'You lie because a man tells you to.'" Bethe remains silent. As Lilly grows, she learns her own evasive maneuvers: "I had tried to climb up ten fire escapes into my room to avoid my parents' questions."[59]

So what does Bethe teach? The first afternoon Lilly sleeps with Hammett, as she moves toward the bed, she says, "I'd like to tell you about my cousin, a woman called Bethe."[60] But what is there to say? Bethe's privacy eludes language. She has already literally silenced Lilly, putting a hand over her mouth when Lilly was on the verge of naming her relationship with Arneggio. Crawling into bed with Hammett, Hellman says nothing. Readers take from this story a lesson about the importance of sexual love to female happiness, about the legitimacy of relationships outside marriage.[61] But equally important are the frequent instructions in the story to mind your own business, don't tell everything you know, keep a secret. Bethe's name serves as a code—for what we never learn, unless simply for writing itself. Above all, nearly mute Bethe is a writing instructor. On Hellman's final visit to Bethe at the plumber's shack, she struggles through a green swamp until she comes in sight of a roof where Bethe stands, hanging clothes from a line that stretched from a pole to an outhouse. "She was naked and I stopped to admire her proportions. . . . She must have heard the sound of the wet, ugly soil beneath me, because she turned, put her hands over her breasts, then moved them down to cover her vagina, then took them away to move the hair from her face."[62] Bethe can stand for a revelation of female sexuality, but that simple reading fails to reveal what Hellman, writing in the 1970s, insists Bethe has to do with her and Hammett.

In the fall of 1937 Hellman became pregnant and pressed Hammett to marry her.[63] Yet their relationship, always unconventional, did not promise domestic happiness. Hammett obtained a divorce from his first wife, Josephine. He even seemed intent on making a family with Lillian, but he continued to see many other women. One day she came to visit him at the Beverly Wiltshire Hotel in Los Angeles only to find him in bed with another woman. She decided that she would never bear his child. Arthur Kober noted her quandary in a diary entry in July: "Lil tells me of her troubles, of Dash's change of feelings. Poor kid doesn't know what to do or where to turn or what to do about."[64] That fall, she set sail for France, where, like many other American women of means, she had an abortion. Her 1937 trip is the source for another of the famous stories in *Pentimento,* that of the antifascist freedom fighter "Julia," who bears a child out of wedlock and loses a leg, her life, and then the baby. Hellman insists that after Julia's death she searched for but was unable to locate the missing child. Biographer and novelist Joan Mellen writes, "It was, of course, Hellman's own baby, baby Lily [*sic*], who cannot be found because she has been aborted."[65] Mellen's incisive reading of the significance of the lost baby suggests another instance of Hellman's evasiveness in life and writing. But "Julia," like "Bethe," speaks to a broader concern. In the story Hellman is supposed to smuggle money to a group of fighters who were once "small publishers" to free prisoners in Germany. Julia is exceptionally hard to pin down in every sense—hard to find, hard to comprehend. Though multilingual, like Bethe, she is occasionally rendered mute, as when, after being severely wounded, her leg is amputated and her face bandaged. Lillian sits by her bed in a German hospital and finds that they cannot communicate: "We sat for a while that way and then she pointed to her mouth, meaning that she couldn't speak because of the bandages. Then she raised her hand to the window, pointed out, and made a pushing movement with her hand." To this melodramatic demonstration of constraint and freedom, Hellman can only say, "I don't know what you mean." From Julia too she receives a letter, now lost. It reports that Julia "had had a baby and the baby seemed to like being called Lilly."[66]

Feminist arguments for abortion have rested on the right of women to control their own bodies. These bodies have not always been their own; whether as the subjects of male artists and writers or as obedient wives and daughters, women have not controlled their meanings and destinies. But Hellman adds a twist: attempts at control result in misrepresentation. The strongest women, fighters against domestic and political authoritarianism, Bethe and Julia, dramatize this lesson. They resist representation only to be subjected to new, always frustratingly inadequate descriptions. Their symbolic muteness draws attention to their place in the stories they generate. They are objects that are supposed to be meaningful. They demand yet evade interpretation. In this way, they stand for the literary text itself. Both prove literally ungovernable. They affiliate with underground or criminal organizations. They violate the law. In doing so they suggest that the first step in interpreting the law is to identify something that is missing but that has analogies in other aspects of law. Problematically abstract concepts such as liberty and privacy come into contact with the problematically concrete, bodily experience of particular women. In the 1960s and 1970s, doing justice to women's claim to reproductive freedom required the overwhelmingly male medical and legal professions to take a leap of imagination, to empathize with kinds of experience outside the reach of then available language.

Responding in a famous 1971 article to Justice Douglas's creation of a right to privacy, conservative legal scholar Robert Bork argued that a judge "must stick close to the text and the history, and their fair implications, and not construct new rights." *Griswold*, Bork argued, is an "unprincipled decision," and he is right.[67] The language ("penumbras-emanations") draws attention to the evasiveness of the text. We may note an analogy between the effort to locate the right to privacy in the Bill of Rights and reproductive freedom in the woman's body. Defining what is interior and what is exterior, what is substantive and what formal, is both difficult (if not impossible) and necessary, just as the principle of "free speech" depends on all the contexts in which speech is not free. The tension between freedom of expression and the right to remain silent makes stories possible. Telling tales is a diversion—in the multiple senses of the word—just as silence is a function of what we cannot or will not say. A simple analogy appears between Judge Bork and Poe's figure for the law, the Prefect and his cohort: "They consider only their *own* ideas of ingenuity; and, in searching for anything hidden, advert only to the modes in which *they* would have hidden it."[68] In solving the case, Poe's detective M. Dupin eschews the Prefect's Procrustean bed of reason—the application of the one principle or set of principles of search—and adopts a poet's method of identification with his subject. In keeping this approach in mind, when faced with a mute figure gesturing to her mouth or her vagina, we may be less inclined to demand, as so many do of Hellman, "What's this mean?" Like *Griswold,* Hellman challenges conventions of reading and writing by assuming that it is possible to imagine live rights only as penumbras, formed by emanations.

Mary McCarthy's Problems with Privacy

In 1984, at the age of seventy-one, Mary McCarthy told an interviewer that she had had "quite a lot" of abortions.[69] Putting aside for the moment questions about her desire to publicize the fact, it is reasonable to ask why she had so many. Why didn't she use contraception? Was it unavailable? Was she unable to ask her partner to wait? McCarthy's fiction and her life give many direct and indirect answers to these questions. If, for Hellman, abortion is the occasion for specific forms of lying and evasion, then, for McCarthy, abortion involves a special form of truth telling, often confession. The two epigraphs to this chapter make this difference plain. In the first, from *An Unfinished Woman,* Hellman sits angry and mute, "refusing answers" in the midst of "good-natured questioning." In the second, from McCarthy's 1955 novel *A Charmed Life,* a wife looks forward to telling her husband about her abortion because "it would be good to have truth between them again." I now turn to that truth as McCarthy imagined it.

McCarthy married four times. She was also openly, even aggressively, promiscuous and sexually competitive. Orphaned at the age of six, she was intensely self-reliant, and she despised those who weren't. A woman competing in a man's world, like Hellman, she kept her name and made her living. In the 1930s, with her long dark hair, vivid smile, unshaven legs, and lacerating pen, she was a tough broad. As her Vassar classmates knew, she began sleeping with actor and playwright Harold Johnsrud before she graduated and married him in 1933. Early in the summer of 1936 they separated. While he toured with a production of Maxwell Anderson's play *Winterset,* McCarthy became engaged to John Porter, the "Young Man" whom she describes in her first published short story, "Cruel and Barbarous Treatment." Porter, a handsome dilettante, "unwittingly effected her transit into a new life."[70]

Sex became a constant subject of her writing. On the train to Reno for her divorce from Johnsrud, McCarthy found herself in the berth and, after a few drinks, in the bed of a businessman from Pittsburgh (the steel man Mr. Breen in "The Man in the Brooks Brothers Suit"). She decided against marrying Porter. After a brief sojourn out West with her grandparents, she returned to Greenwich Village, where her social life really picked up. Serving on the Committee for the Defense of Leon Trotsky, she became the lover of Bob Misch, an advertising man who plied her with black bean soup, claret, and sherry (like Pflaumen in "The Genial Host"). She also began brief affairs with the Marxist author and editor Leo Huberman and with Bill Mangold, a Yale man then separated from his wife. Mangold appears later as the publisher Gus Leroy in *The Group*. She slept with the lyricist Harold Rome and with a little man who made puppets, also a truck driver, and the list goes on. It started to get alarming, she later reports, when "I realized one day that in twenty-four hours I had slept with three different men."[71] One morning she found herself in bed with a man while over his head she was talking on the phone to someone else. "Of all the men I slept with in my studio-bed on Gay Street," McCarthy wrote, "(and there were a lot; I stopped counting), I liked Bill Mangold the best. Until I began to see Philip Rahv."[72]

Rahv, a tall, dark-eyed Jew from the Ukraine, was cofounder and editor of New York's most important intellectual magazine, *Partisan Review*. McCarthy met him at the Trotskyite parties of her friend the novelist James Farrell. Needing a German reader for a new manuscript, she invited him to the Covici Friede publishing office where she worked. Soon they were lovers. He was separated from his wife, whom he lacked the money to divorce. By early summer they had moved into a walk-up on Beekman Place, a posh, tree-lined residential enclave on the East Side. The elegant, modern apartment was owned by some of McCarthy's affluent friends who were traveling in Europe over the summer. McCarthy believed in "free unions," but they had at least one fight when she learned that he had spent a night with Lillian Hellman, who Rahv said had unsuccessfully tried to seduce him.[73] McCarthy became a member of the *Partisan Review* crowd, served as its theater critic, and was a member of the editorial board. During the hot summer months, she and Rahv, Dwight and Nancy Macdonald, Fred Dupee, and William Phillips gathered at the Macdonalds' house in Connecticut to swim naked in the stream and discuss Henry James, Marx, and the war in Spain. In the fall, the *PR* editors found an office for the magazine, and McCarthy found a ground-floor apartment for Philip and herself on East End Avenue across from Gracie Mansion. Soon she was carrying on an affair with Edmund Wilson, the most important American critic of his day, for whom she left Rahv to marry.

McCarthy was not a feminist, and her comment about her abortions can seem provocatively casual, as opposed to the intense sincerity of the testimonials and "abortion speak outs" of the late 1960s. "Saying 'I've had three illegal abortions' aloud was my feminist baptism, my swift immersion in the power of sisterhood," wrote Susan Brownmiller, the radical journalist, formerly a news writer for ABC. "A medical procedure I'd been forced to secure alone, shrouded in silence, was not 'a personal problem' any more than the matter of my gender in the newsroom was a 'personal problem.'"[74] The 1972 debut issue of *Ms.* magazine ran a petition in which fifty-three well-known American women, including Brownmiller, Anne Sexton, Billie Jean King, and Lillian Hellman, declared that they had undergone abortions.[75] Though she favored speaking out over silence, McCarthy was not of that sisterhood. She was not a fan of the Equal Rights Amendment presented to Congress in 1972. During the Watergate Hearings two years later, she befriended Senator Sam Ervin of North Carolina, chair of the Senate Watergate Committee and a hero of many classical liberals since his opposition to Senator Joseph McCarthy in the 1950s. Ervin championed civil liberties yet remained suspicious of civil rights legislation and of federal power, including that of the Warren Court. Likewise, McCarthy refused to be (and had no compassion for) the female victim of the mid-twentieth century, popularized more recently by twenty-first-century movies and television melodramas of highballs, cigarettes, and adultery. Her unfashionable views of sex and politics, her brashness and blindness, insight and inconsistency, are important, however, because they suggest what continues to be at stake in debates about birth control and free expression.

McCarthy's 1984 interview with Carol Brightman, an astute and like-minded scholar one generation younger than her subject, reveals the blind spots of each. McCarthy says she has no interest in feminism and hates self-pity. Brightman then wonders why relations between men and women are so embattled in her fiction and whether the clarity and horror with which she exposes married life in particular might not have much in common with feminism. The observation that the battle between the sexes pervades her fiction, which would seem obvious to most readers, surprises McCarthy. "Really?" she says. Maybe Brightman is just reacting to her critique of the decadence of "bourgeois marriage," not to a conscious depiction of sexual injustice.

> BRIGHTMAN: Well, a good part of feminism is rooted in . . . frustration in personal relationships.

MCCARTHY: I don't believe in equality in personal relationships, whether it's between two men, whatever. It's absolutely meaningless and silly.

BRIGHTMAN: What about the public issues that have been fought over during the last twenty years, the right to a legal abortion, for example?

MCCARTHY: I'm for that. But that has nothing to do with feminism.

BRIGHTMAN: Can you explain why it doesn't?

MCCARTHY: To me, it's just a question of freedom. If men could have abortions I'd be for that.

BRIGHTMAN: Who wouldn't?

MCCARTHY: No, of course I'm for free abortions. I had quite a lot of abortions and I think they are rather damaging psychically, but that doesn't mean that I think people should not be free to have them.[76]

Brightman and McCarthy have a reasonable dialogue about the relative merits of freedom and equality, but in key respects they speak different moral languages, expressing views organized around competing claims (such as individual rights versus the communal good) that reflect their different generational and social positions. "I believe in the institutions of a republic, the protection of laws, starting with the protection of the rights of the individual," says McCarthy.[77] Brightman envisions an egalitarian good life in which the frustrations of sexual relations will be resolved by common agreement. McCarthy's vision seems formal, Brightman's substantive. But one vital question that this interview raises is whether the principles of justice that govern society can ever be neutral with respect to the desires and goals of its citizens.[78] Although it may seem rational to say that the right to an abortion is just an aspect of the larger wish to be free from constraint, McCarthy typically goes overboard in remarking hypothetically that men should be entitled to abortions. In the name of an abstract principle, she ignores the content of an experience that is specific to women. Some constraints are not impersonal or external—the products of rational choice—but deeply personal, even genetic. McCarthy's animosity to Lillian Hellman is rooted in the frustration of the liberal aspiration to neutrality, and this frustration appears particularly in her writings about sex, privacy, and reproduction.

When McCarthy says that she is for freedom and against equality, she means in part that personal relationships are not a public issue. The personal is not the political. Freedom means the ability to throw one's voice into a public arena of rational discourse, assuming there is, or ever was, such a thing. Yet her writing returns constantly to bodies, shame, and the exposure of private lives, raising the question of whether the promotion of free public discourse is compatible with the protection of private autonomy. The "zones of privacy" that the Supreme Court sought to define in *Griswold v. Connecticut* (1965), *Eisenstadt v. Baird* (1972), and *Roe v. Wade* (1973) are spaces of intimacy and trust, supposedly removed from both intrusions of the state and pressures of public opinion. Insofar as they depend on the First Amendment, they are also zones of freedom of conscience. But McCarthy remains deeply suspicious of the modern notion that privacy's function is to shelter the intimate. Like her close friend and mentor the German-Jewish political theorist Hannah Arendt, she yearns for the competitive, aristocratic *polis* of antiquity, when "men" realized themselves in words and action, while women and slaves labored in the privacy of the household. The polis, as Arendt describes it in *The Human Condition* (1958), "was distinguished from the household in that it knew only 'equals,' whereas the household was the center of the strictest inequality."[79] She means that all are equally entitled to display their individuality and thereby to excel. The private is defined by the satisfaction of biological necessity; the public is the realm of freedom. The private-public distinction coincides with the opposition between shame and honor, things hidden and things displayed. Arendt's book and McCarthy's laudatory review ("Arendt's insights into history and politics seem both amazing and obvious") were published at precisely the time the Supreme Court was beginning to hash out the constitutional basis of a "right to privacy."[80]

But McCarthy's review largely neglects Arendt's chapter on "The Public and the Private Realm," which remains the most problematic aspect of the thought of both women. Both regard the public sphere in almost wholly abstract or formal terms, as a realm that is neutral toward substantive moral and religious notions. It is governed by no particular conception of the good; it is alien to compassion and love. But their insistence on radically disembodied rationality and individualistic values also severely restricts their conceptions of justice. In a letter to "Dearest Mary" in 1969, Arendt comments on their shared commitment to the revelatory quality of speech and action that appears only in the agonistic public sphere and their mutual aversion to the private biological and psychological "inner life":

The most important sentence for me and my special
purposes in your essay is: "inside . . . no differences exist; all are alike." And this is literally
true, not merely metaphorically; only what appears
outwardly is distinct, different, even unique. In one
word, our emotions are all the same, the difference
is in what and how we make them appear. To put it
differently, nature has hidden all that is merely
functional and has left it shapeless. What is out-
ward and appears is f.i. [for instance] strictly symmetrical, colored, etc., the inner organs of all living
things are nothing to look at, as though they were
haphazardly thrown together. . . . As I see it, the
difference between man and animal would not
only lie in manifestation, by which I now mean the
deliberate choice of what I want to appear, but in
speech insofar as it is not only communication for
certain purposes. . . . Words by definition survive
and transcend the life-conditioning purposes, at
least so long as the species lasts, words become
part of the world. . . . The "inner life" from this
viewpoint . . . is no less indecent, unfit to appear,
than our digestive apparatus, or else our inner organs which are also hidden from visibility by the
skin.[81]

For Arendt and McCarthy, sexually neutral "man" has no
physical or emotional interior. Not only are all animals alike
on the inside, with their digestive tracts and reproductive
equipment, but an inner life, which includes "our emotions,"
is also indecent, unfit to appear, alien to the transcendent capacity of words, and disgusting. Arendt's public space of ap-

pearance has a twofold character of equality and distinction. It is a level playing field in which excellence shines like a symmetrical and colored work of classical art. The aversion for the private, as unfit to be seen as inner organs, is weirdly overemphatic.

Renewed popular and critical interest in Arendt and McCarthy, whose correspondence was published in 1995, has been inseparable from curiosity about their private lives. The posthumous publication of diaries and letters of these women and their most famous lovers, Martin Heidegger and Edmund Wilson, respectively, have helped to shape their significance for a new generation of readers. Describing her formative relationship with Wilson, whom she represents more than once as having raped and assaulted her, McCarthy rationalizes: "The logic of having slept with Wilson compelled the sequence of marriage if that was what he wanted. Otherwise my action would have no consistency; in other words, no meaning. . . . There is something vaguely Kantian here. But I did not know Kant then. Maybe I was a natural Kantian." As Brightman points out, this preposterous logic is more Catholic than Kantian.[82] McCarthy and Arendt's yearning for meaning without power, by which I mean a principle of validity arrived at without force, seems clearly related to the psychological pressures of their sexual-intellectual experiences. Both fail to acknowledge that the private, too, is a sphere of contest and conflict as well as, potentially, a sphere of freedom. In fact, it is the sphere upon which most of the freedoms enumerated in the Bill of Rights depend. In ancient Greece, Arendt says, the private was merely the sphere of privation, where basic and constant needs, the pains of childbirth and the continuation of the species, were taken care of. Men were not true human beings in private but only a species of animals. Arendt and McCarthy struggled to achieve excellence in a public realm constituted by the New York intellectuals and a wider audience for their books and lectures. Both fought for status in a community in which, as they saw it, men sought to define the world they lived in.

From McCarthy's point of view, it must seem perverse to focus on her abortions, but they were far from trivial. As she acknowledges offhandedly to Brightman, abortion is "rather psychically damaging." She had one child from whose care she was largely liberated, first by Edmund Wilson, who insisted that they hire a nurse so that she could write, and then by arrangements such as boarding schools. Nevertheless, she had "quite a lot" of abortions. In *The Group,* the McCarthy-like Kay Strong, who marries a theater man named Harald upon her graduation from Vassar, is a thin, hard-driving young woman, who talked "airily of oestrum and nymphomania . . . counseling premarital experiment and scientific choice of a mate. Love, she said, was an illusion."[83] She dies in a fall from her window at the Vassar Club, where she moves after divorcing Harald, ostensibly having lost her balance, but a probable suicide. The novel begins with her marriage and ends with her funeral, not unlike *A Charmed Life,* which begins by referring to Martha Sinnott's recent remarriage and ends with her death (through a window) in a car crash on her way to an abortionist in Boston. Kay Strong's strength is not totally illusory, but her name raises questions about why she needs to be strong in the first place.

"This freedom of speech of hers," we are told, "was a kind of masquerade of sexuality." She is both brutally honest and not very truthful. She throws around terms like "significant form" that she learned in freshman English from reading Clive Bell, the English critic who believed that it is only an

object's formal properties that make it aesthetically significant.[84] There is something foolish and naive (and doomed)
about Kay's insistence that society assume a position of neutrality toward the content of speech. The story ultimately does
more than critique the "right to privacy" argument for abortion. It questions the private-public distinction so invidious
to women like her. Although McCarthy privileges freedom
over equality in her interview, her abortions refer back to the
unequal situations from which they arise. In this way she suggests the problem of using the right to privacy as the primary
tool for asserting the right to abortion. In her relentless focus
on verbal irony, her exposure of the difference between the
way things sound and what they mean, McCarthy obligates
us to be close readers not only of her characters' but also of
her own life, starting with the language of love and her own
earliest sexual experience, which she continues to narrate to
the end of her life. Whereas Hellman mostly depicts the effects
or aftermath of abortion, McCarthy repeatedly represents
what comes before it, including, often in harsh uncompromis-
ing detail, the act of sexual intercourse itself.

On a dark November afternoon in 1926, in the front seat
of a Marmon roadster parked off a lonely Seattle boulevard,
fourteen-year-old Mary McCarthy lost her virginity. She recounts the experience more than sixty years later in her memoir *How I Grew.* It was Thanksgiving vacation. She was home
from her first year at the Annie Wright Seminary. She had a
crush on Forrest Crosby, a twenty-seven-year-old with bright
blue eyes and ash-blond curly hair who had met her at a summer resort where she was vacationing with her grandfather.
They dated surreptitiously for a few months and exchanged
letters when Mary was at boarding school. When they met for
their Thanksgiving rendezvous Mary finally realized what

was in the cards, and had been from the beginning. She was scared silly. After pulling to the side of the road, Crosby settled her head on his shoulder. As she chattered about her school friends, he mentioned that his pal Windy had "fucked" a popular Annie Wright senior. At that point, Mary understood, "he was preparing to fuck me." As she tells the story with a heavy emphasis on making the "bare" facts visible, it seems as though nothing is hidden.

> In fact, he became very educational, encouraging me to sit up and examine his stiffened organ, which to me looked quite repellant, all flushed and purplish. . . . Then, as I waited, he fished in an inside breast-pocket and took out what I knew to be a "safety." Still in an instructive mood, even with his erect member (probably he would have made a good parent), he found time to explain to me what it was—the best kind, a Merry Widow—before he bent down and fitted it onto himself, making me watch.
>
> Of the actual penetration, I remember nothing; it was as if I had been given chloroform . . . everything but the bare fact is gone. It must have hurt, but I have no memory of that or of any other sensations, perhaps a slight sense of being stuffed. Yes, there is also a faint recollection of his instructing me to move, keep step as in dancing, but I am not sure of that. What I am sure of is a single dreadful, dazed moment having to do with the condom. No, Reader, it did not break.
>
> The act is over; he has slid under the steering-wheel and is standing by his side of the car and

holding up a transparent little pouch resembling isinglass that has whitish greenish gray stuff in the bottom. I recognize it as "jism." Outside it is almost dark, but he is holding the little sack up to a light source—a streetlight, the Marmon's parking lights, a lit match?—to be sure I can see it well and realize what is inside—the sperm he has ejaculated into it, so as not to ejaculate it in me. I am glad of that, of course, but the main impression is the same as with the swollen penis; the jism is horribly ugly to me, like snot or catarrh, and I have to look away.[85]

This vignette centers on the tension between form and content—signaled by polite, Victorian rhetoric precisely when hinting at a broken condom. In a 1981 review McCarthy describes the convention of milking the reader's anticipation as an *"ars amoris,"* as if it were "foreplay."[86] Her tale of deflowering, however, is not exactly arousing, though it may be educational. Like the condom, the narrative of exposure paradoxically contains Crosby's jism. Birth control is an act of language. Disempowered in one realm, McCarthy asserts control over the sexual act with satire—the paradox being that while birth control aims to prevent biological conception, it frees the woman to be creative. McCarthy's storytelling is both the female prophylactic and the ironically permissive sex manual. It offers what she, as a girl, expected from books: "to see the fig-leaf stripped off sex."[87]

The anecdote is complicated by an internal tension between substance and style, like "jism" and "safety," as well as between the perspectives of the fourteen-year-old girl and the seventy-four-year-old author. The complications point to deeper questions in McCarthy's work about the value of the traditional American notion of privacy, derived from Brandeis and Warren, as the interest in keeping intimate affairs from public view, the individual possessing an "inviolable personality." The narrative climaxes not only when "he" but also "she" holds the man's climax up to the light. McCarthy asks us to imagine that the condom *did* break; she assumes the reader had thought of it before she mentions it ("No, Reader, it did not break"). In short, she asks the reader to imagine the sex as a potential cause not only of pregnancy but also of what might follow for a young girl. Who would be responsible if she became pregnant? She has snuck out of the home of her grandfather, a lawyer who, often in McCarthy's work, embodies the law. She compares him in another memoir to Caesar, "just, laconic, severe, magnanimous, detached. These are the very adjectives I might use to describe Lawyer Preston."[88] He often expressed the hope that she would become a lawyer herself, but she would rather be an actor, a telling ambition in the light of her description of the "act" of sex. She loves the law, though it remains in continual tension with the "wild" side of her nature. It is, however, a particular form of the law. It is laconic, severe, and detached. It embodies the Protestant strain of her background. This model of law is neutral in regard to the substance of controversial moral issues. Protestant grandfather Preston insisted that Mary receive a Catholic education after her parents died because that was what *they* had chosen. McCarthy regards this liberal form of law with a mixture of love and resentment.

The anecdote about losing her virginity forces the reader to ask if it is possible to bracket controversial moral questions. The law regards such questions as a matter of substantive due process, which means pouring into the otherwise neutral due process clause values that cannot be traced to constitutional text or history or structure.[89] It compels us to follow the example of Forrest Crosby and look more closely at the content of the condom, the substance of male sexual expression. To what degree should a right to privacy depend on personal autonomy, to what degree on a right to be left alone, when the relationship is grossly unequal? The sex with Crosby appears to be consensual, but only because the narrator so readily accepts the position of being acted upon. Although she nominally favored "equality before the law and so on," echoing Arendt, she did not believe equality was desirable in private relationships.[90] McCarthy said she liked to wait on her husbands, yet she can seem antagonistic to the self-effacing requirements of love and to privacy itself because of the vulnerability and shame it conceals. Crosby's obscenity and McCarthy's sexual adventurism seem unconstrained by the Victorian mores of Mary's grandparents. But these forms of male and female freedom are qualified and interrelated. McCarthy does not disguise the disparity of power. Nor does she shy from showing force and submission as normal heterosexual practice. She emphasizes that the inequality of the sexes is a source of the enjoyment of the sex itself, at least for Crosby. In describing it, she assumes the role of provocateur. In the explicitness of her sex life, exposing the practices privacy protects, McCarthy dramatizes a critique of the "right to privacy" as it came to be formulated in the 1960s and 1970s.

One way of defining privacy assumes that people should have "independence in making certain kinds of important decisions."[91] Like Hellman, McCarthy came of age between first- and second-wave feminism, and though she sometimes adopts the language of liberal neutrality, she, too, commonly recognizes her inability to disentangle herself from the mixed-up moral values and pressures of her historical moment.

Hellman's response to such entanglements is to omit and conceal; McCarthy's is to expose. Whereas readers commonly complained that Hellman's nonfiction was insufficiently truthful, many complained that McCarthy's fiction was too truthful, uncovering fig leafs that were better off remaining as they were. The libel suit divided their contemporaries between those who felt that Hellman was acting the censor and those who believed that McCarthy was getting a well-deserved comeuppance for malicious acts of exposure. In these ways, their prejudices and passions can seem to mirror each other and, by doing so, reveal irreconcilable contradictions built into the civil discourse of contemporary American public life. They demonstrate the ambivalence surrounding privacy that has dominated American culture since the Cold War. "The problem with privacy in this country," writes Deborah Nelson, "is not that we have too little privacy but that we have both too little and too much at the same time."[92] Privacy is always a problem; it always seems too much or too little, never just right. It becomes visible (as McCarthy's vignette shows) only as a norm that has been violated. Privacy is not something that we can be neutral about.

Like other members of her New York intellectual circle, McCarthy believed that art was an index to the state of society and vice versa. In her most commercially successful novel, *The Group* (1963), particularly in a chapter first published independently in *Partisan Review* as "Dottie Makes an Honest Woman of Herself" (1954), she offers a tale of frustration that centers on female birth control. Dottie Renfrew loses her virginity, procures a diaphragm, and then, like a heroine in Henry James, leaves it under a bench in Washington Square Park. A recent Vassar graduate and like her friends a "great believer in love," Dottie adventurously hooks up with the pornographically named Dick Brown after the wedding of her classmate Kay Strong (the character who resembles McCarthy). Dick is not all phallus. He is also a painter. When he and Dottie have sex in his Greenwich Village walk-up, he treats her clinically and impersonally, stripping her of shoes, stockings, brassiere, girdle, and step-ins, and coaching her: " '*Nothing will happen unless you want it, baby.*' The words, lightly stressed, told her how scared and mistrustful she must be looking. 'I know, Dick,' she answered in a small weak, grateful voice, making herself use his name aloud for the first time." Dottie has multiple orgasms. The gently satirical free-indirect discourse renders her physical sensations vividly. From Dick she learns that she is "highly sexed." However, most of the chapter focuses on anxieties about pregnancy and birth control. "Supposing he had started to have an emission while he was still inside her?" Dottie worries. "Or if he had used one of the rubber things and it had broken when he had jerked like that and that was why he had pulled so sharply away. She had heard of the rubber things breaking or leaking and how a woman could get pregnant from just a single drop."[93]

Dick practices *coitus interruptus,* "a horrid nuisance," and comes on Dottie's belly. He promises that there is not a single sperm swimming up to fertilize her ovum. But the next morning, as he propels her to the door, he says, "Get yourself a pessary." The phrase utterly confounds her (she wonders if it's like Hamlet's rejection of Ophelia: "Get thee to a nunnery"). He explains impatiently, "A female contraceptive, a plug." Understanding dawns: "In a person like Dick, her feminine instinct caroled, this was surely the language of love."[94] Love, however, has nothing to do with it. Like Grandfather Preston, Dick is a "law unto himself," which doesn't mean that he is lawless but that he, too, remains detached from substantive

moral questions. He acknowledges that he thinks of her generically. It is useful to think about this notion of the law by
means of a distinction drawn by the Harvard political philosopher Michael Sandel, who describes two ways of defending
laws against abortion: the "naive" view, which holds that the
justice of laws depends on the moral worth of the conduct
they prohibit or protect, and the "sophisticated" view, which
holds that the justice of laws depends not on substantive moral
judgment about the conduct at stake but on a general theory
of individual rights.[95] Though she tries to embrace the notion
that love and sex can be separated, Dottie, who is a great believer in love, embodies the "naive" view. Dick states plainly
that he does not love her or anyone. He represents the "sophisticated" notion that one can be neutral and independent among
competing visions of the good life.

As Sandel points out, the Supreme Court has struggled
to justify the right to privacy regarding contraceptives between the argument for letting people lead their sexual lives
as they choose and affirming and protecting the social institution of marriage (a tension Dottie feels acutely). In representing these two approaches to "love" and invoking metaphors
of law, Dick and Dottie implicitly raise questions about different aspects of the right to privacy. Dick is a law unto himself
because he identifies privacy with autonomy. He believes in
the right to engage in certain conduct without external constraint. In this sense he is a classic liberal (as well as a self-
described bastard). Dottie, on the other hand, like young Mary
in the Marmon roadster, leads us to question whether moral
language (relating to marriage or not) ought to be entirely
separated from discussions about contraception. Justice Blackmun's *Roe* decision tries but does not fully succeed in dis-
pensing with this moral dilemma; it both acknowledges "the

sensitive and emotional nature of the abortion controversy"
and insists that the Court's task is "to resolve the issue by constitutional measurement free of emotion and of predilection."
The story demonstrates the incompatibility of the naive and
sophisticated perspectives. Although her Daddy had joked
that she ought to have been a lawyer, Dottie often finds herself
wondering what "Dick meant." In discussing sex, he employs
an incredible vocabulary and uses terms from the handbooks,
"orgasm," "climax," and "erectile tissue." Dottie is ashamed of
her ignorance, having only seen a few inexplicit books by
Krafft-Ebing, picked up at a secondhand bookstore. She
nearly chokes on the words "douche" and "birth control."[96]

On Dick's advice she visits a birth control bureau, where
she receives a sheaf of "literature" that describes tampons,
sponges, the collar-button, the wishbone, and butterfly pes-
saries, thimbles, silk rings, and coils, as well as a referral to a
gynecologist. Then she goes to the woman's doctor's office to
get a diaphragm of the kind found by Margaret Sanger in Holland and now, for the first time (circa 1933), imported in quantity to the United States. With her friend Kay, she discusses
the etiquette of contraception (who pays for what, where to
keep the apparatus, how to get rid of it when the affair is over,
and so on). The young women agree not only that getting the
contraception is a bigger step than losing your virginity but
also that no one must find out. The narrative voice tenderly
satirizes their sense of militancy by reinforcing their lack of
real access to the public sphere: "The things you did in private
were your own business, but this was practically public!"[97]
Real names must not be used. It is in concealing her affair and
procuring birth control that Dottie tells her first real lie to her
mother, with whom she has an otherwise extraordinarily
open relationship. The woman doctor, however, asks probing

questions that "like a delicately maneuvering forceps, ex-tracted information that ought to have hurt but didn't."[98] Still Dottie blushes as she feels the interview touching the bio-graphical. The doctor in turn tells Dottie about Sanger and her trip to Holland and how the long fight had been waged through the courts. Dottie had already read about this partic-ular doctor in newspapers that had recounted her arrest a few years earlier in a raid on a birth control clinic. The doctor encourages Dottie to learn how to gain the deepest satisfac-tion from the sexual act. There are no practices, oral or man-ual, that are wrong in lovemaking, she explains, giving Dottie goose pimples. Dottie's trip to the birth control clinic became a cultural phenomenon. Philip Roth cites it in *Goodbye, Co-lumbus* when Neil Klugman urges Brenda Patimkin to get herself fitted for a diaphragm. However, the chapter concludes with what follows Dottie's departure. After visiting the doc-tor, she phones Dick but receives no answer.

Powdered and gloved, Dottie walks across Eighth Ave-nue to Washington Square, where she sits on a park bench, holding her packages on her lap. It is a self-consciously liter-ary episode. Roth would later stage a fraudulent pregnancy test there in *The Facts,* offering homage, like McCarthy, to Catherine Sloper's renunciation of love in Henry James's *Washington Square.* Dottie tries Dick again and receives no answer. Then, in the dark, she begins to cry: "Hoping that she was unobserved, she slipped the contraceptive equipment un-der the bench she was sitting on and began to walk as swiftly as she could, without attracting attention, to Fifth Avenue. A cruising taxi picked her up at the corner and drove her, qui-etly sobbing, to the Vassar Club."[99] Why would she do such a thing? Why throw away the contraception she has obtained with such difficulty, embarrassment, and secrecy and which has been the climax of the story of her first sexual experience? The story shows that a newly evolving notion of privacy rights (in the 1950s and 1960s) based on personal autonomy and the ideal of the neutral state does more harm than good to a young woman like Dottie. She is not, after all, fully independent. Underlying *The Group*, as the title implies, is a critique not exactly of autonomy, which literally means "governed by one's own law," but of a form of individualism based on treating people with complete neutrality. The novel questions a model of autonomy that isolates people in their freedom and offers instead a conception of the individual enabled by a context of particular relationships.[100] Privacy based on the idea of treating people generically (as Dick treats Dottie) needs to be exposed as a way of turning some citizens into passive, dependent objects.

McCarthy opposes the lying, evasion, and silence that Dottie, who eventually confesses to her mother and "makes an honest woman of herself," feels temporarily compelled to commit. Dottie may conceal the contraceptive, but McCarthy does not hide it or any other aspect of the experience. As a result, she was excoriated by her Vassar classmates for exposing their private lives in her novel. Among the bitter reactions published in a *New York Herald Tribune* article entitled "The Group on Mary McCarthy" (a piece McCarthy herself found libelous), one former classmate accused her of having pursued the original Dottie (Dorothy Newton, Vassar '33) into a man's apartment and later into the birth control clinic.[101] Though she denied that the story was anything but fictional, McCarthy appears to believe that if there is no inherent or substantive value to intimacy, then it must be exposed or thrown away.

Despite being disparaged as a "ladies' novel" by many of the critics in her own crowd, including Hellman, *The Group* was a best seller for nearly two years.[102]

In describing sex, McCarthy commonly adopts a tone of clinical detachment tinged with disgust, forced humor, and a barely suppressed desire to wound. "I was able to compare the sexual equipment of the various men I made love with," she wrote at the age of seventy-seven, "and there were amazing differences, in both length and massiveness."[103] Although she liked marriage and domesticity (concluding her life with a long, happy marriage), in her writing McCarthy can seem incapable of intimacy, the feeling of deep engrossment in which people give up their roles as observers and become participants. Of the sex with Crosby she wrote, "It was a kind of hypnotism, which I believe does not go deep either. I obeyed his command to open my legs, having gone too far not to finish the task, but it was chiefly my muscles that submitted; my mind held itself apart, not finding him, to my surprise, very interesting."[104] Of course, Crosby, like Dick Brown, is a banal type, but McCarthy can be no less detached in describing more mature lovers.

As an author she was infamous for satirizing her closest friends, observing them and exposing them without their consent. In doing so she seems hostile not only to the lies and evasions that privacy can protect but also to the notion of personal autonomy or subjectivity that it enables. In choosing to write satirical fiction, McCarthy assumes the role of self-appointed guardian of truth. It is her job to censure folly. McCarthy writes novels because she is interested in exposing what private life conceals, like the protagonist of her first story, "Cruel and Unusual Punishment," an actress in private life addicted to "Public Appearances,"[105] or the terrorists who are the subject of her final novel, *Cannibals and Missionaries*. "Mary," one of her friends exclaimed after reading *How I Grew*, "believes that nothing should be hidden!"[106] Philip Rahv was enraged by her portrayal of him in her allegorical 1948 roman à clef, *The Oasis,* and considered a libel suit. Dwight Macdonald told an interviewer, "When most pretty girls smile at you, you feel terrific. When Mary smiles at you, you look to see if your fly is open."[107]

Although she had sexual relations with many men, at the very end of her life McCarthy wrote that one in particular had been instrumental in "push[ing] me into 'creativity.'" That was Edmund Wilson, who "compelled" her to marry him, then shut her into a little room where he insisted that she write, and later even committed her to a psychiatric ward. McCarthy felt unable to evade these constraints but even perversely seemed to desire them. Regarding herself as a literary construct, she writes in her last book that without Wilson's compulsion, "I would not be the 'Mary McCarthy' you are now reading. Yet, awful to say, I am not particularly grateful."[108] Though she hated pity, the trauma of her marriage to Wilson, like that of losing her parents, shaped her work and her life. She told the story of their relationship in many ways over many years.

One Saturday morning in October 1937, the plump and bulbous-eyed Wilson bustled into the new Union Square office of *Partisan Review.* He was forty-two years old and "breathy." He looked as though he had just bathed, his skin pink and fresh, and he wore a gray two-piece suit. The *PR* boys wanted to impress the famous man. He was by then America's most prominent critic, author of *Axel's Castle* and editor of *Vanity Fair.* Wilson was an influential advocate of modernism and supporter of left-wing causes. In relaunching the journal independently of the Communist Party and with a strong anti-Stalinist line, Philip Rahv, Dwight Macdonald, Fred Dupee, and William Phillips hoped to elicit his support. Mostly he was impressed by the green-eyed McCarthy in black dress and fox stole. He subsequently took her on a couple of dates with her friend and colleague Margaret Marshall. Then Wilson invited the two young women to the small house he rented in Stamford, Connecticut. After Margaret fell asleep in the guest room, Mary followed him into his study to continue a conversation. In the posthumously published *Intellectual Memoirs,* written more than fifty years after their first drunken copulation on the couch, she remained indignant that he misunderstood "my intention." She followed him into his book-lined study only to continue the conversation. She liked talking to him, but he was short, stout, and middle-aged. Nevertheless, he "firmly took me into his arms," and "I gave up the battle."[109]

The same language of physical force and submission appears in McCarthy's 1955 novel, *A Charmed Life,* when Miles Murphy (the character based on Wilson) sexually assaults his former wife, Martha Sinnott (a character based on McCarthy). Like Wilson, Miles is not physically attractive but fat and freckled with a reddish crust of curly hair, a plump face, and eyes like grapes about to burst. Yet he is a man of many women. After an evening of heavy drinking, reading Racine, and discussing ethics at the home of mutual friends and without their respective spouses, Miles offers to drive Martha home. The next thing she knows, they are "making love" on the empire sofa in her parlor.

> She had struggled at first, quite violently, when he
> flung himself on top of her on the sofa. But he had

her pinioned beneath him with the whole weight
of his body. She could only twist her head away
from him, half-burying it in one of the sofa pillows
while he firmly deposited kisses on her neck and
hair. Her resistance might have deterred him if he
had not been drinking, but the liquor narrowed
his purpose. He was much stronger than she was,
besides being in good condition, and he did not let
her little cries of protest irritate him as they once
might have done. . . . The angry squirming of her
body, the twisting and turning of her head, filled
him with amused tolerance and quickened his ex-
citement as he crushed his member against her reluctant pelvis.[110]

The word "violently" applies first to the woman's behavior, a
surprising displacement until the reader discovers that the
free indirect discourse is rendered from the man's point of
view. For instance, "he did not let her little cries of protest irritate him." Like the tale of lost virginity, this narrative focuses on masculine sexual expression, which in this case does
lead to an unwanted pregnancy. But the female voice is not
passive, and the narrator insists that she is not a victim, or at
least not *only* a victim. McCarthy's prose is highly ironic, and
retroactively it works to contain the seepage of male sex.

The passage describing intercourse in *A Charmed Life*
is followed by the woman's self-analysis and lengthy ratio-
nalization, as is the analogous passage in *Intellectual Memoirs,* which even refers the reader to chapter 5 of *A Charmed
Life.* Martha does not feel bad for what they had done, though
neither seemed to have enjoyed it much. It had been a
challenge—having sex with her ex-spouse—that she felt she

had to confront, like being afraid. Although she had struggled, she had also suppressed her scruples "at the blunt simplicity of his onset that took her consent for granted." She simply did not feel that she "had the *right* to refuse him," and the language of rights recurs jarringly throughout the book. Ultimately she decides that holding herself apart like a precious vase not meant for use would be "undemocratic," though this act of adultery will also require her to start "lying and deceiving and thinking of implicating the poor handyman."[111] Similarly, following her autobiographical account of the first sex with Wilson, McCarthy tries vainly to explain her motives to him. But he would not listen to what she "felt sure was the truth; only facts spoke to him, and the fact was that I had let him make love to me. Again I gave up. You cannot argue against facts. And yet to this day I am convinced that he had me wrong: I only wanted to talk to him."[112] McCarthy at least half believes that the truth is not on the side of the "facts," but she also distrusts herself. She tries to separate herself from Wilson's rigidity. She wonders if it is so easy to separate consequences from motivations.

In February 1938 McCarthy and Wilson were married. By the end of March it was clear that Mary was pregnant (like Martha). Wilson boasted that he'd managed it "the first crack out of the box."[113] However, although they both wanted children, he strongly urged her to get an immediate abortion. McCarthy was twenty-five. She refused. They had set up house in Stamford. In 1938 Connecticut was at the center of national debates about birth control. Wilson shut her into a room where he told her that she had to write. She quickly completed "Cruel and Barbarous Treatment." In it the unnamed heroine is incapable of genuine private life: "For the first time, she saw that the virtue of marriage as an institution lay in its public

character. Private cohabitation, long continued, was, she concluded, a bore."[114] This story doesn't dignify the public, but it
demolishes the private, which is only something to be escaped.
Privacy means privation. It is a dangerous place for young
women.

McCarthy's writing returns continually to the origins
rather than the ends of action and, in doing so, reveals the
problems of privacy. Privacy shields the place of rape and bat-
tery. It creates a context for deceit and hypocrisy, protects the
guilty, and increases our vulnerability to shame.[115] It also reinforces women's passive and domestic status, their place as
victims. In returning to the origins of intercourse, McCarthy's confessional writing discovers not just guilt but also her
own agency, recognizing how she empowered beastly father
figures from the monstrous foster-parent Uncle Myers of
her early youth to Wilson. The act of exposure is democratic.
McCarthy's writing focuses intensively on violations of individual autonomy, or of the "integrity of [one's] moral sense,"
which are galling and exhilarating by turns.[116] Politics for her is
personal, not in the 1960s sense that the personal is the political
but in the banal way in which the most passionate political
commitments depend on a personal disappointment, a petty
sleight, or a sexual escapade. Curiously, she asserts control by
denying or disparaging the right to privacy. There is a tension
in her life that most critics and biographers have felt the need to
explain away, between the strong, assertive, and masculine
McCarthy and the kind, domestic, and feminine McCarthy.

Sexual Freedom and Protection

The conflict between sexual freedom and protection from
sexual abuse has been central to American social life from

Hellman's experience at Liveright and McCarthy's with Wilson to the cases of Clarence Thomas and Anita Hill and Bill Clinton and Monica Lewinsky. The experience of sexual harassment and sexual liberation profoundly shaped and was shaped by the lives of Hellman and McCarthy. People hated and loved both women for their sexually provocative lives and writings. Their sex lives were inseparable from their importance as icons of American culture. The conservative journalist Paul Johnson, in an angry and moralistic essay, "Lies, Damned Lies and Lillian Hellman," complains that she was a "five foot four, 'rather homely' girl [with] . . . an assertive sexual personality." He indicts her for her abortions, "female lies" and "sexual promiscuity."[117] As Johnson wrote these lines, Hellman's libel suit was making its way through the courts. In that year, feminist legal scholar Catharine MacKinnon advanced a provocative and powerful argument *against* the choice to pursue the abortion right under the law of privacy, a legal strategy that goes back through *Roe v. Wade* to *Griswold v. Connecticut*. In her view, this approach merely reaffirms the private-public split that feminism sought to contest in the 1960s and the appearance of "male direction in sexual expression." Abortion policy has never addressed the context of how women get pregnant in the first place, but only the consequence of intercourse under "conditions of gender inequality."[118]

MacKinnon's argument against the right to privacy is persuasive. We can find evidence to support her assumptions in McCarthy's life and fiction. McCarthy seemed continually surprised by the consequences of her sexual encounters, which she depicts as largely initiated and guided by men. Many women of her generation, and those among the most highly educated and strong minded, had multiple abortions. "I was all but unique among the women I knew in never having recourse to a back-street abortion," Diana Trilling later wrote.[119] Using contraception means acknowledging and planning and directing sexual intercourse, accepting one's sexual availability. It means appearing available to masculine desire. From studies of abortion clinics, women who repeatedly seek abortions, when asked why, say something like, "The sex just happened." Can a woman be presumed to control access to her sexuality if she feels unable to interrupt intercourse to use birth control?

But MacKinnon's argument is also inadequate. Neither McCarthy nor Hellman ever expresses a puritanical attitude about sex or believes that women need protection from male sexuality or from themselves, in spite of the many pathological qualities of heterosexual sex that they present. In a vital respect, it is the very unpalatable quality of sex that is crucial to their representation of it, the way it brings to the fore more general questions of literary and personal constraint, limitations to freedom, the need for or abandonment of caution. Their sex lives and their writing about sex are not only limited but also enabled by particular, historical forms of censorship, and though we may be blind to contemporary forms of constraint, so are ours. For MacKinnon, sexually harassing utterances immediately violate and subordinate the victim, but Hellman and McCarthy refuse the image of women as passive victims, though they often represent the passivity of women. A great deal depends on interpretation. But their work is infused by the ideology that women's sexuality also deserves expression.

Privacy is the necessary context for love, as law professor Charles Fried has written, for it requires the recognition of persons as ends rather than means. It is a zone or a context or a protection of respect, love, friendship, and trust. "Privacy

is not merely a good technique for furthering these fundamental relations," Fried suggests; "rather without privacy
they are simply inconceivable. They require a context of privacy or the possibility of privacy for their existence."[120] A
threat to privacy, therefore, threatens the integrity of our personhood. Hellman was skilled (perhaps too skilled) at intimacy. McCarthy was not. Both struggled to negotiate a
historical landscape on which the boundaries between the
public and private were undergoing major revision. McCarthy can appear to want to protect a supposedly rational public
sphere from incursion by the private, whereas Hellman can
seem more interested in protecting private freedoms from
public invasion. Hellman's story "Bethe" suggests exactly the
degree to which a threat to privacy can destroy personal integrity when characters turn up in pieces. In *A Charmed Life,*
Martha realizes that to pay close attention to another person
is the prime human virtue: "Without it, there could be no dignity and no reciprocity." But she has a hard time figuring out
the necessary limits or constraints on attention even in private life. From her new husband, she "wished nothing to be
hidden . . . , not even the bad parts of her nature. She respected
his privacy, because he was a man, but for herself, if she could
not be transparent, she did not want love. It seemed to her,
therefore, ominous that the minute Miles reentered her life, a
slight deception began, almost automatically."[121] In spite of
her political comments, Mary McCarthy's fiction shows the
difficulty of addressing female reproductive rights by assuming universal standards of rightness and wrongness.

For most of the twentieth century, abortion was, both
legally and physically, an extremely dangerous undertaking
for a young woman, but it was also common.[122] By 1925, Emma
Goldman's and Margaret Sanger's birth control activism, like

first-wave feminism more broadly, was ebbing. The experiences of women such as Hellman and McCarthy, who came after, show that access to people's bodies and access to information are not two separate or distinct kinds of privacy but are deeply interrelated, even inextricable concerns. Publishing and pregnancy are two forms of reproduction, and their relationship has real (not just literary) ramifications. The women's movement and feminist criticism of the 1960s and 1970s often focused on the ways in which men objectified the world through language; to write from a position of authority, feminist critics argued, is to appropriate certain kinds of experience and even "to dominate it through verbal mastery."[123] As Hellman was writing her memoirs, a furious debate was raging in America over the right to privacy and, specifically, over women's right to make choices whether to terminate a pregnancy. This debate culminated (but did not conclude) in 1973 with the Supreme Court decision on *Roe v. Wade*. In the same year, Hellman published *Pentimento*. Although Hellman had written that by 1925 "the fight for the emancipation of women, their rights under the law, in the office, in bed, was stale stuff," her work—read with that of McCarthy— demolishes the assumption that the fight for sexual freedom has been won, that rights in the office or in bed could be, then or now, taken for granted.[124]

IV
Choice Words and Political Dramas

Pour savoir qui tu es et ce que tu veux faire, il faut que tu décides comment tu te situes dans le monde. In order to know who you are and what you want to do, you have to decide where you stand in the world.
—Simone de Beauvoir, *Les Mandarins,* 1954

EMILE: I know what you're against. What are you for?
—Rodgers and Hammerstein, *South Pacific,* 1949

The ways Americans tell stories about their moral and political choices shape and delimit those choices. On a Tuesday morning in April 1937, a train pulled into Mexico City bearing the seventy-eight year-old philosopher John Dewey, novelist James T. Farrell, and other commissioners and staff of the Dewey Commission of Inquiry into the Charges against Leon Trotsky in the Moscow Trials. Stalin's four show trials in Russia had begun a year earlier. In the first, sixteen prominent Bolsheviks confessed to having plotted with Trotsky to kill Stalin. The court found everybody guilty and sentenced the defendants to death, including Trotsky in absentia. The show trials led to the executions of all the members of Lenin's Politburo other than Stalin himself. Today everyone agrees that they were a monstrous frame-up, part of Stalin's purge of millions of workers, peasants, intellectuals, military officers, and government officials. But in 1937 they were a flashpoint for American intellectuals of the Left. In an "Open Letter to American Liberals," a month before Dewey set out, signers including Malcolm Cowley, Theodore Dreiser, Lillian Hellman, Dorothy Parker, Henry Roth, and Nathanael West attacked the commission for challenging the Soviet party line. The following year a "Statement by American Progressives" aimed to expose "Trotskyist enemies of progress" and assert the "real facts."[1] There was widespread sympathy for the Soviet Union in the 1930s, particularly for the Popular Front against fascism. The signers saw the Trotskyites as aiding a fascist disinformation plot. Choosing sides was a key decision for a generation. "For American liberals and the American liberal movement," as Farrell later wrote, the Moscow Trials "constituted a test and a challenge."[2]

More than thirty years later, in 1979, a few months before shooting the episode for the *Dick Cavett Show* in which she accused Lillian Hellman of being a liar, Mary McCarthy wrote to their mutual friend Dwight Macdonald to protest Hellman's inclusion on the Board of the Spanish Relief Appeal. She complained that Hellman's "loyalty is not to Stalin but to Lillian then and now. . . . She's a deeply unprincipled

woman and won't allow other people the exercise of principle."[3] McCarthy was right. Hellman was unprincipled, and
she was loyal to herself above all. But rather than placing her
beyond the pale of American morality, these qualities place
her at the murky center. Much of American literature, exemplified by authors such as Ralph Waldo Emerson and Walt
Whitman, is untroubled by the idea of putting loyalty to oneself first, being guided by feeling and by the idea that choice is
never entirely free. In his essay "Self-Reliance," Emerson
urges us to trust our emotions. "Do I contradict myself?"
Whitman asks in "Song of Myself," "Very well then I contradict myself." These writers recognize that it is hard, if not impossible, to justify our choices by an appeal either to reason
alone or to fundamental principles. They consider it prefera-
ble to contradict oneself than to be morally rigid, better to act
on whim or instinct than to trust an outside authority or
morals that claim a prior point of origin. Macdonald, a friend
of McCarthy from their days on the board of the anti-Soviet
journal *Partisan Review* in the 1930s, swung between allegiances to the two women.[4] In her 1949 novel *The Oasis*, Mc-
Carthy parodied his contradictory nature: "'Mac,' his supporter
protested, 'you're being inconsistent.' 'What if I am?' he
shouted, waving his arms in the air. 'You know what Emerson
said.' . . . They grudged Mac Macdermott the luxury of being
both right and wrong in the same argument—one opinion
apiece was enough in a democracy."[5] Like Emerson, Macdonald had a tendency to decide first and determine principles
afterward, suggesting that experience becomes morally intel-
ligible in action, or in the stories we tell to justify it.

McCarthy's overemphatic language suggests her own
difficulty with acting in accordance with first principles. In
one of her best known stories, "The Man in the Brooks Broth-

ers Shirt," the protagonist, Meg Sargent, on the verge of an adulterous tryst, asks herself, "How . . . can you act upon your feelings if you don't know what they are?" It is in the act that Meg discovers what they are. In a Catholic girlhood "the Church could classify it all for you."[6] Telling lies was bad, observing the sacraments good. Protestants like Meg's father were supposed to be neutral, a moral position unobtainable for the young woman of the story. "Chance, not choice, governs these insurrections of the flesh, as it does in politics," writes McCarthy's biographer Carol Brightman. "One makes decisions when one chooses to go public: to write and publish."[7] Yet the distinction between private and public, like that between chance and choice, is rarely neat. Although it is true that McCarthy later compares waking up in a man's bed, as if by chance, to discovering herself a Trotskyite, she continually returns to the question of personal responsibility.

In her 1955 novel *A Charmed Life,* one character announces, "You had to be loyal to all sides, to the truth *as you saw it,* which, when you came down to it, means being loyal to yourself." The philosophical protagonist, ironically named Martha Sinnott (sin-not), agrees, only to announce later, "You have to make universals. 'Behave so that thy maxim could be a universal law.' I agree with Kant." Martha's idea of what is morally "right," as opposed to what is useful or "good," is abstract. Miles Murphy, her ex-husband, educated at Heidelberg, the Sorbonne, the London School of Economics, and with Carl Jung in Zurich, has been a playwright, boxer, psychologist, writer of adventure stories, and magazine editor. Critical of Kant's one-size-fits-all proscription, he frowns and replies, "Kant's effort failed—too mechanically monistic."[8] Principles are always complicated by circumstances. Though moral choices are social by definition, however, a keystone of

American moral discourse is that making the right choices means being true to oneself (as urged by the duplicitous Polonius in *Hamlet*: "To thine own self be true"). That language was central to the 2008 political campaign of the "maverick" presidential candidacy of John McCain. It also raised serious questions about his judgment.[9]

Liberal democracies require public figures or those who participate in issues of public concern to justify their choices and explain the reasons for their conduct. In "Self-Reliance," Emerson admonished citizens to speak openly what is in your "private heart" so that "the inmost in due time becomes the outmost." Conforming to the agenda of "a great party either for the government or against it" is to live a lie, because it becomes impossible to "say a new and spontaneous word." Unfortunately, Emerson writes, most people bind themselves to "communities of opinion." "This conformity," he continues, "makes them not false in a few particulars, authors of a few lies, but false in all particulars. Their every truth is not quite true. Their two is not the real two, their four not the real four: so that every word they say chagrins us, and we know not where to begin to set them right."[10] The Hellman-McCarthy case reflects an Emersonian crisis of moral language in America. Lying had a particular meaning to those born in the first decades of the twentieth century, as did Emerson, whose academic canonization owed much to the literary critics of the 1930s and 1940s. At the Cultural and Scientific Conference for World Peace at the Waldorf-Astoria Hotel in 1949, McCarthy publicly challenged left-wing Harvard professor F. O. Matthiessen as to whether Emerson would have been able to live in the Soviet Union. Matthiessen reluctantly acknowledged that he would not. Shaped by the economic and political cataclysms of their day, their generation was both troubled and excited by the competition of political ideas in the new age of mass media. It is difficult, if not impossible, to remain truthful and transparent in a democracy while pursuing what often only a minority regards as necessary ends. How are those ends determined? Who decides?

For sixty years, the United States and the Soviet Union waged a psychological war based on the assumption that the distinction between truth and lies depends on the power of language to persuade. McCarthy's closest friend, the political theorist Hannah Arendt, comments in her essay "Lying in Politics" (in a book dedicated to McCarthy) that the ability to lie is simply the product of human imagination. It is not the lies of the government to which she objects but its mistaken decisions. "We are free to change the world and to start something new in it," Arendt says. "Hence, when we talk about lying, and especially about lying among acting men, let us remember that the lie did not creep into politics by some accident of human sinfulness."[11] The Pentagon Papers, the popular name given to the multivolume "History of U.S. Decision-Making Process on Vietnam Policy," she explains, "tell different stories, teach different lessons to different readers." Russia expert George F. Kennan, whom Hellman knew from her visits to Moscow, developed the concept of "the necessary lie" as a key element in American Cold War diplomacy in a speech to the National War College in December 1947. Trust in public figures eroded in the decades prior to McCarthy's appearance on the *Dick Cavett Show*. The perjury trial of Alger Hiss, the conviction of atomic spy Klaus Fuchs, the founding of the CIA in 1947 and the discovery in the 1960s that it had covertly funded American artists and intellectuals, the Watergate break-in and Richard Nixon's fall, all indicate the practice of what political theorists, such as Karl Popper and Leo Strauss, called "the noble lie" for high-sounding aims such as national security. The US government continues to struggle to rebuild confidence in its statements of intention.

Philosophers have long debated the permissibility of various kinds of lies. The most serious complaint against lying, voiced by Kant, is that it violates the rights of the person to whom it is addressed. Because it subverts the principle of respect for persons, Kant says all lies are immoral and insists on a categorical duty to be truthful. Most people find it impossible to adhere to this basic principle, especially when confronted with a conflicting duty, such as lying to a homicidal maniac who comes looking for their child. Utilitarian thinkers, such as the English social reformer Jeremy Bentham, said that lies could be justified by the goodness or badness of their consequences. Like Kant's obligation to be truthful, however, the utilitarian cost-benefit analysis breaks down in complex cases. In contexts of radical insecurity there can be no easy certainty about the justification of lies. As Arendt wrote in the preface to the first edition of *The Origins of Totalitarianism,* "Never has our future been more unpredictable, never have we depended so much on political forces that cannot be trusted to follow the rules of common sense and self-interest—forces that look like sheer insanity."[12] Twentieth-century developments in advertising, propaganda, espionage, and total war undermined the distinction between personal and political choices, along with boundaries between public and private. The publicity of the Hellman-McCarthy case was not incidental to but emblematic of debates about moral language and their ramifications for civic community. It meant that justification on both sides had to extend beyond citing one's own conscience. Both parties asserted that the other's dishonesty had done real harm to the country.

Hellman and McCarthy used words to justify their conduct in significantly different ways.[13] Both wrote often about the relationship between language and morals and about the problem of translating between languages or making oneself understandable to others. In Hellman's 1941 play *Watch on the Rhine*, the antifascist fighter Kurt Müller (modeled on Gustav Regler, whom Hellman befriended in Spain in 1937) asks his wife, "Heist das auf deutsch 'Idealle'? . . . Is that what I have? I do not like the word. It gives to me the picture of a small, pale man at a seaside resort."[14] As Hellman recognized, particular words contribute to a picture of reality and cannot be understood in isolation from other words and structures of thought. Her 1944 play about diplomats, *The Searching Wind,* opens with a dialogue about the pitfalls of learning too many languages and using them only to gossip rather than to make hard choices. The idea that forms of language are inseparable from the actions into which they are woven was central to the generation of linguists, philosophers, and critics shaped by the social, political, and economic upheavals of the 1930s and 1940s.

By the 1950s, scholars from diverse fields, such as linguist Roman Jakobson and anthropologist Claude Lévi-Strauss (both European émigrés to America), largely agreed that there were relationships between the grammatical categories of the language a person speaks and how that person both understands the world and behaves in it. In perhaps the most important book on moral philosophy in the Cold War period, *The Language of Morals* (1952), Oxford professor R. M. Hare writes, "Thus, in a world in which the problems of conduct become every day more complex and tormenting, there is a great need for an understanding of the language in which these problems are posed and answered."[15] But Hare's method of studying moral language was logical, not historical. Although philosophical discussions of ethical decision-making date back to ancient times, public discourse in America has focused to an extraordinary degree on the language of moral choice and the benefits and drawbacks of consistency. The intensified focus on public decision-making is due to the variables of public opinion and the power of propaganda and advertising to shape it. It is through forms of speech, metaphor, even of grammar, that our world takes shape. This reality of American democratic culture has been reflected since the 1950s in the rise of academic disciplines such as sociolinguistics, political science, and "decision sciences" that investigate how decisions are made by political parties, voters, and branches of government.

At the beginning of his *Politics,* Aristotle says that language is the basic prerequisite for political association. We are political animals by virtue of the gift of speech.[16] We cannot achieve perspective on our lives alone. "The worst crime one human could commit against another," McCarthy herself wrote, was "not to take their words seriously."[17] In this chapter I show that conflicting stories about moral choice reflect what cultural theorist Kenneth Burke called "frames of acceptance" or "the more or less organized system of meanings by which a thinking man gauges the historical situation and adopts a role with relation to it."[18] Burke, America's foremost communist thinker, was neither doctrinaire enough for the Stalinists nor critical enough for the Trotskyites.[19] He wrote for both the pro-Soviet *New Masses* and the anti-Soviet *Partisan Review* and remained suspicious of the rhetoric of each. Whatever their decisions, he remarked, "people are *necessarily* mistaken." In the 1930s Burke often advocated a comic attitude toward history. In recognizing that "*all* people are exposed to situations in which they must act as fools, that *every* insight contains its own special kind of blindness," he believed, "you complete the comic circle."[20] In *Attitudes toward History*, which he wrote as the Moscow show trials were under way, Burke adopted a "comic ambivalence" and recommended the need for compromise, a "comic" way of thinking about political language that aimed to synthesize the conflicting impulses embodied by "man in society, man in drama."[21] To be in society, according to Burke, is to be an actor in a drama. Burke's philosophy of literary form exemplified his age's dramatic way of looking at rhetoric and modes of decision-making. Following him, in this chapter I use the word "drama" to suggest not only dialogue but also that these stories are enacted by the characters themselves. Their language is a form of action, but particular kinds of drama, such as comedy, melodrama, and tragedy, employ different and often incompatible vocabularies of moral decision-making.

In the following pages I focus on three dramas of moral choice that bear historical connections to the Hellman-McCarthy dispute. First is the meeting of Leon Trotsky and John Dewey in Mexico City. Trotsky and Dewey illuminate a basic contrast between two models of moral thinking: one that privileges the notion of the "good" over the "right" and ends over means, and another that denies that there is any meaningful distinction between ends and means. It is tempting to understand the conflict between Hellman and McCarthy in these terms (the good versus the right, ends versus means), but I also show how their lives inevitably complicate these moral frameworks. Second, I look at Hellman's drama of greed and self-realization, *The Little Foxes*, as it relates to contemporary political choices forced by the Spanish Civil War and the Soviet-Nazi Pact of 1939, the genre of melodrama and its limitations in framing moral action. Last, I turn to Harry Truman's devastating decision to drop the atomic bomb and its impact on the idea of choice in public and private life. Many people—from comrades of the Old Left to contemporary historians—have dated the animus between Hellman and McCarthy to the political choices of the 1930s, but as important as the particular choices they made is how they made and represented them—their attitudes toward choice itself. In Hellman's 1951 play *The Autumn Garden,* a young French refugee, who resists the attitudes and language that her American relations want to impose on her, insists, "I do not want the world you want for me."[22] Hellman and McCarthy sought throughout their lives to give shape to a world that they could imagine having chosen, a world that embodied the consequences of their own choices. Together they represent not just different political choices but also different ways that choices are and can be made.

Mary McCarthy among the Trotskyites

In November 1936, the anti-Stalinist radical, Irish American writer James T. Farrell escorted recent Vassar graduate Mary McCarthy to a publisher's party in honor of *New Masses* cartoonist Art Young. Farrell wanted to help the thin, hard-driving, and newly divorced McCarthy to navigate the complex world of Leftist New York intellectual society. She had written favorably of Farrell's novel *The Young Manhood of Studs Lonegan,* and they shared a Midwestern, ex-Catholic background. She had also recently published reviews in the *Nation* and the *New Republic* and was then beginning a job at the left-wing publishing house Covici Friede. The *Nation* and *New Republic* had tacitly sided with the Stalinists and openly opposed the Dewey Commission, as did the *New Masses,* but McCarthy did not seem to hold any firm political views. She had moved to New York in 1933 with her husband, Harold Johnsrud, and had come immediately into contact with communist circles.

In 1934, McCarthy and Johnsrud, with their friends and editors of the magazine *Common Sense,* Selden Rodman and Alfred Bingham, whom Trotsky later characterized as "reactionary snobs," dressed up in evening clothes and demonstrated on behalf of striking waiters in the blue and gold Empire Room of the Waldorf-Astoria Hotel.[23] Urging diners to walk out in sympathy with the strikers, the young activists were supported by bon mots and wisecracks from celebrity authors Dorothy Parker and Alexander Woollcott. A corps of house detectives bore down on them, and a melee ensued. The band tried to drown them out with a furious rendition of "Did You Ever See a Dream Walking?" The *New York Times* called it "an old-fashioned fracas in modern dress and setting." McCarthy parodied this comical display of fashionable politics and moral complacency in her 1963 novel *The Group.* "We've come to stand for something meaningful to other people," proclaims one of the self-satisfied demonstrators, "and when that happens you're no longer a free agent."[24] These young women imagine that their political decisions, which have been determined by history, and their sex lives, which they have freely chosen, have nothing to do with each other. Of course, they have everything to do with each other. McCarthy, with more self-knowledge, reached a political watershed in the summer of 1936 after separating from Johnsrud and nearly marrying another man.

In August 1936, McCarthy missed news of the first Moscow show trial because she was in Reno getting a divorce and did not see the New York papers. Gregory Zinoviev and Lev Kamenev, two of Lenin's coworkers, made degrading confessions and were executed. In July the Spanish Civil War, the first military round between the Soviet Union and the fascist axis of Italy and Germany, a conflict that galvanized liberal Americans, had begun. McCarthy would later write of her pleasurable sense of isolation in Reno, in Seattle (visiting her grandparents and covering a longshoremen's strike for the *Nation*), and then back in New York, where she moved into a one-bedroom apartment on a crooked street in Greenwich Village. She was alone and intensely happy, her heart swollen with Popular Front solidarity. Then she went to the cocktail party with Farrell. In her 1953 autobiographical essay "My Confession" and elsewhere, McCarthy traced her conversion to Trotskyism to that party.

"My Confession," with its self-consciously Catholic moral framework, is an essay about the ethics and the politics of choice. McCarthy's "Confession" evokes the private interaction of priest and penitent to describe experiences that are not only public but also international. As Hannah Arendt had recently written, voluntary self-exposure both produces and is produced by a freedom denied in totalitarian regimes. "My Confession" is a classic liberal reply to the confessional memoirs of former communists Whittaker Chambers and Elizabeth Bentley, who had served as spies in the 1930s, had broken with the party, and then provided sensational public testimony in the late 1940s. Bentley, like McCarthy a Vassar graduate, published her story, *Out of Bondage*, in 1951. Chambers's monumental autobiography, *Witness,* which McCarthy's friend the liberal historian Arthur Schlesinger described as both an "extraordinary personal document" and "an invaluable account of the Communist conspiracy in the United

States," appeared in 1952.[25] For McCarthy, however, these sensational works of "fact-fiction" were too conventionally plotted:

> The diapason of choice plays, like movie music, round today's apostle to the Gentiles: Whittaker Chambers on a park bench and, in a reprise, awake all night at a dark window, facing the void. These people, like ordinary beings, are shown the true course during a lightning storm of revelation, on the road to Damascus. And their decisions are lonely decisions, silhouetted against a background of public incomprehension and hostility.
>
> Is it really so difficult to tell a good action from a bad one? I think one usually knows right away or a moment afterward, in a horrid flash of regret. . . . Too late to do anything about it, I discover that I have chosen. And this is particularly striking when the choice has been political or historic.[26]

As a program for approaching difficult moral choices, McCarthy's dependence on moral intuition has both advantages and drawbacks. On the positive side, relying on intuition implies that she is independent of external influences and is morally autonomous. That is essential in a society that values the freedom of the individual. In this respect, McCarthy contrasts herself with Chambers.

A short and stocky man with a large belly and rotten teeth, Chambers's commitment to radical politics in the 1920s and 1930s, with his later defection and political reversal, defined his whole moral being. In his testimony before HUAC and elsewhere, Chambers seemed to embody what he repeatedly called the "tragedy of history," the need to make a terrible and self-destructive choice. Like Hamlet in his suit of solemn black, he confronted "the agony of indecision." Chambers also compared himself to Sophocles' tragically torn Antigone. Nevertheless, whether as a communist or as an anticommunist, he believed absolutely in the rightness of his choices. Those choices are never free and voluntary but always encumbered by duties he cannot choose to renounce: "I could not separate the acts that I felt that I must perform [denouncing former communists] from my repugnance at having to perform them."[27] Chambers insists that both he and communism are not just eminently rational but so rational that real choice never presents itself. Of his conversion from communism to anticommunism, he writes,

> The torrent that swept through me in 1937 and the first months of 1938 swept my spirit clear to discern one truth: "Man without mysticism is a monster." I do not mean, of course, that I denied the usefulness of reason and knowledge. What I grasped was that religion begins at the point where reason and knowledge are powerless and forever fail—the point at which man senses the mystery of his good and evil.[28]

Chambers feels compelled to sacrifice the iron rules of pure reason for those of pure faith. Like the prophet Jonah, to whom he also compares himself, he places little trust in humanity's capacity for moral choice. McCarthy values individual freedom of choice more highly, but her mode of choice can seem no less arbitrary. One drawback of McCarthy's moral intuition is that, despite her revulsion at Chambers's lightning storm of revelation, depending on intuition also leaves no room for practical reasoning.

However, McCarthy's description of instantaneous moral insight actually conflicts with her story about becoming a Trotskyite because she is not just a narrator but also an actor. Her insight comes only after she demands that Farrell explain things to her. Farrell's account of the party is rich with vigorous arguments, successful persuasions, and frustrating failures that nearly culminate in fistfights.[29] A central subject of McCarthy's essay is the question of whether individuals in isolation from others can be said to make choices at all or whether the deliberative process is not necessarily always social. After repeatedly describing the pleasure of isolation, the joy of being newly single, the narrative shifts to the social dynamics of the party. McCarthy becomes tense and nervous. Sensing the peculiar solemnity of the whispering groups within the group, she finds herself standing bleakly by the refreshment table when Farrell, dimple-faced, shaggy-headed, earnest, and followed by a train of other people, approached her. Making it sound like an invasion, she says he "thrust at her a question." Did she think Trotsky was entitled to a hearing? A circle of listeners closed in.

"What do you want me to say?" McCarthy protested. "I don't know anything about it." A tumult of voices proffered explanations. Feeling out of touch, McCarthy asked what Trotsky had done. Farrell held up a hand, quieting the others and, like a schoolteacher, patiently explained. He said that Trotsky denied the charges and asked if McCarthy thought he was entitled to a fair hearing. "'Why, of course,' I laughed— 'were there people who would say that Trotsky was not entitled to a hearing?'" In a somber voice, Farrell turned to the group and announced, "She says Trotsky is entitled to his day

in court." Four days later she received a letter from the "Committee for the Defense of Leon Trotsky" and discovered her
name in the letterhead. She was outraged and decided within
two minutes to withdraw it and write a note of protest. "The
'decision' was made," she writes, "but according to my habit I
procrastinated." Then she began to receive harassing phone
calls that accused her and the committee of being a "tool of
reaction." Articles and letters appeared in the *New Masses,
New Republic, New York Times,* and *Nation* warning liberals
that Trotsky's request for a hearing was a "sham," complaining of the commission's "hushed adoration" for Trotsky, and
labeling the hearings "the farce of Coyoacan."[30]

Procrastination saved McCarthy from joining this
sorry band of Stalinists. Rather than wrestling with her conscience at the crossroads of choice, she felt, almost passively,
as though she had been saved from choosing because she
simply could not give in to the pressure tactics of the anti-
Trotsky forces without making an inquiry into the "rights and
wrongs" of his case. "Most ex-Communists nowadays," Mc-
Carthy remarks, "when they write their autobiographies or
testify before Congressional committees, are at pains to
point out that their actions were very, very bad and their motives very, very good. I would say the reverse of myself, though
without the intensives. I see no reason to disavow my actions
which were perfectly all right, but my motives give me a little
embarrassment."[31] McCarthy presents a different dramatic
form or framework than Chambers for understanding what
people do and why they do it. She says not that motives have
nothing to do with actions but that attributing motives involves questions of emphasis between what was done, when
and where it was done, who did it, and how and why they did
it. Conceptually speaking, the action precedes the motivation—

that is, we define the motive only after we have defined the action.

In her fiction McCarthy explores the difficulty of isolating motives from actions. Her characters' and her own aspiration to neutrality and independence of judgment is continually and ironically frustrated. For instance, at the end of her Cold War satire, *The Groves of Academe,* a novel about a literature instructor who is dismissed from a liberal arts college and then claims that he is the victim of a communist witch hunt, the college president asks the sort of question McCarthy posed to Hellman: "Are you a conscious liar or a self-deluded hypocrite?" The instructor, Henry Mulcahy, quotes the paradox of the liar: "A Cretan says, all Cretans are liars." He straightforwardly explains that the problem is subjective: "We're none of us certain of our motives; we can only be certain of facts.... I'm not concerned with truth ... I'm concerned with justice."[32] In a choice between truth and justice, he chooses justice. More provocative than the idea that truth defers to justice is the implication that the choice between truth and justice itself is a red herring because ultimately it is impossible to separate facts from values or the content of stories from the way they are told. Like Hellman, Mulcahy is a deeply unprincipled man. In the end, McCarthy forces the reader to ask whether rights can be justified in a way that does not presuppose any conception of a greater good or whether the principles of justice that govern a society can ever be truly neutral with respect to the competing moral convictions of its diverse citizens.

Taking as her subject the accidents and mistakes that lead to significant historical results, McCarthy's writing and her worldview are basically comic. Comedy is what happens when people try to translate some pure aim or vision into a material result. Doing so necessarily involves elements alien to the original, "spiritual" (as Chambers imagined it) motive.[33] In "My Confession," as an actor in her own comedy, McCarthy observes herself acting, commenting on the peculiar blend of the irrational and the rational, a mish-mash of motives that evokes the original meaning of the word "satire" (from *satira,* "medley"), along with the satirist's role as a self-appointed corrector of folly. She acknowledges that if Chambers's and Bentley's "decisions partook of the sublime . . . mine descended to the ridiculous."[34] The job of the satirist, as McCarthy says at the essay's outset, is to protest. After the conversation with Jim Farrell at the party for Art Young, McCarthy's contrarian nature, more than anything else, drove her to side with the Trotskyites. In "My Confession," "The Man in the Brooks Brothers Shirt," *The Groves of Academe,* and other works, McCarthy's descriptions of how she did or didn't make choices, of motivations and actions, causes and effects, means and ends, whether in going to bed with a stranger or joining a political campaign, were shaped by and helped to shape the meaning of the Dewey Commission's examination of Leon Trotsky in Mexico City. McCarthy finally calls as a witness to her side Trotsky himself, a "man of words" who in his own autobiography declined to view his life as a tragedy. Manipulating the historical record to suit her own personal narrative, McCarthy focuses on the role chance rather than choice played in Trotsky's life, too. During Lenin's last illness he went duck shooting, contracted influenza, missed Lenin's funeral, remained bedridden during the political struggle that followed, and was driven from power.

Stalin's archrival and Lenin's second in command, as well as his closest collaborator, Trotsky was the organizing genius of the Bolshevik Revolution, the founder and commander of the Red Army. Then, in 1929, Trotsky was expelled from the Communist Party and shortly thereafter from the Soviet Union. After years of exile in Turkey, France, and Norway, he moved to Mexico in 1935. There he and his wife, Natalia, lived at the home of the painters Diego Rivera and Frida Kahlo. The American Committee for the Defense of Leon Trotsky was led by Farrell and the radical Marxist George Novack, its secretary, who had also been at the party for Art Young. When Farrell was unable to win the signature of a party guest for Trotsky, he would sic the more intense Novack on him or her. Together, they had helped to secure Trotsky's asylum in Mexico (when unable to do so in the United States). They would arrange for the work of the Dewey Commission six months later to be carried out for eight days at Rivera and Kahlo's red and blue villa in Coyoacán, a bohemian enclave on the edge of Mexico City.

The commission offered the only significant opportunity for Trotsky, then in his sixties, to defend himself in the court of world opinion. The hearings, which began on the morning of April 10, 1937, were an international sensation intensified by a multitude of photographers, the gray-haired Dewey's incisive questions, Kahlo's beauty, and Trotsky's intellectual range and the brilliance of his defense. A police guard stood outside the house. Visitors were searched for guns, and Trotsky himself was said to be armed. The forty-foot room in which the hearings were held, and which Trotsky ordinarily used as his study, had French windows that faced the street. These were covered and further protected by six-foot barricades of cemented brick and sandbags. On the first day, Dewey appeared in a blue suit and, after thanking Mexico for allowing the meeting, described the function and reason for the hearings. He concluded by saying: "I have given my life to the work of education, which I have conceived to be that of public enlightenment in the interests of society. If I finally accepted the responsible post I now occupy, it was because I realized that to act otherwise would be to be false to my life work."[35] Unlike Dewey's sense of responsibility for public enlightenment and fostering the interests of a democratic society, Trotsky's life work had been world revolution. In the course of the hearings, his statements often ran counter to Dewey's democratic ideals. Dewey, who subordinated himself to his role, did not hesitate to challenge Trotsky's belief that a law of history determines the particular way in which class struggle is to be carried out or to question particular details of his testimony. At such points, Farrell reports, there was a "revelation of temperament in intellectual exchange"; they "so clearly and so dramatically represented two worlds."[36]

In bringing together two of the twentieth century's most important yet most temperamentally different thinkers—the polemicist Trotsky and the pragmatist Dewey—the hearings offered more than a choice between Bolshevism and liberalism. The event showed, as Dewey the educator perceived, that it is only in *pursuing* justice or the interests of society that we discover what those things are. Dewey later said that he had always disagreed with Trotsky and that after the Coyoacán hearings he disagreed more than ever, implying that he decided first and determined the principle afterward.[37] In short, it is the work of education—for Dewey, the testing of beliefs— that establishes what justice or the "interests of society" are. As Mary McCarthy said, it is possible to know right away that the Moscow Trials are unjust, that Trotsky deserves a hearing, or that Bolshevism leads to evil, but the truth of these "facts" becomes clear only in the process of verifying them. The Trotsky hearings dramatized a conflict between Trotsky's philosophy—that the ends justify the means—and Dewey's philosophy, which denied that there is any meaningful distinction between ends and means. Trotsky's and Dewey's moral differences illuminated not only their own choices but also the larger debates of their day about how to make choices.

At the first hearing Trotsky appeared in a gray tweed suit. He was strongly built, about five feet ten, with blue eyes, round spectacles, and a burning intensity. Farrell compared him to a tightly drawn bow. The even-tempered Dewey, always spick-and-span, modest in word and deed, was America's outstanding liberal. He had visited the Soviet Union with a group of educators in 1928 and had approved of its aims, which amounted to the remaking of a socialized human nature. Nonetheless, he was glad that the experiment happened in Russia rather than in America, whose freedoms he personally cherished and helped to foster. Many had tried to dissuade Dewey from making the arduous, not to mention politically and personally dangerous, trip to Mexico. Stalin's agents were everywhere and would assassinate Trotsky three years later with an ice ax. But Dewey insisted on the journey, which he regarded as a mission of truth and fair play. On the train, he read versions of the first two trials, in which he found many inconsistencies, and Trotsky's writings, whose advocacy of world revolution he did not find sympathetic.

During the hearings, Dewey appreciated Trotsky's brilliance but lamented that his extraordinarily fluid intellect worked only within the framework of fixed absolutes. The differences between their morals are clearly illustrated in two short essays published within a year of the hearings in the magazine the *New International.* Trotsky's blistering polemic "Their Morals and Ours" first appeared in English in the February 1938 issue. He dedicated the essay to the memory of his thirty-two year-old son, Leon Sedov, who died under suspicious circumstances in a Paris hospital while Trotsky was writing it. The essay argues that the supreme law of history is the law of the class struggle and that the end of human history should be complete human liberation. He looks to the future to justify his position. Most important, he directly addresses the most popular and imposing accusation against Bolshevik "amoralism," the maxim that "the end justifies the means." Sarcastically parroting his opponents, he acknowledges that there is no "principled" difference between Trotskyism and Stalinism. Morality is simply a function of class struggle. The Moscow Trials are, he says, the corruption of the "end justifies the means." Ends and means are constantly changing places. Democracy in certain periods is the "end" of the class struggle; only later it may be transformed into its "means." For Trotsky, morality is a product of social development. It serves social interests that are contradictory. He criticizes Kant's categorical imperative because it is a shell without content. "In all decisive questions people feel their class membership considerably more profoundly and more directly than their membership in 'society.'" In his view, the power of man over nature should be increased so that the power of man over man can be abolished. Liberal, Kantian morals are merely the abstract and formal conceptions of the bourgeoisie and other "non-decisive groups in class society."

The editors of the *New International* invited Dewey to respond, and he did with a short piece entitled "Means and Ends" in August 1938. Although for Dewey the meaning of any action, or the justification of any means, was inseparable from its consequences or ends, he believed that the end also must be justified. Dewey pointed out that Trotsky used the word "ends" in two different senses. On the one hand, Trotsky meant the final justifying end; on the other hand, he used this word to signify the means applied for the attainment of the final justifying end. Class struggle was a means, but the end of history to which it pointed, human liberation, was as yet mere metaphysical speculation. The end can be identified only once it is achieved, and then it is no longer an end but a means to something else, a circularity that Trotsky can take only as far as the historical law of class warfare will let him. No end is absolute. Deterministic systems of thought such as Marxism deny the basic feature of personhood, our capacity to choose our own ends. Dewey puts it this way: "The belief that a law of history determines the particular way in which the struggle is to be carried on certainly seems to tend toward a fanatical and over-mystical doctrine of the use of certain ways of concluding it." The problem with Trotsky's way of thinking is that "the means were deduced from a supposed scientific law instead of being searched for," as Dewey had searched in traveling to Mexico City. Dewey admired Trotsky's courage and dialectical sophistication; but, as he later told Jim Farrell on the train back from Mexico, he thought him "tragic. To see such brilliant native intelligence locked up in absolutes."[38]

The philosophy that the ends justify the means was essential not only to popular conceptions of communism but also to the most basic accusation of anticommunists that communists were liars. They would say anything to achieve their end, the goal of a global classless, stateless society, itself the ultimate lie. In his essay "Dewey in Mexico," Farrell compares the liberal philosopher to Émile Zola standing up and declaring that a powerful empire had lied. "In our age, many serious and liberal men of intelligence have despaired of truth," writes Farrell, "of the viability and effectiveness of truth in the struggle against totalitarian lies. The Moscow Trials produced one of the most monstrous of all totalitarian lies. And it was with Dewey's own method of free inquiry that this lie was exposed."[39] Reactions to the Moscow show trials and purges centered on this expedient attitude to the truth. "If the charge [against the former revolutionaries] was true," wrote Chambers, "then every other Communist had given his life for a fraud. If the charge was false, then every other Communist was giving his life for a fraud."[40] Dewey's disciple, the philosopher Sidney Hook, a former radical Marxist turned Cold War hawk, had helped organize the hearings as leader of the American Committee for the Defense of Leon Trotsky. He argued that the "natural pragmatism of the human mind" required training in the use and analysis of language to overcome totalitarianism's "degradation of the word."[41] When McCarthy accused Hellman of being a liar in 1979, the comment evoked this moral universe of the 1930s and the Cold War. Hook emphatically makes this point in a vitriolic 1980 article, "The Scoundrel in the Looking Glass," in which he accuses Hellman of defending the Moscow Trials, attacking the Dewey Commission, spinning a "myth about her past that has misled the reading public of at least two countries," having "duped a generation of critics devoid of historical memory and critical common sense," and being an eager but (ironically) "unaccomplished liar."[42]

Along with Hook and Chambers, foremost among communist turncoats intent on exposing communist "verbiage," lies, and slander was Arthur Koestler.[43] Koestler had been born in Budapest in 1905, joined the Communist Party in 1931, written a Soviet propaganda book in 1932, traveled to Spain as a communist spy in 1936, been imprisoned, and then resigned from the party in 1938 following the last of the show trials and the execution of Nikolay Bukharin. But it was the Soviet-Nazi Pact of 1939 that demolished his faith. In the fall of 1938 Koestler began his harrowing novel *Darkness at Noon,* which tells the story of the imprisonment, interrogation, and execution of an old Bolshevik who confesses to fraudulent charges. The book was published in 1940. The vividly imagined character of Rubashov resembles both Bukharin and Trotsky with the latter's goatee and pince-nez. He allows no place for personal feeling—or even the "grammatical fiction" of the first-person singular pronoun—in his hyperrationalist, utilitarian system of thought. Rubashov embodies the problem of treating human beings as means rather than ends.[44] He has accepted and continues to accept an ideology of lies. He must capitulate to the logic of No. 1 (Stalin) and his interrogators by the force of his own reasoning.

> The ultimate truth is penultimately always a falsehood.... It is said that No. 1 has Machiavelli's *Prince* lying permanently by his bedside. So he should: since then, nothing really important has been said about the rules of political ethics.... Politics can be relatively fair in the breathing spaces of history; at its critical turning points there is no other rule possible than the old one, that the end justifies the means.... We were neo-Machiavellians in the name of universal reason—that was our greatness ... our sole guiding principle is that of consequent logic.... History has taught us that often lies serve her better than the truth; for man is sluggish and has to be led through the desert for forty years before each step in his development.... We admitted no private sphere, not even inside a

man's skull. We lived under the compulsion of working things to their final conclusions.[45]

Like Trotsky and Chambers, Rubashov subordinates individual tastes to the laws of history. There is something of this compulsively syllogistic thinking that remains to Koestler himself even after his conversion. Although his faith in communism failed and he overtly rejected utilitarian thinking and abstraction, his universe remained Manichean, divided between the moral and the immoral.

Koestler's weird, intergalactic satire *Twilight Bar: An Escapade in Four Acts* testifies to the consistently utilitarian undercurrent in his thought. He began the play in Russia in 1933 and completed it in England in 1944 after his turn from communism. In this drama, aliens have divided the cosmos into "good" and "bad" planets, based strictly on "logical" calculations of happiness and suffering. Those where pain outweighs pleasure will be liquidated. The decision on earth hangs in the balance. The problem is not that earthlings choose the wrong side of the battle (capitalism versus communism, workers versus establishment) but that people won't choose a side at all because they aren't willing to make a change for their own happiness.[46] Whatever the motives, choosing happiness is the only moral option. But it is the eleventh hour, and the earth must improve its Happiness Quotient to survive. A driving force behind and a contributor to the collection of autobiographies of excommunists, *The God That Failed*, Koestler, the former communist agent, became an American propagandist through the CIA-financed Congress for Cultural Freedom. In 1948 he came to New York, where at a party thrown by *Partisan Review* editor Philip Rahv, he met Mary McCarthy, tried to sleep with her—pinning her down, like a "garage mechanic," when she visited his hotel room—and quickly insinuated himself into the incestuous milieu of the anticommunist Left, which took up the banner of ideological warfare on behalf of the US government.[47]

I conclude here with Koestler's expedient attitude toward lying and his assimilation into the anticommunist milieu in which McCarthy, Rahv, Macdonald, et al. were prominent members because it speaks to one of this book's central concerns: the tension between freedom of expression and the specific, historical forms of constraint that enable or abridge it. In telling his personal "story" in *The God That Failed*, Koestler referred to the "necessary lie, the necessary slander" of communism, which "may all sound monstrous and yet it was easy to accept while rolling along the single track of faith."[48] In 1949, faith in freedom seemed no less necessary, when ends and means became confused. Arthur Schlesinger wrote that liberal resistance to communism required both privacy and freedom of expression (and funds), recognizing that these requirements were necessarily in tension with each other.[49] This is not to say that the languages of liberalism and Bolshevism were simply based on different and untranslatable but equally valid moral propositions. A conversation of this nature about moral language (and the well-known "linguistic turn" of Cold War American intellectuals) under the Soviet regime is inconceivable.

Principles may originate in the private hearts of individuals, but Hellman and McCarthy knew that they were also shaped by hidden loyalties and by policy-makers who intervened in what appeared to be open debates. In *Scoundrel Time*, the memoir that most infuriated anticommunist liberals, Hellman inveighed against the propaganda programs supported by the CIA: "I had believed in intellectuals, whether they were my teachers or friends or strangers whose books I had read. This is inexplicable to a younger generation, who look upon the 1930's radical and the 1930's Red baiter with equal amusement."[50] Of course, her profession of shock is disingenuous, a rhetorical ploy that conceals her own covert affiliations. At the Waldorf-Astoria Hotel in late March 1949, the Communist Information Bureau assembled a Cultural and Scientific Conference for World Peace in the heart of New York to shape Western opinion. *Life* magazine labeled Hellman the conference "Mastermind," and she was widely perceived to have played a key organizational role.[51] McCarthy was among the leading anti-Soviet protestors. Lines of nuns, kneeling on the sidewalks, blocked the entrances to the hotel, praying for the souls of the nearly one thousand delegates making their way to the opening banquet of the conference in the hotel ballroom. It was a world, Arthur Miller wrote in his memoir *Timebends,* "of symbolic gestures and utterances."[52] The so-called battle for men's minds, epitomized by the clashes within and around the hotel on those dreary spring days of 1949, is one frame in which to picture the lies and libel of which McCarthy and Hellman accused each other.

In 1980, a legal feud about lying tapped into deeper questions about the possibility of free and democratic expression when statements of political belief came with strings attached whether by the CIA or the Cominform. Personal decisions were shaped, often in unconscious ways, by government dictates. "What kind of freedom," asks one Cold War historian, "can be advanced by such deception?"[53] Lies unbalance the playing field of debate. But it is useless to imagine a field in which everything is illuminated. Although I do not wish to appear as an apologist for Lillian Hellman's political choices or to suggest that she and McCarthy simply made different but morally equivalent decisions, I do want to show that both represented moral choice in a way that can still be instructive. Hellman was never a doctrinaire communist in the way that Chambers and Koestler had been; nor does the term "Stalinist" mean much applied to her, as it might, say, to Klaus Fuchs. As I show in the following pages, Hellman's melodramatic imagination, combined with a failure in means-ends reasoning, contributed to what can be understood as a powerful and serious critique of liberalism. From the 1930s to the 1970s Hellman's and McCarthy's generation found it both increasingly necessary and increasingly difficult to talk about moral decision-making. Current distortions of national conversation on health care (among many other subjects), the deployment of dramatic effects, such as Representative Joe Wilson's shout—"You lie!"—to the president of the United States before a joint session of Congress on September 9, 2009, indicate that we are the inheritors of those difficulties.

Lillian Hellman and the Limits of Melodrama

After the Trotsky hearings, the Stalin-Hitler pact of 1939 presented American intellectuals of the Left with their most vivid moral crisis. On September 30, 1938, in a move designed to push the Nazi military regime eastward toward the Soviet Union, British prime minister Neville Chamberlain and French prime minister Édouard Daladier signed the Munich Agreement, ceding the Sudetenland to Germany. Their policy of appeasement, supported by Franklin Delano Roosevelt and numerous other world leaders, was regarded by the USSR as fundamentally anticommunist and anti-Soviet. In what one historian calls "a melodramatic telegram" to Moscow, the

Soviet Ambassador in London wrote: "International relations
are entering an era of the most violent upsurge of savagery
and brute force and policy of the mailed fist."[54] In December
1938, Soviet chargé d'affaires Georgei Astakhov signed a new
trade agreement with Germany in Berlin. The following
March, Stalin delivered a speech to the Eighteenth Communist Party Congress in which he denounced Western appeasement of Hitler and declared a policy of noninvolvement in
intercapitalist quarrels. In August 1939 British-Soviet-French
triple-alliance negotiations broke down. Within weeks Soviet foreign minister V. M. Molotov and Nazi foreign minister
Joachim von Ribbentrop had signed a nonaggression pact. On
September 17, 1939, German and Soviet troops entered Poland. Historians continue to debate the nature of the Soviet
decision to make a pact with Nazi Germany, but to Lillian
Hellman and many others, 1939 was to be "the holocaust year
of our century." In retrospect, she wrote, "I knew the hurricane was somewhere off the coast and death around the
corner."[55]

For Hellman personally, however, 1939 was a banner
year. Her best and most successful play, *The Little Foxes*,
opened at the National Theatre in New York on February 15.
Set in 1900, the domestic drama evokes the contest between
Democratic populist William Jennings Bryan and Republican empire-builder William McKinley, the great advocate for
business consolidation and world markets. But it also dramatizes the global struggles of the 1930s. It depicts the forging of
an alliance between a mercantile family of the industrializing
"New South" and a northern businessman with a fondness
for the German composer Richard Wagner. The avaricious
Hubbard siblings, Ben, Oscar, and the steely Regina, require
the financial backing of Regina's ethical yet weak-hearted

banker-husband Horace, and they are willing to do anything to get it. When Horace refuses to invest in the proposed cotton mill, the brothers conspire to steal his railroad bonds. Horace discovers the theft and informs Regina that he will say he made them a loan so as to cut her out of the ill-gotten profits. In a climactic personal dispute, Regina gives Horace a coronary and watches him die rather than hand him the medicine sitting nearby. She then blackmails her brothers to ensure that she receives the biggest piece of the pie. The play culminates with the realization of her daughter, the strong-willed ingénue Alexandra, that what her loving servant, a former slave, Addie, has said is true: "There were people who ate the earth and other people who stood around and watched them do it."[56]

The central role of Regina Hubbard was played as a melodramatic villain by Tallulah Bankhead and somewhat more moderately in the 1941 film by Bette Davis. Reviewer Brooks Atkinson admired this vivid work of theater for characters "etched in hatred." He described Bankhead's performance as an indictment of a social evil: "In Miss Hellman's excoriating drama of greed in a family of rugged individualists, Miss Bankhead plays the part of a heartless, ambitious woman who sacrifices her husband and family for the chance of making a fortune. From any humane point of view it is an odious part."[57] Facing her ruthless mother in the end, Alexandra resolves, "I'm not going to stand around and watch you do it. I'll be fighting as hard as [Uncle Ben will] be fighting."[58] Hellman's work consistently advocated the need to take action in the world and forcefully critiqued contemporary liberals who, in her view, failed to do so. "I felt shame and sorrow," she wrote in 1967, "at all liberal impotence in the face of the hurricane."[59]

A crucial question remains: What will Alexandra be fighting *for?*[60] To liberals it might seem that what matters most to a free person ought to be not the things she chooses to do (the "good") but her ability (the "right") to choose them. Yet it is Alexandra's mother and enemy, Regina, who speaks for this view. She says at the end of the play, "Do what you want; think what you want; go where you want. I'd like to keep you with me, but I won't make you stay. Too many people used to make me do too many things."[61] That doesn't sound evil. We might also ask how Alexandra can be regarded as an agent of choice before knowing the particular ends she has chosen; the lights go out on the play before she has gone anywhere or done anything. In fact, she is not an agent of choice but the exponent of an unquestioning morality with an inevitable end. Melodramatic plots restrict individual choice in order to restore traditional ethical imperatives as an immediate political concern. Atkinson comments that "the devastating conclusions are foreordained by play construction rather than by free will."[62] *The Little Foxes,* which indirectly dramatizes the political choices of the 1930s, explores the limits of melodrama, a genre that privileges the "good" over the "right" and divides the moral world into an opposition that seems to ordain a particular choice. Prioritizing plot over character, melodrama shares the ethic of Bolshevism: the end justifies the means.

Hellman was a staunch antifascist, a sympathizer with the Soviet Union, which she visited in 1937 and to which she would return on a diplomatic mission during the war, and a political loose cannon. The success of her provocative first play, *The Children's Hour,* when she was twenty-nine, and new relationships, especially her romance with the detective-writer Dashiell Hammett, coincided with the beginning of what became known as the Popular Front period (1934–39), the formation of broad alliances of diverse political groups from the center and left, organized by the Stalin-led Communist International in response to the growing threat of fascism around the world. Always motivated more by personal loyalties than by any clearly considered political program, Hellman had been a militant organizer in 1936 of the Screen Writers Guild, a "fellow traveler" if not an official member of the Communist Party in the late 1930s, a participant in and supporter of Franklin Roosevelt's New Deal programs, and an advocate for Loyalist forces in Spain.

The Spanish Civil War had begun with a failed coup d'état by a group of army generals on July 17, 1936. The following day General Francisco Franco led an insurrection against the legitimately elected Republican government. The Republicans were supported by the Soviet Union, the Nationalists by Germany and Italy. The United States remained neutral, but American volunteers to the Abraham Lincoln Brigade, like other international brigades, fought for the "Loyalist" Republican side. In the midst of the military conflict, authors and journalists such as Arthur Koestler, George Orwell, John Dos Passos, Martha Gellhorn, Ernest Hemingway, and Lillian Hellman contributed to propaganda efforts. In July 1937, at the home of Frederic and Florence Eldridge March, Hellman attended a showing of *The Spanish Earth,* a propagandistic film about peasants who "work the land for the common good" and fight against "professional soldiers" who try to "impose their will" on the poor.[63] She had collaborated on the story for the film with Hemingway and director Joris Ivens. With her friends Dorothy Parker and Archibald MacLeish, she had founded an organization called Contemporary Historians to support the project. Hemingway, who narrated the movie, made a compelling appeal at the Marches' house on behalf of the Loyalists. Hammett pledged a thousand dollars. Hellman claims in *An Unfinished Woman* that she attended the fund-raiser after having been to Spain, but she had not been to Spain before the movie was made, and it is difficult to reconstruct the extent of her involvement in the war effort. Martha Gellhorn, Hemingway's lover at the time (later his wife) and a figure in his 1937 autobiographical play about the war, *The Fifth Column,* would pick apart the details of Hellman's story. "I can hardly bear to discuss Miss H's ego trip to Spain," she complains, while doing so with relish.[64] Two months after seeing *The Spanish Earth,* Hellman made the trip to witness the conflict herself. She wrote: "I had such strong convictions about the Spanish war, about Fascism-Nazism, strong enough to push just below the surface my fear of the danger of war."[65]

The problem with Hellman's politics, many felt, was simple-mindedness. "Her view of the world was melodramatic," writes one biographer.[66] "If you didn't share her passionate concerns or subscribe to her solutions, you were not stupid—you were a villain," writes another.[67] But Hellman's passions were unpredictable. Later she would be a great admirer of the independence of Marshal Tito of Yugoslavia, the first communist leader to defy Stalin's authority, a position that resulted in Yugoslavia's expulsion from the Cominform, the official forum for the international Communist movement.[68] She also moved easily between the radical Left and the foreign policy establishment, maintaining close ties to Averell Harriman, the ambassador to Russia during her second visit there, and Robert A. Lovett, the assistant secretary of war, whom she invited as her special guest to the opening of her play about diplomats, *The Searching Wind,* in 1944. Her antifascist melodrama *Watch on the Rhine,* written and produced with the Soviet-Nazi Pact still in effect, was chosen for a command performance in Washington for President Roosevelt's birthday in 1942. He was surprised to learn that she had begun the play a year and a half before the war because he had heard of her communist sympathies.[69] (The timing of *Watch on the Rhine* was cited in her defense before the House Un-American Activities Committee and against her by the *New Masses.*) As Irving Howe wrote of Hellman in the 1970s, "I find myself disturbed by the way she clings to fragments of old dogmas that, at other and more lucid moments, she knows she should have given up years ago."[70]

Hellman claimed to have first thought of writing *The Little Foxes* on a plane coming out of Spain in 1937.[71] In her month there she made radio broadcasts and speeches, visited hospitals, and dined on sardines with government officials who urged her to plead their case to Franklin Roosevelt. The Spanish Civil War was a precursor not only of World War II but also of the murky ideological struggle of the Cold War. Hellman's account of her experiences is shaped by these internal contradictions: "A great many people have told me a great many things—atrocities on one side and the other; nuns and priests torn by the limbs in Republican villages; peasants and intellectuals burned alive on Franco's side; why what government fell when; the fight among the Anarchists and Communists and Socialists; who is on what side today and who wasn't yesterday—but this is not the way I learn things and so I have only half listened."[72] Soviet policies were neither benign nor honest. Communists were killing Trotskyites and anarchists, not just fascists. Andrés Nin, formerly a member of Trotsky's staff in Russia and founder in Spain of POUM (Workers' Party for Marxist Unification), was tortured and

murdered by the Republican government. Spanish radical
José Robles, a friend of Dos Passos from his days of teaching
at Johns Hopkins in the 1920s, fell out with Soviet emissaries
and was executed in 1937, causing a rift between Dos Passos
and Hemingway around the time of Hellman's visit.[73] Hellman treats Dos Passos's defection unsympathetically. In *An
Unfinished Woman,* she claims that at dinner in Madrid,
Hemingway and Dos Passos had an ugly fight because Dos
Passos didn't bring any food and ate everyone else's. She disparaged anyone who failed to support the causes she adopted.
Telling her story about Dos Passos in 1949 at a cocktail party,
she infuriated Mary McCarthy. It was one of their few face-
to-face encounters, a Sarah Lawrence College reception in the
sun room of the college president. McCarthy denounced Hellman for slander and, by her report, left Hellman trembling in
fury and surprise.[74]

Although the account of her personal experiences in
Spain in *An Unfinished Woman* details the difficulty of knowing what was going on, for the most part it seems to the Lillian Hellman of the memoir that the choice between the two
sides was so obvious as not to be a genuine choice at all. At a
dinner party in London the evening after departing from
Spain she was asked about the political choice offered by the
Civil War.

> Louise told the table I had just come from Spain. A
> man to her right said the English version of "Re-
> ally" several times and then, "I've never been able
> to fathom the issues."
>   Louise, nervous, said, "Perhaps Lillian will
> tell you."

The man said, "Which side did you choose to visit, Miss Hellman? Each has an argument, I dare say."

I said, "I chose Franco, of course. He's got more money."

Louise's husband said, "Now, now, no harm intended."[75]

Although Hellman implies that there is no moral choice in the conflict between Franco and the impoverished Loyalists, her language works against itself. The "English version of 'Really'" suggests multiple versions not only of that word but also of what's real. Hellman's rage for a particular moral order then turns comical. In a rampage of anger following this exchange, she leaves the table so fast that she turns over her chair. She returns to the hotel and throws herself down upon her bed so hard that she slips to the floor and sprains her ankle. Melodrama can be both materially destructive and self-injurious. Political passion unleavened by the virtues of social intercourse—courtesy, gentleness, sociability—leads to a serious failure in self-government of individuals and societies. Later in the book, she derides the mode of decision-making that makes her feel "a hatred for the side of me that either falls into action or avoids it without thought, aimless, giving in and over to people or places, or slamming doors in anger or fear, all the same coin."[76] She returns home to the United States to fund-raise for the Abraham Lincoln Brigade and is so distraught at the surrender of Barcelona to Franco's forces on January 26, 1939, weeks before the opening of her play, that Tallulah Bankhead takes her to her dressing room and gives her a shot of brandy "to ease her anguish."[77]

Nevertheless, in 1939, as Russia and Germany devoured Poland and her play about opportunistic alliances earned raves and enabled her to purchase a 130-acre estate, this passionate antifascist did not protest. As Carl Rollyson has written, "This period of two years, which ended when German armies invaded the Soviet Union in June 1941, is the most telling episode in her political life." It is telling because of how she and others continued to tell and retell it years later. During these years, Hellman hewed out positions that were not only radical but seemed intended to provoke fights—and they did. For instance, well into the run of *The Little Foxes,* on November 30, 1939, Russia invaded Finland. Bankhead "thought the Russian invasion the brutal act of a bully" and wished to arrange a benefit performance for Finnish relief, as every other Broadway theater had done with the exception of those run by Herman Shumlin, the impresario, director of *The Little Foxes,* and Hellman's lover at the time. Bankhead's proposal was vetoed by Shumlin and Hellman, who commented, according to Bankhead, "I don't believe in that fine, lovable little Republic of Finland that everybody gets so weepy about. I've been there and it looks like a pro-Nazi little republic to me."[78]

Hellman's support of Soviet policies, from the Moscow Trials in 1936 to her sponsorship of the pro-Soviet World Scientific Conference for World Peace in 1949, constitutes her most severe failures of judgment in five decades of public life, and it continues to rankle not only enemies but also admirers. She spent much of her last decades glossing this period in a way favorable to her reputation. Recalling her visit to a Moscow theater festival in 1937 in *An Unfinished Woman,* she wrote, "I did not even know I was there in the middle of the ugliest purge period, and I have often asked myself how that could be. I saw a number of diplomats and journalists but they talked such gobbledygook . . . that one couldn't pick the true charges from the wild hatred."[79] No doubt it was difficult to tell truth from falsehood in the gobbledygook of the moment, but this remark and many others like it have been regarded by Hellman's critics as self-serving claptrap. When McCarthy said on the *Dick Cavett Show* that every word Hellman writes is a lie, including "and" and "the," it was commonly assumed that she was talking about Hellman's writings on international themes, from the self-aggrandizing and allegedly plagiarized story of the antifascist "Julia" to her tendentious account of the communist witch hunts in the 1950s. Howe traced Hellman's 1980 libel suit against McCarthy to those long-standing political differences of the American Left: "The question involved—of one's attitude toward communism—is probably the central political-cultural-intellectual problem of the 20th century. I think for many of us those disputes were the formative passions of our lives—for good or bad, it's made people what they are today."[80]

"Good" and "bad" are words that recur throughout Hellman's writing. She and her characters frequently use morally charged and seemingly simplistic language and invite others to apply it to them. Critics have disparaged the plays as they have her politics in the same terms. "As melodrama," one writes, "*The Little Foxes* teeters between the slick and the substantial. By the slick I mean a skill in theatrical manipulations which make our responses too easy. . . . By the substantial I mean a sense of reality which has some continuing power to gain assent. The slick predominates."[81] But, as Hellman well knew, different forms of expression are appropriate to different historical realities, and melodrama, a term dismissively associated with sensationalism and simplemindedness, also shines a light on individuals' capacity for moral action. *The Little Foxes* has vestiges of the populist impulses of the genre's postrevolutionary French origins. The Chicago businessman Mr. Marshall takes the Hubbards for southern aristocrats, only to be corrected: pathetic Aunt Birdie is an aristocrat who yearns for the good old antebellum days on her plantation, Lionnett, but the "story" Uncle Ben (and the play) tells is of the adaptable new breed, the bourgeoisie, which Marx and Engels described in the *Communist Manifesto* as putting "an end to all feudal, patriarchal, idyllic relations."[82]

Hellman asserted that *The Little Foxes* was a melodrama in that historical sense, staging a radical conflict between old and new social orders. "Melodrama is an interesting word because it has come to have a corrupted modern meaning. It used to be a good word," she wrote. "If you believe, as the Greeks did, that man is at the mercy of the gods he might offend and who will punish him for the offense, then you write tragedy. The end is inevitable from the beginning. But if you believe that man can solve his own problems and is at nobody's mercy, then you will probably write melodrama."[83] But if *The Little Foxes* is a good melodrama—the story of a godless world in which individuals must solve their own problems—what specifically is its subject? Is it, as Atkinson supposed, the social evil of rugged individualism? Is it the corruption of a brilliant woman by her desire for financial independence, the defeat of the weak-hearted Old South, the growth of Alexandra as a feisty figure for America in time of war? Is it an allegory of capitalist alliances, of the will to power, of the relationship of greed to violence? All of these themes are part of its story.

Most important, it is a story about the use and the limits of melodrama in fashioning a worldview. It adopts a moralizing attitude to the history of both the Progressive Era (when the play was set) and American isolationism in the late 1930s (when it was written). Each act ends with a scene of striking moral clarity. At the end of the first act feeble Aunt Birdie is struck hard across the face by her brutal husband, Oscar, an act of violence the young Alexandra dimly perceives. At the end of the play, Alexandra stares down her mother, who has manipulated the death of her tender-hearted father, before Addie, the black housekeeper who serves as judge and moral touchstone in the play, puts out the lights. In the movie, Addie embraces Alexandra. Nearly every critic comments on Hellman's excellent craftsmanship, but it is always a backhanded compliment that implies, as Atkinson patronizingly remarks, that the play "does not have the general significance [Hellman] intends" or that the form isn't significant. The force that drives the play is the energy of Regina's desire, which has nothing to do with affection for her husband or child. When she makes her financial demand of the paterfamilias, her tough brother Ben, he is taken aback: "What a greedy girl you are! You want so much of everything."[84] The melodrama reaches its limit when it confronts the problem of limiting Regina's desire as a consumer and, by extension, her autonomy. It suggests that the fate of this civil society is bound up with the quality of its citizens' character, that respect for individual freedom of choice must be tempered by self-restraint and a sympathetic imagination.

Rather than leaving for Chicago, Regina retreats into the interior of the house, seemingly freed from her maternal function but without having extricated herself from her southern home. In the end it is Alexandra who picks up the rhetoric of self-realization. "I am going away from you," the newly mature young woman tells her mother.[85] Ironically, however, neither of these women goes anywhere. As Addie puts out the lights, Regina heads to her bedroom and Alexandra stands still in the living room. This conclusion does not mean that the characters might not do what they propose in another play. But the final tableau does dramatize their limitations in this one. In these two limited individuals we can read a divided consciousness, an attraction to forms of self-realization in the "good" and the "bad," also in the public and the private, ends and means, idealism and pragmatism. These polarities characterize Hellman's writing from her melodramas to her autobiographies, genres that, in their self-consciously rhetorical dimension and investment in the individual personality (Miss H's ego trips), have more in common than may first meet the eye. Alexandra's liberation has been enabled partly by her benevolent father, the banker, who leaves her a substantial bequest of capital. But she has also benefited from the capitalistic machinations of the Hubbard clan, suggesting paradoxically that proprietary capitalism is the means rather than the end of social-democratic promise.[86] In other words, filthy lucre may tie people down, but it is also the source of a certain kind of freedom. As an interpretation of the Progressive Era, *The Little Foxes* centers on the idea that reason and desire, capitalism and socialism, individualism and the social good, seem to be but are not the terms of an either/or choice. Regina and Alexandra, different though they are, both benefit from the incorporation of large-scale production defined by Hubbard Sons and Marshall. But the limitations of the form leave these "unfinished women" poised between understanding their fundamental motives and achieving their goals, dramatizing in deeply personal terms a still unfulfilled need to take action in the world. *The Little Foxes* is both a reaction against and an endorsement of the liberal marketplace and the individualistic ethics it promotes.

In 1944, Hellman told Margaret Case Harriman that "she would like to be a liberal if she could tell, these days, exactly what the hell a liberal is."[87] Thirty years later, reflecting on the Cold War in *Scoundrel Time,* Hellman wrote: "My belief in liberalism was mostly gone. I think I have substituted for it something private called, for want of something that should be more accurate, decency."[88] Hellman was not alone in imagining decency and liberalism to be antithetical, if we think of liberalism broadly as privileging the freedom of individual choice. But decency, along with other moral virtues, has posed an enduring problem for liberal society. *The Little Foxes* imagined this yearning for a social democracy attuned to the necessity of balancing liberty, equality, and fraternity with commitments to rights and traditions. Though excoriated by liberals, with reason, for simplifying and distorting history, Hellman implies that there need not be a moral choice between political engagement and the value of private pursuits, if we think of these choices not in the abstract but on a case-by-case basis. Unlike Alexandra, or Hellman at her most self-righteous, we should act not in pursuit of long-term ends, like human liberation, but of proximate goals such as improving education for the poor, and so limit the melodrama. Birdie and Uncle Ben are not the only models of behavior to choose between, nor are the radically self-interested Regina and the sick but benevolent Horace. Every choice is imperfect, and that is why the play concludes with the lovely Alexandra poised on the cusp of choice, between negative and positive freedom.

American critics generally employ the term "melodrama" to delimit moral agency, to restrict forms of choice, much as

"Progressive" historiography of the early twentieth century returned repeatedly to a primal scene of industrial capital preying on the small producer or freeholder.[89] "It is useful to be aware of the limits of melodrama as an aesthetic and cultural form," says Yale professor Peter Brooks, because melodrama "cannot figure the birth of a new society."[90] Melodrama seems to promote the notion that freedom or "rights talk" must compete with equalitarian ideals. The language of containment and the reduction of moral choices to either/or antitheses bespeak the Cold War when melodrama became an academic subject. Articles on its hyperdramatization of forces in conflict and the history of its origins in the bourgeois revolutions of the late eighteenth century appeared in liberal, anticommunist journals such as *Partisan Review*. Critics defended this "bad" and "dirty word," which had become a term of abuse like "communism," with varying degrees of historical self-consciousness.[91] Classical liberalism, unlike the melodramatic imagination, imagines a world without a purposive moral order, leaving conceptions of the good to individual choice. In such a world without end, Cold War critics imagined, we are free to construct principles of justice unconstrained by any prior order of value. Melodrama is end-driven. In taking morality from the hands of greater powers and handing it to the humble, it shares the world-healing preoccupations of Marxism.

Hellman's plays continually acknowledge and exploit their own rhetorical limitations, but they do so in order to inject the language of personal outrage, moral indignation, and virtue into an ostensibly neutral public discourse. The final scene of *The Little Foxes* represents the total failure of moral language, as Kober recognized in his 1941 letter to Hellman about the screenplay: "We must find a way to pictorially dramatize this idea at the end of the story."[92] The failure is not the fault of Regina alone but of the breakdown of her relationship with Alexandra. Freedom and virtue do not walk hand in hand. Regina continually offers to talk, and Alexandra as persistently refuses. "What do you want to talk to me about, Alexandra?" The daughter replies, "I've changed my mind. I don't want to talk." Regina says they can wait until morning to talk about whether Alexandra would like to go to Chicago. "It won't make any difference," says Alexandra. "And there isn't anything to talk about."[93] This failure of speech represents the limits of melodrama. Regina is stripped of her attachments, but rather than being liberated she is disempowered. Having denied the value of her formative relationships, she discovers that her end does not justify her means. Having secured her rights without any consideration for the good, she has not actually made a choice of ends but simply matched the desires she already had, regardless of their worth, with the best available means of satisfying them. Regina and Alexandra depend upon each other, as rights depend upon the good. Like Regina, most of us desire the freedom to choose our own ends, but like Alexandra we must recognize an obligation to fulfill certain ends that we have not chosen, ends given by our membership in a family, a culture, or a people.

Just Decisions and the Atomic Bomb

Different forms of storytelling don't just encourage people to make particular choices; they also establish what choices are available and the way choice operates: by chance or intuition, by a cosmic imperative, by momentary passion, or through rational deliberation. Conflicts often arise between people and even within individuals because they use different terms to describe or understand their choices. Whittaker Chambers believed that his decision to expose Alger Hiss as a communist spy was tragic, but his Columbia University classmate, Lionel Trilling, perhaps the most important American literary critic of the Cold War, described him as a "tragic comedian" who brought an "aura of parodic melodrama" to the historical stage.[94] Comedy is rational. It exposes rigid habits of thought and behavior. Melodrama is charged with emotion. But, Trilling implies, it too is a way of confronting the imperfect world. Tragedy, however, suggests the suffering of the individual human soul or, as he writes in *The Liberal Imagination* (1950), "the mind embracing its own pain."[95] In these ways real-life people imagine themselves and others in literary terms. Using this language indicates literature's rhetorical function, the way it models the action of persuasion and identification. The postwar period involved a reassessment of previous attitudes toward history and especially, as Kenneth Burke wrote in *A Rhetoric of Motives* (1950), the "*partisan* aspects" of rhetoric, the way individuals become identified with groups that are at odds.[96] The principal scene of fighting moved from actual battlefields to the realm of language, psychological warfare, propaganda, and cultural persuasion. In large measure, this shift was a product of the logic of the atomic bomb.

The term "cold war" was coined by George Orwell in a 1945 essay entitled "You and the Atomic Bomb" to describe the end of large-scale wars at the expense of a "peace that is no peace."[97] Orwell's title alone indicates the sense of radical disproportion between the bomb and the intimately addressed, individual reader. Partisans cannot simply bare their fists to fight, as Alexandra melodramatically pledges to do at the end of *The Little Foxes*. That is what makes the Cold War cold. The

Alexandra-type heroine of Hellman's 1951 play *The Autumn Garden* chooses not to defend the earth from ravenous foxes but to preserve her own interests from hidden slanderers by means of words—with blackmail—more like the villainous Regina. In that play, a motley group gathers after the war at a resort on the Gulf of Mexico; nearly all are worn-out. "Rhetoric is concerned with the state of Babel after the Fall," Burke says, evoking the postlapsarian and conversationally challenged world of *The Autumn Garden*.[98] These characters are sad and enfeebled, but are they tragic? It was widely believed that the language of tragedy had never been more pertinent than to the contemporary moment, as one scholar noted, "when we feel that our lives are perched precariously on the brink of continual disaster." The meaning of tragedy was more than an academic debate, for "a failure to understand what tragedy is about can have important and undesirable consequences for our grasp of reality."[99]

In what follows I describe forms of storytelling—and tell some stories—that reflect shifts in the relationship between stories and the world occasioned by the conclusion of the war, the explosion of an atomic bomb over Hiroshima, and their impact on models of moral choice. Although there have been other valuable studies of the impact of the atomic bomb on Cold War narratives of apocalypse, utopianism, and "containment," what interests me is the relationship between these forms of language and liberal models of decision-making.[100] The radical reassessment of the relationship between storytelling and reality is captured most provocatively in a short 1946 essay by Gertrude Stein called "Reflection on the Atomic Bomb." "They asked me what I thought of the atomic bomb," Stein writes without saying who "they" are and instantly unhinging the reader from anything concrete. "I said I had not been able to take any interest in it." Such a flippant sentence can make it sound as if the bomb is trivial, but it seems more likely that the bomb is too much of whatever "it" is to really think about it in any ordinary sense. Instead Stein digresses. She says she likes to read detective and mystery stories, unless they are about atomic bombs. What is the use of reading a story about something as destructive as that, which leaves nothing to be interested in? Of course, she does not really digress, because storytelling is her subject and atomic bombs are things that it seems impossible to tell stories about. Living people are interesting, not the ways of killing them. She concludes, "Everybody gets so much information all day long that they lose their common sense. They listen so much that they forget to be natural. This is a nice story."[101] Stein, like John Dewey, saw the world aesthetically, shaped by human imagination, not driven by ends but always in progress. She appealed to writers after the war, such as Hellman, who taught her work in a Yale University seminar, and to the US State Department, which paid for Virgil Thomson's adaptation of *Four Saints in Three Acts.* In 1966 Hellman devoted the opening class to Stein's 1926 lecture "How Writing Is Written," emphasizing her "inner time sense" and her resistance to simplistic interpretation.[102] Her resistance to conventional literary forms exemplified the Cold War preoccupation with the choice between freedom and necessity.

In 1946, a young sergeant in the 128th Infantry Regiment of the 32nd Infantry Division of the US Army was shipped to Japan, where his troop train went through the recently devastated city of Hiroshima. He was tall, with long, gangly limbs, angular features, and a blond crew cut. The twenty-five-year-old John Rawls had considered studying for the Episcopalian priesthood. When he entered Princeton in 1939, his first semester as an undergraduate coincided with the German attack on Poland. Many members of his class immediately signed up for the Reserve Officers' Training Corps (ROTC). Rawls did not. After he graduated in 1943, he entered the army as an enlisted man and, following basic infantry training, completed a course in the Signal Corps.[103] When he reached Japan, he had already served nearly two years in New Guinea and the Philippines. By June 1945 his experiences in the Pacific war had led him to reject his belief in orthodox Christianity and to consider the idea of the supremacy of a divine will to be evil. Formerly a philosophy major at Princeton, Rawls returned there for graduate work in 1946. His first publication, an article entitled "Outline of a Decision Procedure for Ethics," was published in 1951. It aimed to discover a reasonable method for settling disputes. Rawls would go on to become America's foremost liberal, political philosopher, teaching for many years at Harvard. He published his major work, *A Theory of Justice,* in 1971. Before Rawls, American moral philosophy had a utilitarian bent, more oriented toward notions of the common good; after Rawls the emphasis shifted toward thinking about rights, the protection of individual liberty, and the social and economic bases of equality.

In 1995, shortly before suffering the first of several strokes, Rawls wrote a short essay called "Fifty Years after Hiroshima." With so much historical perspective, Rawls wondered, what was to be said about the choice to drop the bomb? Was it a great wrong or was it justified? He answers this question unequivocally: "I believe that both the fire-bombing of Japanese cities beginning in the spring of 1945 and the later atomic bombing of Hiroshima on August 6 were very great wrongs."[104] A decent democratic society must respect the human rights of the members of the other side, both civilians and soldiers, not only because they have these rights but also to teach the enemy soldiers and civilians the content of those rights by their own example. Just peoples by their actions and proclamations foreshadow during the war the kind of peace they aim for and the kind of relations they seek among nations. By respecting rights, they show in an open and public way the nature of their aims and the kind of people they are. Practical means-ends reasoning requires decision-makers to balance the immediate aim of victory in war with not causing more harm than good.

Truman's decision to drop the atomic bomb on the Japanese denied choice not only to the civilian casualties of the bomb but also to the Japanese command structure, which had no warning of the catastrophic new weapon that had only recently been tested in Los Alamos, New Mexico. The decision not to warn the Japanese or give them a choice to surrender before the bomb was dropped was one subject of the policy debate. Yet it becomes clear in Truman's memoir of this period, *A Year of Decisions, 1945,* and in those of other key actors, that the order to proceed with plans to drop the atomic bomb took on a momentum of its own (indeed, it had taken on that momentum before Truman became president in 1945). That direction was one result of American diplomats' increasing frustrations with and skepticism about the Soviet Union as a partner in finishing off the Japanese and securing the peace. Drawing on metaphors of playwriting, acting, and the stage, Kenneth W. Thompson wrote in his 1962 book *American Diplomacy and Emergent Patterns* that diplomats must "carry the marks of men of action; they must both be and appear decisive, matter-of-fact, and to the point."[105]

Although he realized that the atomic bomb would inflict damage and casualties beyond imagination, Truman never expressed doubt about this single choice. On learning of the weapon shortly after taking office, he appointed a committee to study the implications it would have for the United States. The scientific advisers reported that there was no acceptable alternative to bring an end to the war. Because of his dependence on advisers, writes Hannah Arendt in *Crises of the Republic,* the president, "allegedly the most powerful man of the most powerful country, is the only person in this country whose range of choices can be predetermined."[106] However, as Truman later wrote, "The final decision of where and when to use the atomic bomb, was up to me. Let there be no mistake about it. I regarded the bomb as a military weapon and never had any doubt that it should be used."[107] Truman's decision to drop the bomb raises questions about a procedural political system that is nominally neutral toward competing versions of the good.

Like Whittaker Chambers, Truman invokes the politically expedient language of choice to describe what sounds like an absolutely necessary act, one determined by the force of circumstances beyond his control. In announcing the foreign policy initiative that became known as the Truman Doctrine, he said: "At the present moment in world history nearly every nation must choose between alternative ways of life. The choice is too often not a free one. . . . I believe that we must assist free peoples to work to their own destinies in their own way."[108] But what does choice mean if it is not free? The rhetoric of tough choices ("The buck stops here," a phrase printed on a sign on his desk) defines the Truman presidency, but the emphasis on the president's decisiveness suggests something unusual that needs to be asserted (in an aggressively monosyllabic form) or a way of limiting the struggles with choice that characterized everyone else. He insists that "there be no mistake about it." But in doing so, he implies that many are in danger of making precisely that mistake.

Among Truman's advisers, the bomb's most potent attribute was its shock value. Secretary of War Henry L. Stimson said, "There must be administered a tremendous shock." General George C. Marshall "was emphatic in his insistence on the shock value of the new weapon."[109] The basic question, which preoccupied nearly every postwar artist and intellectual, is whether total war of this magnitude is justifiable. One of Hellman's closest friends, the journalist John Hersey, whom she met in Russia in 1944, suggests in *Hiroshima,* his Pulitzer Prize–winning reconstruction of the stories of diverse survivors, that even the Japanese themselves debated this impossible question: "It seems logical that he who supports total war in principle [as the Japanese did] cannot complain of a war against civilians. The crux of the matter is whether total war in its present form is justifiable, even when it serves a just purpose. Does it not have material and spiritual evil as its consequence which far exceed whatever good might result? When will our moralists give us a clear answer to this question?"[110] The unanswerable rhetorical questions with which this passage ends indicate the limitations of postatomic moralists, including Hersey himself. *Hiroshima* implicitly critiques our capacity to make judgments because the process of moral reasoning only *"seems* logical." As literary critic Alan Nadel suggests, the book's first section—entitled "A Noiseless Flash"—"calls into question the cause-and-effect relationship, as old as thunder and lightning, between sound and light," as well as the relationship between historian and subject.[111] Hellman was horrified by Hersey's book, as she had long been revolted by the suffering of individuals in war.[112] To what degree, she and her contemporaries wondered, can freedom be administered by shock? Jean-Paul Sartre had raised this question in his 1943 adaptation of the *Oresteia*. "La liberté fondu sur moi comme la foudre [Freedom hit me like a thunderbolt]," says Orestes, anticipating a radically ambivalent notion of freedom as a tragic postwar reality.[113]

The decision to drop the bomb on Hiroshima was of such magnitude that it seemed paradoxically to cause every other kind of choice to become both meaningless and meaningful at the same time. In *Time* magazine, James Agee wrote, "The bomb rendered all decisions made so far, at Yalta and at Potsdam, mere trivial dams across tributary rivulets. When the bomb split open the universe and revealed the prospect of the infinitely extraordinary, it also revealed the oldest, simplest, commonest, most neglected and most important of facts: that each man is eternally and above all else responsible for his own soul."[114] Mary McCarthy learned that a single atomic bomb had been dropped on Hiroshima while shopping in a little general store on Cape Cod. She later remembered saying to herself, as she stepped up to the counter, "What am I doing buying a loaf of bread?"[115] Yet she accommodated herself to this reality by insisting that small-scale choices gained importance.

The story of reading about the bombing of Hiroshima in a tiny general store, for McCarthy, is a key instance of the democratic equality of empirical facts, of the vitality of local detail in "the actual world," as opposed to thinking in cosmic terms of worldwide disaster. It is the former that imparts the "air of veracity" to novels, as she argues in "The Fact in Fiction," an essay based on a series of talks in Yugoslavia, Britain, and Poland, where she met her future husband James West, in 1960. Like her friends the historian Arthur Schlesinger (who arranged her 1960 tour), Arendt, and Macdonald, she participated enthusiastically in the internationalizing initiatives of the State Department in the postwar period. Hellman attacked this group in *Scoundrel Time:* "They went to too many respectable conferences that turned out not to be under respectable auspices, contributed to and published too many CIA magazines."[116] This critique had merit and it struck home, but it was not entirely fair. Between the years 1944 and 1949, Macdonald's journal *politics* formulated a communitarian alternative to both Marxian socialism and Cold War liberalism. As Gregory Sumner suggests, it aimed to rescue the individual from the "collective abstractions and messianic ideologies" of the Left and the Right and to promote a new internationalism.[117] For Arendt, Macdonald, and McCarthy, the bomb was the climactic expression of the enormous bureaucracies of the mid-twentieth century. Their mission was to formulate a new humanism centering on the individual human will. "After the war was the very best period, politically, that I've been through," McCarthy, a frequent contributor, later wrote. "It seemed possible still, utopian but possible, to change the world on a small scale."[118]

Tragedy, according to Schlesinger's 1949 testament to American liberalism, *The Vital Center: The Politics of Freedom,* is the condition of democracy. In contrast, totalitarianism imposes certitude, eliminates conflict, and seeks to liquidate the tragic insights that give man a sense of his limitations. America's heightened responsibility for making choices in the postwar world of "falling dusk" leads Schlesinger to declare this "age of anxiety" the most exciting time in which to live: "no time more crucial or more tragic."[119] The condition of tragedy is not therefore simply that of defeat, but it indicates what literary scholar Murray Krieger called "the crisis-mentality of our time."[120] *Crisis* derives from the Greek word for decision, choice, or judgment. The postwar period was characterized by a profound reassessment of systems of thought that dictated rationalistic solutions to all social questions, not only totalitarian but also, as Daniel Bell argued in *The End of Ideology*, humanistic; that is, intellectual systems that could claim *truth* for their views of the world or that had a particular end in view. For Bell and others, "ideologists" dressed up their choices in heroic moral terms but evaded the "ethics of responsibility" rooted in the self-interest and particularity of the marketplace.[121] His is not an argument for capitalism per se but for constant social self-criticism based on a desire for consensus. The "end" of ideology is a double entendre. It does not only mean that ideology is over, though that may have been the hope of many postwar Americans, but rather refers to the fact that ideology is always goal driven, concerned with ends rather than means. What Bell and other classical liberals of his generation envision is a society without any particular end or model of the good but rather a society that can secure the means whereby every individual can pursue his or her own ends.

To Americans after the war, tragedy represented a troublesome set of democratic negotiations, as it did in ancient Athens. As Sidney Hook writes, the tragic sense is characterized by the phenomenon of moral choice rooted in a historical reality of tremendous complexity, which permits no systematic solutions but constantly demands local action: "Acute ethical problems arise when in the pursuit of the good we do things which appear not to be right, as e.g., when in order to avoid the dangers of war a nation repudiates its treaty obligations or when in order to win a war non-combatants are punished who are in no way responsible for the actions of others."[122] One freedom limits another. It is sometimes necessary to burn down a house to a save a village. No matter how we choose, Hook writes, we must butcher some ideal, which accounts both for the agony of choice and for the inescapable irony in the fact that many of the rights we presently enjoy are owed to ancestors who, in the process of winning them for us, deprived others of their rights. Moral choices involve figurative and literal acts of violence, but citizens still have to perform them. They always involve questions of intention, responsibility, regret, and remorse. Laurence Olivier reflects this view when he begins his 1948 Oscar-winning movie *Hamlet* not with the words of Shakespeare but with his own line: "This is the tragedy of a man who could not make up his mind."

Freedom of choice is more than freedom from restraint; if it were only that, our freedoms would inevitably be restricted by the unbridled actions of others. Society needs to limit some freedoms in order to protect others, but Western societies seemed to have more and more trouble making those choices. Sartre held that the most important thing about the human condition is that in conflicts of obligations, we choose and make values for ourselves. We cannot choose *not* to be free, Sartre believed, but only to deceive ourselves about the extent of our freedom. For Sartre, awareness of this total freedom can lead to the Hamletlike state of anguish that Olivier realizes in the figure of a man on a precipice. He is both attracted to and repelled by the abyss. Immensely popular in the United States in the 1940s, Sartre's plays were produced on Broadway; his articles appeared in American journals; and he gave highly publicized lecture tours. Yet in the journal *politics* McCarthy critiqued the productions of two of his plays in 1949 for promoting but not really demonstrating a model of democratic decisiveness. Although his aesthetic is one of action, she writes that *Red Gloves* (*Les Mains sales*), his play about the politically engaged intellectual in the early 1940s, faced with choices between fascism, revolutionary socialism, and liberalism, ends up merely as a "triumph of equivocation." McCarthy complains, "It takes no stand whatever (not even a neutral one) on the Communist question, while going through all the motions appropriate to an act of judgment."[123] She suggests that the play does not demonstrate the full exercise of rational choice. The same could be said for *No Exit* (*Huis Clos*), in which one character insists on self-determination, yet when faced with an open door refuses to walk through it. The argument for action in the play does not justify the result.

In 1951, when Hellman completed *The Autumn Garden,* she and Hammett were under close FBI surveillance. In the following two years, they would both be called before the House Un-American Activities Committee. Hammett went to jail in July for refusing to provide information on fugitive communists. Alger Hiss, whom Hellman subsequently befriended (and defended in *Scoundrel Time*) and who supported her suit against McCarthy, had been found guilty of perjury in 1950. Caught up in the subsequent sweep of the State Department, Hellman's lover John Melby, a career diplomat she had met in Moscow in 1944, had become increasingly involved in the Truman administration's military buildup in the face of Soviet and North Korean collaboration. Melby, who played a key role in American relations with China, led the survey mission to Southeast Asia to determine how the United States could best aid the area in resisting communism.[124] His relationship with Hellman doomed his diplomatic career. Hellman blamed American liberals for failing to defend those in political trouble. "I am still angry," she wrote in

1976, "that their reason for disagreeing with McCarthy was too often his crude methods." Means and ends took on new meaning during the communist witch hunts led by Joseph McCarthy and Richard Nixon. Hellman would trace the "double-talk" of Watergate days to the cynical manipulation of language in the 1950s. In *Scoundrel Time,* she writes, "We, as a people, agreed in the Fifties to swallow any nonsense that was repeated often enough, without examination of its meaning or investigation into its roots."[125] Close reading is integral to moral decision-making.

Set in Constance Tuckerman's boarding house in September 1949, *The Autumn Garden* features Constance's French niece, a caddish painter and his faded wife, a sharp-tongued grandmother, her ineffectual daughter and effete grandson, a wise drunk, named Crossman for the editor of *The God That Failed,* and a tired general who is a veteran of the European campaign.[126] The general longs to divorce his batty wife, who seems to think he fought in the Pacific (the "old soldier" of the Pacific campaign, Douglas MacArthur, declared his intention to "fade away" in 1951). He avoids her by retreating to the waterfront to study his Chinese grammar. Their absent son works on the atom bomb and represents, ironically, the general's current domestic impotence. *The Autumn Garden* moves beyond tragedy and the melodramatic means-ends distinctions of the prewar period and evokes the comic insight that everyone acts the fool. In a speech at a "Women for Wallace" lunch on February 10, 1948, Hellman insisted that to avoid simplistic alternatives between liberals and reactionaries, Democrats and Republicans, peace and war, "we must alter our comedy values." She complained that the "smashing of the atom" had become not a viable new source of energy but only "a threat to the lives of human beings."[127] With the exception of the European refugee, the self-reliant Sophie, this group lacks energy.

The play concludes with an ironic quotation of Emerson's famous proposition to "believe that what is true for you in your private heart, is true for all men." The jaded Ned Crossman laments, "I've kept myself busy looking into other people's hearts so I wouldn't have to look into my own. . . . I fooled myself. And I've never liked liars—least of all those who lie to themselves." Constance, the woman who craves his love and whom he calls Con, comforts him: "Never mind. Most of us lie to ourselves. Never mind." Her attitude too is a muted echo of Emerson: "Every word they say chagrins us, and we know not where to begin to set them right." This comedy is "topsy turvy," as the general's wife says, because it is about the failure of conversation and, as a result, of consent. "Would you mind telling me what you're talking about?" one character asks another, after a bewildering use of pronouns.[128] These people fail to share words. Comedy conventionally concludes with marriage in order to ritualize the choice to affirm a social bond, but here it is impossible to marry or to divorce. What tires the general is not the war but domestic affairs. The seventeen-year-old French refugee flees not from but back *to* Europe because of the unwanted advances of a married man. The play shows that the exercise of choice based on private judgment requires social protections. To live together in a civil society, individuals cannot be trusted to serve as both judge and executioner but must forge a shared language that will enable them to unite with others and to carry out laws justly. The community fails to protect the choices of individuals; so they require extralegal means, such as blackmail.

The drama brings all of its characters to a crossroads, where each must assess his or her life. Marriage is the social unit that stands for all others. After twenty-five years of married life, General Griggs wants out, but his wife, Rose, refuses. In the end, rather than fight, they give up on choice.

> GRIGGS. What point did you come to about my decision?
>
> ROSE. Decision? Your decision—
>
> GRIGGS *(tensely)*. Please stop playing the fool. I'm afraid of you when you start playing that game.[129]

The dialogue, or its failure, echoes a similar scene in *An Unfinished Woman*, in which Hellman and Hammett reached a crossroads before his trial in 1951 (when they, too, had been together twenty-five years). Hammett was never able to discuss matters that were important to him, and Hellman had to cope with his silence: "When we were a few steps from Sixth Avenue, he stopped and said, 'Lilly, when we reach the corner you're going to have to make up your mind that I must go my way. You've been more than, more than, well, more than something-or-other good to me, but now I'm in trouble and a nuisance to you. I won't ever blame you if you say goodbye to me now. But if you don't, then we must never have this conversation again.'"[130] Hellman resented the failure of moral conversation, much as she herself contributed to it.

The Autumn Garden asks who has the authority to make moral choices about interpersonal relations and how that standing is acquired. Critics (including Hellman) commonly note that Hammett was a shaping force behind the general's statement that he has failed to decide the shape of his own life: "That big hour of decision, the turning point in your life, the someday you've counted on when you'd wipe out your past mistakes . . . it just doesn't come suddenly. You've trained yourself for it while you waited—or you've let it all run past you and frittered yourself away."[131] But instead of centering on the general's discovery that he wasted his life, I want to focus on Sophie, the young, multilingual refugee who uses her gift for languages to choose the world she wants for herself. She is an ironist. She has to make a change because the incontinent painter Nick Denery, himself returned from Europe, gets drunk one night, forces his way onto her bed, and falls asleep. When he is discovered there in the morning by the garrulous Rose Griggs, the spread of gossip in the small town condemns innocent Sophie. But she is more agent than victim. As she tells her less pragmatic and more consistent Aunt Constance, "I will speak whichever way you think most fits the drama."[132] She does not hope for radical social reformation like the melodramatic Alexandra. Instead Sophie uses melodramatic language ironically when she learns that her current position cannot continue: "I am utterly, utterly miserable." She is "ruined." Nick's wife Nina accuses her of "adding considerable drama" to a "foolish incident." But Sophie knows that "little is made into very much here."[133] In the absence of legal and political protections, Sophie turns to the linguistic currency that is accessible to her. For her there is no morally relevant distinction between means and ends. She insists that language has cash value. A word is good because of what it can do for you.

Sophie demands "blackmail" and not "largesse" from Nick and Nina to finance her return to Europe. She wishes to make a distinction, to define herself as self-reliant and not as a beneficiary of others. Nina can't understand. "You are serious?" she asks. "Just for a word, a way of calling something, you would hurt my husband and me?" Sophie replies, "For me it is more than a way of calling something."[134] Having lived in occupied territory both in France and in the Tuckerman home, she recognizes that the consent implied by even temporary residence is not sufficient for establishing oneself as a member of society. She draws attention to the crucial distinction between what John Locke called "express" and "tacit" consent when she insists that Nina acknowledge giving her the check as a payment for blackmail and for no other reason. What language can we legitimately claim our own? This question, which assumes that words can be personal property, is the basis of several Hellman lawsuits, her frequent threats to sue, and her final libel suit against McCarthy.[135] Her legal battles included fights with film directors who sought to make use of her life and Hammett's, legal maneuverings of Hammett's daughters for possession of his literary estate after his death, and a suit against an ex-lover who published her letters. It also characterized Hellman's attitude toward the text of *The Autumn Garden,* as director Harold Clurman remarked: "The play's words belonged to *her* and only she had the right to deal with them [e.g., to make cuts]."[136] Blackmail is a central and recurrent preoccupation in Hellman's work that implies, like lying, a misuse or perversion of language to ends for which words were not initially intended. The liar or blackmailer takes an utterance that has particular value in one context and removes it to another context in which it has different value. Lying and blackmail are *in-appropriate* in the sense that they are instances of language appropriated and made one's own and, as a result, involve a shift in social power. Unlike lying, however, blackmail, in the simplest terms, involves an exchange of money. It is the buying and selling of language.

Language is a tool. Sophie will dictate the terms under which money is given because, as she recognizes, words are never innocent. A good actor as well as a translator, conscious of the value of every word, Sophie knows that her own personal property consists only of language. She is the drama's embodiment of self-reliance and moral choice, and she will be leaving America. The drama reframes Hellman's critique of the shortcomings of American liberalism in 1951. It has been read as a "modern tragedy . . . in the Chekhovian sense."[137] But Chekhov called *The Cherry Orchard,* which Hellman's play resembles, a comedy, as she well knew. Describing *The Cherry Orchard's* "sharp comedy" in her introduction to the 1955 edition of Chekhov's letters, Hellman comments, "Nowhere else does Chekhov say so clearly that the world these people made for themselves would have to end in a whimper."[138] It is a line borrowed from T. S. Eliot's post–World War I poem "The Hollow Men": "This is the way the world ends / not with a bang but a whimper." Of course, Eliot did not mean to evoke an atom bomb, which did not exist in 1925, but Hellman's figure of speech can't avoid doing so. In the spirit of the Cold War, she leaves out the bang and concludes with the lie. "Most of us lie to ourselves," says Constance in the play's last line. "Never mind."[139]

To say that most people lie and then to give up is a damning expression of apathy and moral resignation. Clurman later wrote in the *New Republic* that Hellman was "just with her characters," whom she regarded with "an astringent, almost cruel clarity. But she [was] unable to reveal in their weakness that which still makes them part of what is blessed and great in life."[140] Unlike Chekhov, he complained, she did not make her characters "forgivable." Clurman gives a liberal critique of the play, but Hellman's play is a critique of liberalism. It focuses

on key, even prosaic, liberal values: the importance of personal choice and respect for the instrumental role of words
in shaping the attitudes of free people. Persuasion can be
directed at people only insofar as they are free, but none of
these characters proves capable of choice. Sophie, the strongest among them, reacts to social constraint and injustice by
asserting a claim to her own language, not by trying to establish new grounds for consensus. Constance's final line expresses an element of Hellman's (and certainly of Hammett's)
thought in those dark years, when they were shadowed by the
FBI and prying neighbors. But in the broader context of the
play it also indicates a searching self-criticism, for it represents a retreat from collective responsibility and from history.

Lillian Hellman and Mary McCarthy were extraordinary because they represented a level of political activism,
combativeness, and genuine risk-taking—on both sides of the
Old Left—that most Americans avoided during the socially
conservative postwar period. Critic Deborah Martinson
comments that "following *Autumn Garden,* politics usurped
[Hellman's] energy." *The Autumn Garden,* however, depicts a
world characterized by exhaustion, where the sons of the dysfunctional older generation work on the atom bomb and the
family has disintegrated. It is not, as Martinson describes it,
a world "tinged with hope for a meaningful future."[141] None
of the couples in the play presents a positive, working model of
a civil union, established by consent, contested and reaffirmed
through conversation. The attitude of the play is neither tragic
nor melodramatic. Nor, despite its comic elements, is it a comedy. Instead it adopts a form that combines burlesque and
elegy. In assuming this attitude toward history, *The Autumn
Garden* offers a powerful critique of American liberals' turn

from the communal good to a notion of individual rights independent of any substantive vision of the good. The characters' failure of conversation betokens a society that has lost the capacity for self-renewal.

V

Criticism versus Libel

The libel here labeling the plaintiff as a "dishonest writer,"
"every word she writes is a lie," crosses the boundary
between opinion and fact. Conceivably there are those
who believe that constitutional protection should be
broadly applied where one author/critic sets out after another
author/critic. And there are those, too, I suppose, that
consider the plaintiff-author endowed with an adequate verbal
arsenal to respond in kind and, indeed, with ample access
to print and other media to vent just such a response. . . . At this
stage of this lawsuit, the language complained of does not
clearly pass the test as an opinion.
—Justice Harold Baer Jr., 1984

As the dominance of television has grown, extremely important elements of American democracy have begun to be
pushed to the sidelines. But the most serious loss by far has
been the playing field itself. The "marketplace of ideas" so
beloved and so carefully protected by our Founders was a
space in which "truths," in John Stuart Mill's words, could
be discovered and refined through "the fullest and freest

comparison of opposite opinions." The print-based
public sphere that had emerged from the books, pamphlets,
and essays of the Enlightenment has, in the blinking eyes
of a single generation, come to seem as remote as the
horse and buggy.
—Al Gore, *The Assault on Reason*, 2007

I n the first chapter, I wrote that Justice Harold Baer raised
questions in the Hellman-McCarthy case that are central to both law and literary criticism. For instance, what
is a critic? "The fact is," said McCarthy's friend Dwight
Macdonald, "Mary's a critic with a right to make judgments."[1]
Macdonald thought the case should have been dismissed on
those grounds. But, if McCarthy spoke as a critic when she
called Hellman dishonest, what was the source of her critical
authority? Was it fact or opinion? Baer found that "the language complained of does not clearly pass the test as an
opinion," or what the law defines as literary criticism. The
Hellman-McCarthy case blurred distinctions between literary, political, and personal criticism at a time (1940s–80s) of
intense reevaluation of the relationship between people, texts,
and language. The very notion that these categories—literary,
personal, and political—should be kept separate had become
the subject of major critical debates during Hellman and Mc-
Carthy's lifetimes, as literary critics moved increasingly out
of the public sphere and into universities. In 1949, W. K.
Wimsatt and Monroe Beardsley advocated an "objective"
form of criticism of any "verbal situation," which did not require any knowledge of authors' intentions or of readers' reactions.[2] Their famous essays "The Intentional Fallacy" and

"The Affective Fallacy" focused on the difficulty of defining a discrete object of judgment and the problem of establishing "critical" standards. The Cold War sense that people were not what they seemed, that texts might be censored, abridged, or misleading, released what historian Ann Douglas describes as "a flood of hyperinterpretation, of which New Criticism's ascendancy in the academy was but one manifestation."[3] Defamation and lying also became increasingly prominent literary and political topics in these years, with the founding of the Central Intelligence Agency in 1947 and the targeting of writers and their work in communist witch hunts.

A new symbolic couple emerged on the American cultural landscape. Blanche DuBois, the neurasthenic southern belle in Tennessee Williams's 1947 *Streetcar Named Desire,* calls it "slander" when her brother-in-law Stanley Kowalski repeats "vicious stories" about her behavior as a public school teacher. Blanche and Stanley's competing tales result in the destruction of Blanche's reputation and her life. Like Whittaker Chambers and Alger Hiss in 1948 and McCarthy and Hellman in 1980, Stanley and Blanche dramatize both a contemporary crisis in everyday language and the evolution of public disputes about fairness, lying, and libel that reverberated through the courts, the halls of Congress, works of popular culture, and journals of literary criticism. What does it mean to criticize as opposed to libel someone, to express an opinion as opposed to a fact? When does it become a problem to intentionally inflict emotional distress? After Stanley calls Blanche a liar, he acquires "proof from the most reliable sources" and claims that he has "thoroughly checked on these stories." He assumes an "impressive judicial air" when he interrogates her and appropriates the old papers of her lost estate for a "lawyer acquaintance who will study these out."[4]

Similarly, in Robert Penn Warren's 1949 novel *All the King's Men*, political hatchet man and history student Jack Burden discovers that "the man of idea" and "the man of fact" were doomed to destroy each other, "just as each was doomed to try to use the other and to yearn toward and try to become the other, because each was incomplete with the terrible division of their age."[5] In a rebuke to Republican vice president (and Chambers champion) Richard Nixon, the intellectual and eloquent Democratic presidential candidate of 1956, Adlai Stevenson (a Hiss character witness in 1949), said that the United States was in danger of becoming "a land of slander and scare," the world of Stanley rather than Blanche.[6]

The fascination with this paradigmatic couple—and the language of defamation that characterized it—reflects a reformulation of the fact-opinion distinction that was the basis of the fair-comment privilege and a source of enormous confusion. In libel law, this confusion led to extensive discussion in *New York Times Co. v. Sullivan* (1964) about the difficulty of determining truth and about how the First Amendment rejects "any test of truth."[7] At the same time, however, the Court (perhaps inconsistently) did adopt a test of truth—namely, a rule that the speaker is liable for defaming public officials if the statement was knowingly or recklessly false. After 1964 *both* the subjective state of mind of the speaker and the objective truth or falsity of the statement had to be taken into account, but the Court struggled particularly with the objective truth or falsity of statements. Although "fact" and "opinion" were not clearly defined, unless some form of factual information could be guaranteed, meaningful public discourse would be impossible. So, one pragmatic response was to treat the validity of facts, in what the Supreme Court has called "public discourse," as at least theoretically determinable without reference to the standards of any given community. The inevitable result of this sensible approach—indicated in the 1988 libel suit filed by Moral Majority leader Jerry Falwell against pornographer Larry Flynt's *Hustler* magazine—has been to isolate the domain of "public discourse" from civility rules that define the identity of communities, leading to an increasingly uncivil public sphere.[8] In *Hustler Magazine, Inc. v. Falwell,* the Court unanimously ruled that no matter how outrageous or malicious an attack on a public figure may be (*Hustler* suggested that Falwell had sex with his mother), it is protected by the First Amendment unless it is knowingly or recklessly false.

In the decade following the publication of the Hiss-Chambers case, Wimsatt and Beardsley's essays, *All the King's Men,* and *A Streetcar Named Desire,* literary critics, like judges, increasingly questioned the relationship between the author, the story, and the person affected by it. Hellman and Mc-Carthy represent the development of the contradictory Cold War couple in conjunction with the rise of a new medium: television, which dramatically expanded the boundaries of public discourse. In addition to raping Blanche, Stanley's other signal act of violence is to throw a radio out the window. Of course, the character doesn't know that radio will be super-seded by a new technology, but he is far readier than Blanche for the postwar, televised world. In the following pages I il-lustrate both the failures of conversation in such intransigent couples and the role of broadcast media in shaping and per-petuating those failures. Like so many others in fiction and fact, the Hellman-McCarthy case was about the fine line between severe denunciation and actionable libel. Each of the half-dozen cases I discuss here revolves around ambiguous charges of public harm, represents a personal reputation destroyed or damaged by allegations of lying, and deploys the literary language of figurative truths and falsifying "stories."

The Fairness Doctrine

In their valuable 1936 book *Hold Your Tongue! Adventures in Libel and Slander,* lawyers Morris Ernst and Alexander Lindey comment: "Since every citizen of a modern civilized state is talking, writing, or reading nearly all the time he is awake, the law of libel touches an enormous area of life."[9] There is, as their jaunty title suggests, a dramatic dimension to defamation. Once the terms libel and slander are tossed around anything might happen. In 1980 Ernst was listed in Mary McCarthy's deposition as one of those whom Hellman had dishonestly maligned but who were no longer around to answer her "intemperate charges."[10] A complex figure, Ernst had been both the general counsel for the American Civil Liberties Union and a supporter of FBI chief J. Edgar Hoover. Hellman knew him well. In the 1930s she had supported his campaign for free speech. He had successfully defended James Joyce's *Ulysses* from obscenity charges in 1933 and had challenged Connecticut's birth control law in 1940. In 1942 Ernst visited Hellman's Pleasantville farm shortly before she attended a command performance of her antifascist play *Watch on the Rhine* with Franklin Delano Roosevelt. She charges in *Pentimento* that he told Roosevelt that she had paid for communist war protesters to picket the White House. "I didn't know Mr. Ernst's reasons for that nonsense story," she explained to FDR, "but Ernst's family had been in business with my Alabama family long ago and that wasn't a good mark on any man." Roosevelt laughed and said he'd "enjoy passing that message on to Mr. Ernst."[11]

When their war of words made its way from the media to the courts, both Hellman and McCarthy were well past their prime as cultural arbiters, but their battle was emblematic of a central tension in American liberalism between freedom of expression and the protection of privacy, personal rights and social obligations, and it marked the evolution of literary celebrity beyond the media of print, photography, and the movies to a cultural landscape reshaped by television. It raised questions about what interests might be at stake in challenging an author's reputation, beyond the emotional distress of one individual. Reputation involves a private interest, but as the courts have found, it is also a social asset that exists beyond a single person.[12] Although the law treats an invasion of privacy and injury to reputation as separate matters, both redress "dignitary harms" and seek to uphold norms of civility. Dating back to Warren and Brandeis's famous 1890 article "The Right to Privacy" and Hellman's 1934 play *The Children's Hour,* many have recognized a profound analogy, if not confusion, between defamation and an invasion of privacy. What are the limits of decency that cannot be abridged without damaging the social order? To what degree should the law safeguard the interests of individuals, enabling them to receive and to express respect, as constitutional law expert Robert Post puts it, "in the maintenance of rules of civility"?[13] The Hellman-McCarthy case cast a spotlight back to the formative disputes of current American life and specifically to the question of what it means to "tell stories" rather than to lie. Libel law is nebulous and inconsistent. Its very complexity indicates the importance of thinking about the boundaries of personal attack in historical terms. Justice Baer makes this point explicitly in the Hellman-McCarthy case, pointing out that what constitutes a statement of fact in one context may be treated as a statement of opinion in another. Writing in an age of burgeoning mass media and, during the Cold War, of limitations on freedoms of expression, Hellman, McCarthy, and their contemporaries had a keen interest in defining the line between telling stories and telling "the truth."

Today public communication has become inseparable from the media, and personal comment is the culture's stock and trade. Debates over fairness on radio and network television may seem quaint in the age of satellites and the Internet, yet television continues to be the dominant medium by which Americans consume information. Recently libelous right-wing radio broadcasts have raised old specters, not only of 1930s demagogues, such as Father Charles Coughlin, but also of government regulation by which, as journalism professor Fred Friendly remarks, "a well-intentioned law can be manipulated to mute 'noxious views,' as perceived by one group of politicians."[14] In issuing stinging personal attacks on public figures, current shock jocks have provoked debate over the regulation of free speech and instigated calls to reinstate a seemingly anachronistic policy that dates to the height of the Cold War. In 1949 the Federal Communications Commission established the highly controversial "Fairness Doctrine," which, though concerned more with tone than defamation, required broadcasters to air coverage of controversial issues of public importance and to make space for contrasting viewpoints. Of course, the reply time guaranteed by the FCC Doctrine did not necessarily ensure fairness. It was abolished in 1987, after President Ronald Reagan vetoed a bill that would have extended it to cable television. Due to the efforts of current members of Congress, it has become a political hot potato once again. Complaining of the "outrageous lies about Obama and health care," one recent commentator demands: "It's long past time for the FCC to open hearings on bringing back the Fairness Doctrine—and to take testimony about exactly how it has been abused since being lifted—actually, even the idea of fairness has been openly mocked."[15] Others have noted that the Fairness Doctrine itself has been abused by political groups of all stripes, that it has been employed by the state to intimidate the media, and that the ever-expanding marketplace of ideas is better off without it.[16] (President Obama does not favor reimposing it on broadcasters.)

When McCarthy called Hellman's every word a lie in a *Paris Metro* interview in 1978, Hellman did not take legal action. She did when the charge was later made on television. However, when Hellman sued Dick Cavett and PBS along with McCarthy in 1980, she had been offered an opportunity to appear on Cavett's show to rebut McCarthy's charge. Knowing a good deal about image-based advertising campaigns, she declined. The debate over fairness on television situates the significance of the Hellman-McCarthy case in a history of failed American dialogues from the late 1940s to the present. Other failures of conversation explored in this chapter are Chambers and Hiss, Norman Mailer and Gore Vidal, and presidential candidate John Kerry and Swift Boat Veteran for Truth leader John O'Neill. The language of libel, if not actual libel suits, characterizes each conflict, as do questions about the public interest and valid criticism—literary, political, and personal—what common law courts have called "fair comment." The media shapes the meaning of language that might otherwise be innocuous, proving instrumental in determining whether the language causes harm.

When an author or public figure places his or her work before the public, he or she invites attack, and the author may seem to have no right to complain of adverse criticism. Critical opinion that falls beneath the legal umbrella of "fair comment" is not libelous. Fair comment is a "qualified privilege" to make critical statements. It deals only with language that invites public attention, rather than with an individual's private life; it does not attack the person, personality, or motives of the author; it uses facts as a starting point (though gross exaggeration does not necessarily make comment unfair); and it does not serve as a pretext for the gratification of private spite.[17] Since *Times v. Sullivan* in 1964 and *Gertz v. Robert Welch, Inc.* in 1974, this privilege has been largely obsolete.[18] After 1964 public figures who were plaintiffs in libel suits had to show "actual malice," which means proving that the defendant intentionally made false statements or recklessly failed to verify alleged facts. (A key to Hellman's position that she was a private figure was that she did not want to prove "actual malice" on McCarthy's part. Moreover, the judge agreed with Hellman that she was a private, not a public, figure; so, the relevant standard would be not "actual malice" under *New York Times,* but "negligence," which means that the speaker did not reasonably believe that her statement was true.) If this description of qualified privileges, fair comment, actual malice, and the status of public figures seems extremely complex, that is because it is. Legal scholars, too, say that a great deal of the law of defamation "makes no sense."[19] But long before these milestone cases, much of America's most important and exciting criticism was anything but "fair" or absent of "malice," according to these definitions. Severe denunciation is the critic's province, but it may also be libel. It is for the law to decide when the critic ceases to criticize and begins to defame.

There have been a number of cases in which talk show hosts have been sued for defamation, though the courts have been reluctant to hold talk show hosts liable for the defamatory statements of guests. In *Adams v. Frontier Broadcasting Company,* the Court discussed the importance of the talk show format to free speech and suggested that the reputation of private individuals must cede to this consideration. The Court therefore refused to hold the radio station liable for the impromptu and defamatory remarks of a caller: "Programs such as this are the modern version of the town meeting in vogue earlier in our country's history, and they are utilized in a similar way to afford every citizen an opportunity to speak his mind on any given issue."[20] Of course, there is a big difference between talk shows and the town meetings of a bygone day; namely that the talk show is a commercial medium. However, the extent of mediation—the degree of editing or of the host's involvement in the dialogue—has been a factor in defamation cases. The *Dick Cavett Show* offered an important forum in the late-twentieth-century marketplace of ideas. Cavett would claim in his defense in the Hellman-McCarthy case that his interviews are protected by the "right to neutral reportage," but his argument fell flat because New York does not recognize a constitutional privilege of neutral report and, as the judge replied, because "the policy arguments for protecting reports of newsworthy events begin to fade as the events reported bear a greater resemblance to entertainment rather than to news."[21]

Cavett may not technically be a critic, but he both offers a venue for criticism and guides critics, as he did with McCarthy and many others, onto provocative ground. He has enticed his guests to make statements of malice and to attack personalities.[22] Critics themselves shape trends in consumption, which is one reason for their being invited onto talk shows, but they are also consumers. They therefore occupy a particularly prominent but also fraught and tenuous terrain of public-private discourse. When, in Samuel Beckett's play *Waiting for Godot,* the two tramps insult each other, they shout "Moron!" "Vermin!" "Abortion!" and so on, until Estragon shouts "Crritic!" at which point Vladimir "wilts, vanquished."[23] The critic is bound to displease somebody. Television viewers and consumers are themselves critics in an implicit and sometimes in an explicit sense. Who does not pass judgment or express an opinion about people or texts on a regular basis? Today Amazon.com permits anyone to be a published critic, and the anonymous reviews posted online can seem dangerously close to libel, as do posts on countless media blogs. It has been argued that the web has proved better at spreading deceptions than the truth.[24] Providers, such as the *New York Times,* often protect themselves from lawsuits by refusing to edit submissions, leaving only the author of the content liable. But, as legal scholar David Roberts puts it, "Anyone who publishes criticism of another person enters a field in which he might, given certain conditions, be charged with defamation," and the test of "whether a comment is defamatory is not directly in the intention of the writer, but in the apprehension of the reader."[25] In *Philadelphia Newspapers, Inc. v. Hepps* (1986), the Court held that, at least in cases involving matters of public concern, the plaintiff has the burden of proving the *falsity* of the statement, instead of the defendant having the burden to prove its *truth.* That case was decided after the Hellman dispute ended in 1984, but the principle was implicit in *New York Times* and *Gertz.* In an age of rising numbers of libel suits, it protects the critic at least from having to prove his or her own innocence.

Although a venue for critical debate, American media, even nominally public media such as PBS, manage consensus and promote consumer culture.[26] In this respect the American public sphere is profoundly different from the classical models to which it has been compared. The Greek ideal of a realm of freedom and permanence that served as a model for Justice Brandeis's conception of public discussion is vitiated not only by the mediated nature of American public discourse but also, of course, by the fact that the integrity of the Greek public sphere depended on slave labor and the exclusion of women, precisely those confined to the private sphere who sought to overcome their state of *privation* in postwar America. As politicians and protestors, celebrities and critics sought new ways to manipulate their own publicity, the cultural conflicts of the Cold War period led to violent assaults from multiple directions on the integrity of the idea of the public and exposed both the complicity and the limitations of commercial media in partisan initiatives.

It is now a commonplace that American public and private spheres were transformed by television in the decade following World War II. RCA black-and-white sets entered the market in 1946, though only about eight thousand families had televisions by the year's end. In January 1947 the opening of Congress was televised for the first time, and the long-running radio show *Meet the Press* made its television debut. That October the House Un-American Activities Committee opened public hearings on communism in the film industry, which were covered by television crews from NBC, CBS, and ABC. In 1960, when Richard Nixon and John F. Kennedy engaged in the first televised presidential debate, nearly 50 percent of American families, or around forty-six million, owned televisions.[27] But the history of television has not only served to spread access to information. In the late 1940s, J. Edgar Hoover exerted his influence on the Federal Communications Commission (formerly the Federal Radio Commission) to deny licenses to applicants who "have affiliated themselves sympathetically with the activities of the communist movement."[28] Hoover sent the FCC unsolicited memoranda regarding licensing applications. Private sponsors too sought to avoid controversy. In 1949, the FCC took the view that station licensees were "public trustees" and therefore had to present contrasting points of view on topics of public importance. In the following decades the FCC established rules limiting personal attacks and political editorializing, but they were selectively enforced and attempts to define the "public interest" were notoriously unsuccessful.[29] In 1985 the FCC issued a "Fairness Report," which asserted that the doctrine did not work and might be in violation of the First Amendment.

The first case of dueling televised hearings featured the antiphotogenic Whittaker Chambers and media darling Alger Hiss. Yet, as Susan Jacoby notes, "the Hiss affair was the last political drama in American history in which television exerted almost no influence," because fewer than 10 percent of Americans owned television sets.[30] On August 3, 1948, an overcast Tuesday morning, Chambers, a former communist operative, appeared in a rumpled gray suit before the House Un-American Activities Committee. Seated at the witness table, surrounded by flashbulbs and microphones, he named Hiss, formerly a highly respected figure in the State Department, then president of the Carnegie Endowment for World Peace, as a fellow communist. Hiss vehemently denied the charges. He was dignified, and his testimony was convincing. It nearly paralyzed the committee but for the exertions of a little known freshman congressman from California, thirty-five-year-old Richard Nixon, who was insulted by Hiss's lofty demeanor and condescending treatment of committee members. Nixon would spearhead the investigation with a zeal that seemed to transcend (or sink beneath) the public interest. As HUAC's chief investigator, Robert Stripling, wrote only a year later, "Nixon had his hat set for Hiss.... It was a personal thing. He was no more concerned about whether or not Hiss was [a communist] than a billy goat!"[31]

The relative credibility of Hiss and Chambers became a major topic of public debate. Republican congressman Karl Mundt commented that "the committee and the country must be badly confused about why these stories fail to jibe so completely."[32] Nixon proposed that Hiss and Chambers confront each other. Two weeks later, the two men were brought together in a suite at the Commodore Hotel in New York. Louisiana representative F. Edward Hébert succinctly expressed the period's pervasive suspicion of duplicitous language: "It is the most fantastic story of unfounded—what motive would Chambers have or what motive—one of you has to have a motive." Chambers was sympathetic to Hébert's "bludgeoning instinct for truth." A southern Democrat, Hébert also believed that Nixon and Mundt were motivated by political partisanship and only wanted to drag the hearings out (and he was right). The congressman's outburst represented, Chambers later wrote, "the rumbling of the nation itself, a little entangled in its own language, a little foiled, but with a rough grip of reality."[33] To the slim and dashing but cautious Hiss, Hébert remarked, "Whichever one of you is lying, is the greatest actor that America has ever produced." Hollywood actors and writers had been blacklisted earlier that year. The first congressional witnesses in history to appear on live television, Chambers and Hiss were both practiced liars.[34]

Hiss challenged Chambers to repeat his charge outside the committee so that he could sue for libel, and later that year Chambers deliberately went on the radio program *Meet the Press* to make the same assertion. The program was hosted by the anticommunist publisher Lawrence Spivak, and it aired live on August 27 at 8:00 p.m. across the nation. "Millions who heard it, or heard of it," Chambers recalled in his 1952 autobiography, *Witness,* "caught only its surface meaning: Whittaker Chambers had deliberately opened himself to a libel suit by Alger Hiss. But I like to believe that some who heard it, heard at the same instant, its inward meaning. That meaning was that God . . . *wanted no slaves.*"[35] By "inward meaning," Chambers presumably means something independent of historical context, public norms, and, in a word, of interpretation, a notion of semantic autonomy at odds with the unruly processes of democracy; the practical problems of interpretation, however, understanding relationships between literal or "surface" and ideological or spiritual meanings, the said and the unsaid, are central public concerns. The Hiss-Chambers case dominated US news for more than a year, as did the libel suit Hiss brought against Chambers. Hiss's professional reputation, the complaint charged, had been willfully and knowingly damaged to the amount of fifty thousand dollars. When the Associated Press subsequently asked Chambers what he thought of that, he replied, "I welcome Alger Hiss's daring suit. I do not minimize the ferocity or the ingenuity of the forces that are working through him."[36] Two days later Hiss's attorneys added another twenty-five thousand dollars to the suit. Chambers's attorneys formally pled "the truth" in response. The libel suit was finally thrown out with prejudice when Hiss was convicted of perjury.

The disintegration of distinctions between public and private life in these decades made it hard to be critical, to make judgments both about politics and about art, because public and private figures have different burdens of proof. A lie would simply be called a falsehood if there were not a perceived intent to mislead. As Chambers's Columbia University classmate Lionel Trilling put it in *Sincerity and Authenticity*, the time was characterized by an increasingly overt conflict between the "honest soul" and the "disintegrated consciousness."[37] Trilling's 1947 novel, *The Middle of the Journey*, a roman à clef about the failure of liberal discourse in America, features one character named Gifford Maxim who is clearly derived from Whittaker Chambers. Like his literary criticism, Trilling's one novel raises questions about the status of private versus public figures and what it means to be a "political person." These questions touch on the challenge and significance of determining authors' intentions. They are impossible to answer in the abstract because the conception of the private individual and the impulse to reveal one's self are a response to the public that society creates. As Chambers enacted the struggle between the honest soul and the disintegrated consciousness, Trilling argues, the very notion of sincerity, the unmediated exhibition of the self, began to lose urgency, while the idea of authenticity gained political power. Despite the many roles he played, Chambers insists repeatedly that he possesses something authentic that passes show. He, too, had committed perjury before HUAC, yet in an article on the case for the *New York Review of Books* Trilling called him a "man of honor." After reading Trilling's article on the beach in Martha's Vineyard, Lillian Hellman, a Hiss supporter, wondered how he "could have come out of the same age and time with such different political and social views from my own."[38] In fact, they were not so different.

Passing judgments on a society in order to change it calls for something more serious, as recent political campaigns have put it, than just words. At the same time, however, the practice of democracy in America requires people to shape their speech by their apprehension of public opinion. Trilling's perception of a moral life revising itself reflected debates about the law of libel that, like Chambers, reopened wounds of the 1930s, raising questions about hidden intentions, covert politics, private lives, and public exposure. In 1974 the landmark case *Gertz v. Robert Welch, Inc.* set a new standard of liability for private libel actions. It rejected yet another major libel decision (*Rosenbloom v. Metromedia, Inc.*) that had extended the *New York Times* decision beyond public officials and public figures to private figures and forged a standard of "negligence" rather than "actual malice." In *Gertz*, a libel action brought against the publisher of a magazine described the plaintiff as a "Communist-fronter," "Leninist," and participant in various "Marxist" and "Red" activities. In this case the Court decided not to define too precisely the distinction between public figure and private person, preferring "broad rules of general application."[39] As a result, determining whether a plaintiff is a public figure is very difficult and has been described as being "much like trying to nail a jellyfish to the wall."[40]

The problem of determining what Americans should be able to say about each other became harder in the decades following World War II because technological, political, and social transformations changed the way people thought about the boundary between private and public life. Lying also assumed new importance in public policy in the doctrine of plausible deniability promulgated by President Truman's National Security Council in 1948 and questions about what presidents from Truman to Eisenhower to Reagan did or did not know about secret Cold War operations. CIA involvement not only in the surveillance of the most intimate details of the lives of citizens but also, as revealed twenty years later, in Cold War cultural production and "psychological warfare" provoked complex questions about liberal discourse, the necessity of openness, and personal accountability. The decades following World War II saw an intense and largely successful assault on the idea that a text means what its author meant and led to forms of criticism that could seem increasingly arbitrary, extravagant, and destructive.

Conversation on the *Dick Cavett Show*

In the 2004 presidential election, a political advocacy group named the Swift Boat Veterans for Truth spent twenty-two million dollars attacking the military credentials and, by extension, the life story of the Democratic nominee, Senator John F. Kerry. Questions about truth in political campaigns, about sincerity and authenticity, and the so-called character issue did not arise for the first time in 2004. But to many citizens, American political discourse sank to a new low. Distinctions between truth and lies seemed to disintegrate, while the lines dividing partisans hardened. Was the attack on Kerry malicious or courageous? Did it expose lies or invent new ones?

Kerry's supporters subsequently assembled a dossier to expose every one of the Swift Boat group's charges as a lie. Kerry himself signed forms authorizing the US Navy to release his record and hired a researcher to comb the naval archives in Washington. In 2007 he personally accepted from the Texas oilman T. Boone Pickens, who had bankrolled the anti-Kerry group, an offer of one million dollars to anyone who could disprove a single charge lodged by the Swift Boat Veterans for Truth. True or false, however, the charges stuck, and they have been credited in part with Kerry's defeat. This

successful character assassination seemed especially perni-
cious because the large amount of money spent by an "independent" group (that is, not a national political party or one
directly linked to a specific candidate) appeared to subvert
even-handed debate, allowing only the privileged few—those
with very deep pockets—access to "free speech." "They spent
something like $30 million, and we didn't. That's just a terri-
ble imbalance when somebody's lying about you," Kerry later
said, slightly exaggerating, in a 2006 *New York Times* interview. "They lied and lied and lied about everything. How many
lies do you get to tell before someone calls you a liar?"[41]

It is commonly supposed that disputes over stories
about public figures need to be resolved in the marketplace of
ideas. As Justice Oliver Wendell Holmes put it in 1919, "The
best test of truth is the power of the thought to get itself accepted in the competition of the market."[42] That's how democracy works. But this interpretation of the First Amendment's
protection of free speech was not legal doctrine at the time of
Holmes's writing, and his pragmatic understanding of truth
continues to be contested by liberals and conservatives, who
have tended to differ over whether truth is embedded in local,
partial perspectives or independent of them (these traditional divisions were complicated by the second Bush White
House's combination of hostility to open dialogue and belief
that it made "reality").[43] The notion, forwarded principally by
Holmes and arguably by Justice Louis Brandeis in the years
between the two world wars, that "truth" was best tested in
the marketplace of ideas was a protest against the intolerance
of their own day.[44] And although their dissenting opinions
became law nearly twenty years later, they did not clarify the
crucial legal distinction between "fact" and "opinion" upon
which judgments of truth or falsehood (or lies) depend,

particularly in cases of libel. Holmes himself qualified his marketplace metaphor by remarking further, "That at any rate is the theory of our Constitution. It is an experiment, as all life is an experiment." An experiment is the action of trying something, or putting it to proof; a test or trial. When Holmes says that "all life" is an experiment, he means that the truth of lives and, by extension, of ideas becomes evident only in the testing.

However, it is also vital to note that when Holmes said that "the best test of truth is the power of the thought to get itself accepted in the competition of the market," he was talking about social and political *ideas,* not facts that bear on individual reputations. Indeed, in *Abrams* he said that he was talking only about cases "where private rights are not concerned." During his years on the Supreme Court, he once expressed some doubt about the utility of libel law, in *Peck v. Tribune Co.* (1909), but he did not argue that it was inconsistent with the constitutional protections for freedom of speech or that the truth of defamatory statements should be determined by "the market."[45] As for Brandeis, many people would question the suggestion that he thought that truth of any sort "was best tested in the marketplace of ideas." Although he joined Holmes's dissent in *Abrams,* when Brandeis himself wrote about freedom of speech, he spoke in much more civic republican terms. Brandeis was, in fact, one of the seminal advocates of protecting another personal right, the right to privacy, from violations by the press. What I wish to suggest is that, over time, liberals have come to extend the "marketplace of ideas" notion to libel law.

The reputations of public "officials," including elected representatives, and of public "figures," including those who arguably thrust themselves to the forefront of particular public controversies in order to influence the resolution of the issues involved, may be damaged, and therefore they can sue. But the burden of proof for a successful defamation claim differs in public and private cases. Public figures must show what the *New York Times* decision called "actual malice," the knowing or reckless misrepresentation of fact, on the part of the parties who allegedly libel them. Private figures do not. John Kerry reportedly considered filing a libel suit against the leader of the Swift Boat Veterans for Truth, John O'Neill. "I don't know if they will actually go forward," a Kerry adviser told the *New York Post*. "But consideration is serious. If Kerry plans on running again in 2008 . . . it would make sense that he'd file the suit."[46] Kerry did not sue; nor did he run again in 2008. Libel, however, is a significant marker of changes to American society because, since the 1960s, it has made its way from the state common-law courts to the federal courts, from lawsuits that involved only disputes between individuals to lawsuits that have also involved the state in questions of free speech and public debate. The history of libel in America chronicles the breakdown of distinctions between the public and the private as well as between truth and falsehood.

The animus of John O'Neill, a Swift Boat veteran, trial lawyer, and coauthor of the 2004 book on Kerry *Unfit for Command*, can be traced back to June 30, 1971, when, following Kerry's testimony before the Senate Foreign Relations Committee, O'Neill was recruited by the Nixon administration, which Kerry had directly criticized, to debate the twenty-seven-year-old former navy lieutenant on the *Dick Cavett Show*. (The *Cavett Show*, really the title of numerous shows hosted by Cavett over the years, was then running on ABC, where it competed against the *Tonight Show Starring Johnny Carson*, before Cavett moved to CBS, then to PBS, and later to other venues.) Cavett did not give his regular monologue or invite other guests onto that "serious" episode. Instead he read testimonials that praised his show's treatments of disputes about Vietnam before introducing the representative of Vietnam Veterans for a Just Peace (O'Neill) and Vietnam Veterans against the War (Kerry). After reading from the letters that responded to previous episodes devoted to the war, Cavett started the debate with a coin toss. O'Neill, who won, began to speak of wanting a "just and lasting peace, in Southeast Asia" but quickly moved to a personal attack on Kerry, who had accused members of the US military of committing crimes in Vietnam. "Never in the course of human events," said O'Neill, "have so many been libeled by so few."[47]

Accusing Kerry of libel assumes a particular plot of rhetorical ground, not to mention being ironic, since, unlike O'Neill, Kerry did not turn personal in the debate. By sleight of hand, O'Neill invoked a law designed to repair the reputation of a private party to subvert a political critique of official conduct. O'Neill's accusation implies that Kerry's falsehoods are both misrepresentations of fact and that the people that Kerry has criticized are not public officials but private citizens. Perhaps Kerry's critiques helped to lower the esteem in which those serving in the war were held by society at large, but O'Neill's off-the-cuff charge also indicates the degree to which libel is happening all the time, whenever people criticize or speak ill of others (without justification), as well as the danger of using libel to curtail political debate.

Cavett's status as a talk-show intellectual has always been a selling point, but its market value also indicates an inherent compromise in his apparent promotion of disinterested debate, as his somewhat awkward transitions to commercials in that exceptional episode with Kerry and O'Neill implied. For example, after O'Neill concluded an extended comment, Cavett said: "Mr. Kerry, I expect you do have something to say to that. We have a message however from Calgon. Here is how a bath can smooth and soften your skin, leaving you radiant and refreshed with Calgon Bath Oil Beads. . . . [After the break:] I must apologize for the fact that we do have to keep stopping. It's a commercial medium, and sometimes those things aren't going to mesh very well."[48] Would an advertisement for a different product provide a better "mesh"? Are the cosmetic benefits of Calgon Bath Oil particularly incongruous in a debate about the Vietnam War? Cavett draws attention not only to the commercial medium that structures the debate but also, in denying its relevance, to the content of the commercials. He raises and skirts the question of how the medium affects the way the audience and the contestants think about their subject. The woman softening her skin in the privacy of her bath is connected to the veterans' debate by the television camera and a technological environment that abridges the distinction between the public and the private.

Generally, Cavett's program featured a range of guests wider than those of other talk shows. Cavett often staged odd, provocative groupings, such as Salvador Dalí and silent-screen star Lillian Gish with baseball great Satchel Paige, or both Muhammad Ali and Joe Frazier, whom Cavett provoked by asking if they did, in fact, hate each other; the fighters lifted him into the air between them like a wishbone for being, as Ali put it, an "agitator." Cavett discussed taboo subjects like pornography. He also fostered a more fluid and intimate environment by reading and responding to questions of audience members at the beginning of each show. The Kerry-O'Neill episode was set on a narrow, carpeted platform with three leather armchairs around a small circular coffee table. Cavett was in the middle. O'Neill wore a white suit, his black hair closely cropped. He appeared tense and angry. Kerry, in a light gray suit and blue shirt, his thick hair an unruly mop and an arm slung across the back of his chair, seemed both more focused and more relaxed. He was also more persuasive. The debate infuriated President Nixon, who discussed it with his chief of staff, H. R. Haldeman, in a conversation recorded on the Watergate tapes. "Well, is there any way we can screw [Cavett]?" Nixon asked. Haldeman replied, "We've been trying to."[49]

In addition to the occasional political debate, Cavett's show has been the scene of notable, if not entirely rational, confrontations between literary figures, including a famous fight, six months after the O'Neill-Kerry debate, between Norman Mailer and Gore Vidal on December 1, 1971. Mailer was seething from Vidal's review of his book *The Prisoner of Sex*, in which Vidal had attacked Mailer's attack on women's liberation and compared Mailer (who had stabbed his wife) to the convicted psychopath Charles Manson. Vidal had emerged only a year earlier from a libel suit filed by the conservative writer William F. Buckley Jr., whom he had critiqued in an *Esquire* review (*Esquire*, co-named in the suit, settled out of court for legal expenses). Cavett, a small man in a tight-fitting gray suit and long blond sideburns, began the episode by referring to the fact that Mailer had punched a guest (the Puerto Rican boxer José Torres) on a previous show, and he directed his monologue at the many critics who "knock television" because they think "it lacks culture." He cited, among others, an article in which Buckley called him a "jovial dwarf" to show that television had figured in the thoughts and writings of "people in the literature profession." Later he described

Vidal, who came to pitch his new play, *An Evening with Richard Nixon,* as having given more people apoplexy than any other guest. He asked who Vidal thought was the most honest politician in his lifetime. Vidal, who had been a politician himself, replied, "A politician is not meant to be honest but to keep dishonesty within bounds. . . . A real politician obscures everything. He corrupts the language." Language (which, with sexual assault, would be a major theme of the evening) was, he concluded, "the principal rapee of [the Nixon] administration." Mailer was the last of the three guests to arrive, and he had, as he put it, stopped off beforehand at one of his favorite watering holes. When he slowly swaggered on from the wings in black Italian boots, a navy pin-striped suit, an unruly bush of gray hair, and several drinks under his belt, Cavett and Vidal had already been joined by the elegant and elderly Paris columnist for the *New Yorker* Janet Flanner.

Mailer refused to shake Vidal's hand and kept his back to the audience until compelled to take a seat. Balled up furiously in his chair, Mailer said, "I would like to get into a discussion with Gore," but "he's shameless in intellectual argument. He is absolutely without character or moral foundation." A long silence ensued, and Cavett explained, "I wanted to give you [Vidal] time to defend yourself. Do you feel that you have been attacked?" Vidal tried to bring the conversation into focus, referring to his and Mailer's published exchanges, noting that Mailer had come out against things he took seriously—women's liberation, masturbation, contraception, abortion—and that Norman was taking the whole thing too personally. After an exchange between the men of barbs barely veiled as literary criticism, Janet Flanner pitched in: "You men insult each other not only in public but act as if you were in private.

That's the odd thing. You act as if you're the only people here." "Aren't we?" Mailer replied. "*They* are here," said Flanner, gesturing at the studio audience.[50]

Mailer's pose, ignoring the audience, acting as if he were not acting, is symptomatic of the disintegration of the public-private distinction in America in this period and of the role of the media in shaping that landscape, especially when it is being pointedly ignored (though Mailer did turn later to members of the audience and demanded to know why they were taking the side of the other guests). Mailer contributed vitally to that disintegration in his own quasi-journalistic work. For instance, *Armies of the Night: History as a Novel / The Novel as History,* a narrative of the 1967 March on the Pentagon, tells the story of "Mailer," the author as a character who self-consciously, even clownishly, invites public consumption and critique of his own egotism. "He" had lived in the sarcophagus of his public image since the age of twenty-five in constant battle with "assorted bravos of the media and the literary world [who] would carve ugly pictures on the living tomb of his legend." Given the ambiguity of historical events in the electronic age, he writes, "egotism may be the last tool left to History."[51] The viewers of the *Dick Cavett Show* are critics, as their responses to the Kerry-O'Neill debate (in letters) and the Mailer-Vidal sparring session (in shouted responses) clearly show. But they are also consumers, and as Mailer the showman well knew, the *Dick Cavett Show* is inextricable from its advertising and, so, its privatized functions. Gore Vidal appeared on Cavett's show both as an author and as a critic, and he was a negative, even antagonistic reviewer not only of Mailer's book but also of Mailer (on other occasions, both before and after the *Dick Cavett Show,* Mailer headbutted and punched Vidal and threw a glass at him), exciting the ire that, Cavett knew, made for good TV.

Ten years later Mailer, of all people, tried to arbitrate between Hellman and McCarthy following the feud that erupted over McCarthy's comments on the *Dick Cavett Show.* In "An Appeal to Lillian Hellman and Mary McCarthy" published in the *New York Times,* Mailer, who was a friend to both with an astute appreciation of their personal and literary differences, sought to act as peacemaker.

> Anyone, who knows literature or who has worked in literature for his or her life, is not going to be surprised that Mary McCarthy and Lillian Hellman do not like each other. McCarthy's work has been a constant illustration to us that honor is a pose, a kind of scaffolding of identity—and identity is the central spiritual problem of our time. . . . Lillian Hellman, on the other hand, has spoken to our disappearing sense of honor, our individual and national honor. . . . Such differences are profound. They produce mortal insults and lawsuits. I think the latter is a disaster. If Lillian wins then every writer will have to feel that much more tongue-tied at daring to criticize another American writer without qualification. So I do wish that Lillian would drop the case. But I do not know if she can. The insult has been too personal. Men used to kill each other in duels, now women try. To say what Mary McCarthy said, knowing with her critical sense that her words had to be deadly to Lillian's honor, was a barbarity and a brutality.[52]

This open letter was followed by another failure of public conversation between Hellman's friend, and eventually one of her
literary executors, the critic Richard Poirier and Mailer. Poirier, who had written admiringly of both Hellman and
Mailer in his 1971 book *The Performing Self: Compositions and
Decompositions in the Languages of Contemporary Life,* complained that "the proposition that writers who have antithetical or dissimilar views of the world necessarily 'detest' each
other would not at all get the assent he imagines from 'anyone
who knows literature.'"[53] Mailer replied with a blistering letter to Poirier, which was unprintable in the *Times* but which
he sent to Hellman, McCarthy, and several others. "I have to
hand it to you," he said. "There was the need only to attack
my letter, but you also had to attack me ... precisely what
McCarthy did to Hellman. It makes me want to be wealthy
enough to sue you. I would lose the case of course, but have
the pleasure of seeing you broke after paying your lawyers."
Poirier was an English professor. Hellman herself then responded with a letter to Mailer (whom she called Normie),
telling him he should have kept his mouth shut.[54]

The threat of financial punishment had become increasingly potent, even when the jury award might be uncertain.
As in the Hellman-McCarthy case, for instance, a judge ruled
that the 1971 Buckley-Vidal libel suit would have to go to trial
to determine as a matter of fact whether Vidal's article was
defamatory. Buckley, satisfied with making a public point and
teaching Vidal a lesson, settled out of court for $115,000 in
lawyer's fees and an editorial statement from *Esquire* dis-
avowing the article. Arnold Gingrich, publisher of the magazine, said: "We simply felt that under the adversary system,
nobody wins but the lawyers. This agrees to call off the mutual
spending of money." Although *Esquire* covered the settlement,

Vidal bore the cost of his own attorney's fees, estimated at $75,000.[55] The $2.25 million lawsuit Hellman filed against McCarthy, Cavett, and PBS was divided into $1.75 million for "mental pain and anguish" and being "injured in her profession" plus $500,000 for "punitive damages." How did she arrive at these amounts, and might a jury have reckoned her injuries and the need for punishment at such numbers? As Rodney Smolla notes, the dollar amounts alone indicate that libel suits had become a new American status symbol, and juries in the 1970s and 1980s were increasingly awarding them (though they tended to be reduced by trial judges or on appeal).[56] The point is that American citizens themselves found these lawsuits sympathetic and, in the scales of justice, increasingly favored the rights to personal and professional reputation, dignity, and privacy over media criticism and adverse comment. The pendulum for and against critics, reviewers, and the media has swung both ways, but its tilt in 1980 indicates the culmination of a crisis that had percolated throughout the lives of Hellman, McCarthy, and their contemporaries. Although the judge ruled that McCarthy's remarks were potentially defamatory, it seems clear now that the case epitomized the failure of public discussion in America. Against that failure, had the case gone to trial, the jury would have been asked in a broad sense to balance Hellman's interest in reputation against the First Amendment protection of free speech and of civil liberties. From a legal standpoint, the jury would have been asked to decide (1) whether Hellman had proven all the elements of the tort and (2) whether she had also met the constitutional standard applied to the case. So, for example, when Justice Baer held that Hellman was a private figure, the jury would have been asked to decide whether McCarthy reasonably should have known that her statement was false. But as a practical matter, when the jury decided these issues, it would certainly have been influenced by its view on the larger question of whether McCarthy's right to free speech or Hellman's right to reputation should prevail in this case. Hellman's lawyer and friend Ephraim London (who reputedly did not charge her for the legal work) was, like her, a celebrated advocate of the First Amendment protection of free speech and of civil liberties. He answered critics that Hellman's libel suit was an assault on precisely those values by saying, "The First Amendment guarantees the right of free speech; it doesn't guarantee the right to lie about someone."[57]

Libel and Literature

"How can one do full justice to the words used in court: 'The truth, the whole truth, and nothing but the truth?'" asks philosopher Sissela Bok. "These words," she says, "mock our clumsy efforts to remember and convey our experiences. The 'whole truth' has seemed so obviously unattainable to some as to cause them to despair of human communication in general." It is worth noting that Bok wrote these words in 1978, a moment of epistemological crisis not so much for philosophers as for average citizens, and Bok's *Lying: Moral Choice in Public and Private Life* was a popular trade book that has since gone through multiple reprintings. What makes lying a moral problem, she observes, is the question of intention. A falsehood becomes a lie if the speaker or writer intends his or her comment to mislead. As Bok points out, "It is to this question alone—the intentional manipulation of information—that the court addresses itself in its request for 'the truth, the

whole truth, and nothing but the truth.'" But then she re-
verses ground, suggesting that the problem with deception is
not in the source but in the effect. The problem with lying is
that it is a form of assault on human beings, as violence is, and
that knowledge of our vulnerability underlies our demand for
truthfulness. The point is that lying, unlike some other forms
of falsehood, causes harm to other persons, whether in practice, or as Immanuel Kant believed, in principle. It is a moral
concept which is concerned with right conduct.[58]

The law does not protect deliberate falsehood, which
would almost always constitute malice, both under the common law and under modern First Amendment doctrine. A
speaker can make a negligent misstatement without any "deliberate falsehood" or intention to deceive. The problem is
proving that a falsehood is deliberate. That is why Hellman
sought private-figure status, because then she would have to
show only negligence, not "actual malice." As deliberate falsehood in libel law that means malice, in life-writing it means
intention. On January 28, 1973, President Richard Nixon, the
man who did as much as anyone in the second half of the
twentieth century to undermine the public's trust in the veracity of its public figures, had a conversation with his counsel John Dean that was later submitted as a transcript to the
House Judiciary Committee in its impeachment inquiry. It
was about the threat of libel and the press's willingness to
print "this Watergate junk."

> PRESIDENT: Well, it is God-damned near impossi-
> ble for a public figure to win a libel case any more.
>
> DEAN: Yes, sir. It is. To establish (1) malice, or reck-
> less disregard of—no, they're both very difficult.

PRESIDENT: Yeah. Well, malice is impossible, virtually. This guy up there, "Who me?" Reckless disregard, you can, maybe.

DEAN: Tough. That's a bad decision, Mr. President.
It really is. It was a bad decision.

PRESIDENT: What the hell happened? What's the
name of that—I don't remember the case, but it was
a horrible decision.

DEAN: New York Times v. Sullivan.[59]

Nixon and Dean confuse the lingo: under *New York Times,*
"malice" and "reckless disregard" are not two different standards; reckless disregard is one way of showing "actual malice." But the confusion of the nation's chief executive (and
chief liar) indicates the slippage between the technical language of the law and that of common usage. After the *Rosenbloom v. Metromedia* decision in 1970, the Supreme Court, in
a move that mirrored similar debates in literary criticism,
shifted its emphasis in cases of libel from the character of the
plaintiff or the type of person injured by a statement to the
matter of the statement itself. But the structure of cause and
effect is as inseparable from libel as it is from lying. *Rosenbloom* held that all statements on matters of public concern
are subject to the *Times* standard, regardless of the public or
private status of the plaintiff, but as an indication of the fluid-
ity of this debate, the *Rosenbloom* decision was rejected four
years later by *Gertz,* after which the level of protection turned
on *both* the status of the plaintiff (public figure or official versus private figure) and the nature of the statement (matter of
public concern or not). The conflict, which came to a head at
that same historical moment, between Hellman and McCarthy

epitomizes a clash between two kinds of language: one that faithfully reports on matters of fact and one that is shaped by an individual's consciousness and desires and therefore colors and distorts the facts. The academic field of law and literature also arose in the 1970s, at the same time as these moves in the courts on libel.[60] I will not enter the debate about the relationship between style and substance in jurisprudence, other than to say that cases of libel have raised particular questions about reading, such as the challenge of balancing journalistic demands of fact-checking and readable prose, and that in response to these irresolvable, literary questions, the language of the courts has been remarkably capacious.

To the extent that judges use the language of literature— metaphorical, figurative, and rhetorical terminology—they appear to use it as examples of language that is too loose to be taken seriously. In the context of defamation, figurative language is not to be regarded as a statement of fact. But in the 1990s, the courts resisted an artificial distinction between fact and opinion, faced with the challenge of distinguishing between the provable and the unprovable, readily understood meaning and language that is "figurative, rhetorical, or hyperbolic."[61] Of course, there is no such thing as "pure" opinion, an opinion unmixed with fact. The problem is indicated by the fact that, in each individual case, as the courts also found, the determination of whether the statement is factual or figurative cannot be separated from "the general tenor of the article." How exactly is the general tenor to be determined? Here the Court has been less helpful, and the questions that have arisen are directly related to contemporary literary studies. In his seminal book *Renaissance Self-Fashioning*, published in 1980, the same year as Hellman's lawsuit, English professor Stephen Greenblatt explains the "function" of literature in three ways: "as a manifestation of the concrete behavior of its particular author, as itself the expression of the codes by which behavior is shaped, and as a reflection upon those codes." His own "interpretive practice," which he continually roots in autobiography, Greenblatt says, "must concern itself with all three of these functions."[62]

In 1949, a young Belgian literature instructor with a broad forehead, thick brown hair, and a mischievous smile took a teaching position at Bard College, a small, artsy liberal arts school whose wooded campus borders the Hudson River and the Catskill Mountains. Bard had taken in a number of European refugees after the war. Paul de Man had been recommended for the job by his friend the novelist and memoirist Mary McCarthy, who had taught there herself in 1945–46. He had emigrated from Europe in 1948, and McCarthy met him at the apartment of her friend the journalist and editor of *politics,* Dwight Macdonald, on East Tenth Street in New York. McCarthy liked him. She and her husband Bowden Broadwater often had de Man to their farmhouse in Portsmouth, Rhode Island, and shared holidays with him. In that rustic setting he seemed cheerful and helped with the dishes and the scythe. McCarthy found him highly intelligent and lively to talk with, though she later wondered if that was because "he *always* agreed with us, which made us slightly suspicious."[63] She noted odd discrepancies in his stories, especially about his wife and children, who were in South America. In a letter years later to his biographer McCarthy recalled: "He was extremely evasive about such things.... In the end it became clear to us that Paul was a pathological liar or what is called a mythomane."[64] *Mythomane* is a French psychological term for a chronic but often unconscious, unintentional liar. In addition to marrying one of his students while still married to his first wife, de Man trashed the home he had leased, ran up telephone bills, failed to pay his rent, stole from his landlord, and then seemed to disappear. He was fired in 1951. He turned up on McCarthy's radar years later at Yale University as one of the leading literary scholars of his generation.

With his friend Jacques Derrida, Paul de Man became associated with a way of reading called deconstruction, a term Derrida coined in his 1967 book *Of Grammatology* to challenge theories of intentional meaning. Derrida suggests that the written text does not have a clear or unitary origin (for Derrida, the author's absence is a condition of writing) and that meaning is not present in the text, an assumption he exposes as metaphysical speculation. Deconstruction draws from structural linguistics the insight that every term has a binary opposite but concludes that, insofar as two opposites are inextricable, texts can mean the opposite of what they or the author seem to intend (for example, to assert that America is a democracy compels us to consider ways in which America is not democratic). It is a mode of analysis that not only exposes contradictions in literary and philosophical language but also dissolves any distinction between literary and nonliterary writing.

De Man, deconstruction's most elegant practitioner and renowned teacher, extended these literary insights into the sphere of ethics, in effect by claiming that they did not extend to ethics. In *Allegories of Reading* (1979), he shows that language is always unreliable, that distinctions between literal and figural, "private structures" and "public effects," break down, and that local difficulties of interpretation make historical reflection impossible. In his chapter on Rousseau's *Confessions,* he locates the episode in which the young Rousseau

stole a ribbon and blamed a servant girl, "a truly primal scene
of lie and deception," as "the core of his autobiographical narrative." For de Man, the story subverts assumptions about the
elusive author and exemplifies the "possible 'excusability' of
lies."[65] In a famous passage, he describes the moral ramifications for political and autobiographical texts of this depiction
of lying, which he understands as a product of figurative language but not of a responsible individual. Confession exists
only as a "verbal utterance." Wrongdoing is reduced to a problem of interpretation within the story: "It is always possible to
face up to any experience (to excuse any guilt), because the
experience always exists simultaneously as fictional discourse
and as empirical event and it is never possible to decide which
one of the two possibilities is the right one. The indecision
makes it possible to excuse the bleakest of crimes because, as
a fiction, it escapes from the constraints of guilt and innocence."[66] Fictional discourse here sounds like the kind of
mythomanie that characterizes Blanche DuBois's hallucina-
tory yet hyperlinguistic consciousness in *A Streetcar Named
Desire*. Dissolving disciplinary boundaries, de Man focuses
on grammar and rhetoric, the internal structures of literary
language, and figurative speech that suggests the indetermi-
nacy of all texts. The story of language's inability to tell one
story subverts value judgments and inverts structures of
cause and effect. If texts seem to present answers, deconstruction uncovers questions.

De Man died in 1983, a year before Lillian Hellman. Five
years later American readers discovered that he had written
anti-Semitic articles for the Nazi collaborationist journal *Le
Soir* while he was still in Belgium between 1940 and 1942. The
brouhaha that Derrida called the "trial of Paul de Man" subsequently took place both in the national media and in the

more rarified realm of academic publishing and conferences, where de Man's friends—many of them, like Derrida, Jewish—struggled to defend not only the teacher's reputation but also, as poet and critic David Lehman writes, "the entire critical movement he had championed."[67] Lehman, who covered the story for *Newsweek* and later wrote a book about it, felt like an attorney faced with hostile witnesses in his many interviews with professors who regarded journalists as enemies and journalism as an enterprise inherently hostile to deconstruction, which it is. The journalists, like Stanley Kowalski, insisted on biographical facts but masked their own rhetoric, while the professors, like Blanche, denied the alleged ethical truth of the stories yet paradoxically asserted that there was a deeper truth about the person.

The intensity of the dispute had much to do with the tension arising from perceptions of journalistic simplifications and academic mystifications, rival communities of opinion. There was a danger in the de Man case, with its charges of calumny, as in *Times v. Sullivan,* that some inaccuracies in the early press coverage would be marshaled to curtail further public discussion. In light of de Man's past, critics wondered if his theory of language wasn't self-serving. De Man had critiqued Wimsatt's understanding of intentionality as a psychic or mental content that is transferred from the mind of the author to that of the reader like wine from a jar to a glass.[68] The concept of intentionality, he believed, is not psychological but structural. What this means is that we are all intentional critics when we recognize coherence in the texts we read, a purpose in the way they are put together. Doing so does not limit our range of interpretation. As de Man had put it, "The question of authorship never receives a satisfactory answer, although it would seem to be a settled matter."[69]

Questions about deliberate falsehood and damaged reputations alone prove difficult to answer not because it is hard, if not impossible, to pinpoint the author's intentions but because the intention of the utterance is structurally inseparable from how it is received. The meaning of a defamatory statement is determined from the point of view of the reader. So, in cases of libel, rather than focusing exclusively on the text or attempting to parse the intentions of the author, the Court reads the statement in the way it would have been read by the average person: "The publication will be tested by its effect upon the average reader" (*James v. Gannett Co., Inc.*).[70] In short, under the Court's doctrine, a defendant can be held responsible only if the statement is false and defamatory *and* the defendant had the requisite state of mind *and* it has the requisite effect upon the reader. In construing the meaning of a defamatory statement the courts look not simply at the words but at their context in order to determine how an "ordinary" reader would read them. Like the generation of critics that followed Wimsatt and Beardsley in the 1970s, courts have found that interpretation of the text itself will be profoundly affected by the context in which it appears: "Words standing by themselves may be incapable of a defamatory meaning, yet the same words, if found in bad company, may, from that circumstance, be held to be defamatory. The contrary is also true: Words seemingly defamatory may be innocent in context."[71] Also, "Challenged statements are not to be read in isolation, but must be perused as the average reader would against 'the whole apparent scope and intent' of the writing."[72] The assignment of meaning is essential for determining liability. Although generally the Court stays away from the interpretation of meaning in literary texts, in cases of libel the Court does so because they are deemed to be of "important public interest."[73]

Libel and slander raise the question of justice in story-telling, about appropriate self-expression in public, about reputations and how people represent one another and themselves. The philosopher Richard Rorty has written that the "vocabulary of self-creation is necessarily private, unshared, unsuited to argument. The vocabulary of justice is necessarily public and shared, a medium for argumentative exchange."[74] He urges us to drop the demand for a theory that unifies the public and private and embrace the position of a figure he calls a "liberal ironist." Well below the level of theory, in cases of libel, the private language of self-creation and the public language of justice necessarily, if uncomfortably, are linked. "Irony" comes from a Greek word that means "dissimulation." Rorty does not mean that we should have a society of liars or that we should raise our children in such a way that will make them continually dubious about their process of socialization (both Hellman and McCarthy represent numerous ironical children of this sort). But Rorty does believe that ironists have something to have doubts about because our society is basically rhetorical. Everyone has the power to re-describe it. That is the essence of our democracy.

Rhetoric is used whenever people try to produce an effect on others with their words. As University of Chicago professor Wayne Booth wrote in 1974,

> In reading any irony worth bothering about, we read life itself, and we work on our relations to others as they deal with it. . . . But it is also clear by now why irony causes so much trouble. An aggressively

intellectual exercise that fuses fact and value, requiring us to construct alternative hierarchies and
choose among them; demands that we look down
on other men's follies or sins; floods us with emotion-
charged value judgments which claim to be backed
by the mind; accuses other men not only of wrong
beliefs but of being wrong at their very foundations
and blind to what these foundations imply—all of
this coupled with a kind of subtlety that cannot be
deciphered or "proved" simply by looking closely at
the words: no wonder that "failure to communicate" and resulting quarrels are often found where
irony dwells.[75]

In this aggressively intellectual way, Lillian Hellman, with all
of her personal failings, was an ironist. In this respect as well,
her dispute with Mary McCarthy is a far cry from the recent
scandals of autobiographical hoaxes perpetrated by the likes
of James Frey (*A Million Little Pieces*, 2003) or JT LeRoy
(*Sarah*, 2000). Although Hellman's name has been invoked in
these cases, and similar calls for fact-checking by publishers
have arisen, the comparisons are superficial and trivialize the
deeper issues at stake in the Hellman-McCarthy libel suit.[76]
The Hellman-McCarthy case, as I have aimed to show, can
teach us about how competing philosophies of language, of
education and interpretation, are crucial to American under-
standings of privacy and all that follows.

Political opponents can legitimately claim that Hellman
took elements of "Julia" from the lives of other people and
misreported what Hemingway or Dos Passos "really" said in
Spain. But the stories Hellman told were, in a vital sense, *her*
lives. The value of her works, which are remarkable and de-

serve serious literary criticism, arise from provoking readers to examine the key distinctions upon which both liberalism and libel depend: the public and the private, fact and opinion. This is not to say that she should not be held accountable for historical untruths, distortions, slander, or weak arguments, but that the fusion (and confusion) of private-public, fact-opinion, literal-figurative in her work is a product not only of her readers' interpretation but also of the writing. It also points to the limitations of the kind of autobiographical theory of the mid-1970s that defined the genre in quasi-legalistic terms as a contract between the author, the character, and the reader (the truth, the whole truth, and nothing but the truth).[77] In her life-writing Hellman intentionally raises important historical and theoretical questions about readers' emotional investment in and the function of the idea of the author.

I want to tell one last story about an example of Hellman's self-conscious storytelling. In the first of her memoirs, *An Unfinished Woman,* which won the National Book Award in 1969, she describes a fight she had with Dashiell Hammett, her partner of many years in a rocky on-again, off-again relationship. Unhappy with Hammett's heavy drinking, she made an angry speech one night: "It had to do with injustice, his carelessness, his insistence that he get his way, his sharpness with me but not with himself."[78] As often in her writing, the author transfers characteristics of herself, author and protagonist, onto another figure. In the midst of this scene, with Hellman drunk and Hammett drunker, she notices that he is grinding a burning cigarette into his cheek. She asks what he is doing. He says that he is doing it to himself to keep from doing it to her. It is a richly circular moment of convoluted angry gestures, self-expression, repression and public-private concern (with injustice), confusion of oneself and another, a failure (with Hammett) and an achievement (with the reader) of intimacy. Hellman and Hammett never spoke of this self-defacing, disfiguring action again, but she thinks back to it as an author in her narrative reconstruction of the event and speculates. She imagines herself in his opposition to her, his feeling ashamed of his behavior but his having won the game/argument by it, and so she feels ashamed.

Hellman concludes with the following observation about moral language and the problem of removing one crucial word from its context: "Unjust. How many times I've used that word, scolded myself with it. All I mean by it now is that I don't have the final courage to say that I refuse to preside over violations against myself, and to hell with justice." Read in context, the line "to hell with justice" sounds bracingly ironic. It demands that we reexamine relations not only between characters within the story but also between ourselves as readers and the narrator-author who resists carelessness, sharpness, and violence. It uses moral language to damn "justice," which may provoke us to ask what justice is. It blends an ostensible statement of fact about a domestic quarrel with emotionally charged values about right behavior and personal violation. But ultimately how the reader interprets these subtle lines will depend upon a degree of sympathy and a capacity for identification, without which they are just words.

Conclusion

I have to say it is difficult for me to talk to you because I feel
really duped. But more importantly, I feel that you betrayed
millions of readers. I think it's such a gift to have millions of
people to read your work and that bothers me greatly. So
now, as I sit here today I don't know what is true and I don't
know what isn't. So first of all, I wanted to start with *The
Smoking Gun* report titled, "The Man Who Conned Oprah,"
and I want to know—were they right?
—Oprah Winfrey to James Frey, 2006

On January 11, 2006, after a week of bad publicity,
James Frey, self-described drug addict, alcoholic,
and criminal, and author of a controversial memoir entitled *A Million Little Pieces,* appeared on
CNN's *Larry King Live* to defend his veracity. On January 8,
2006, *The Smoking Gun* website had published an exposé, "A

Million Little Lies: Exposing James Frey's Fiction Addiction."[1] It alleged that Frey manipulated details of his life to render himself more compelling as a "tragic victim" and to sweeten the "melodramatic narrative." Instead of spending months in prison, as he claimed, Frey had spent a few hours in a holding pen. Yet, in plain but graphic language, the memoir traffics in his heart of darkness. It opens with the young author-narrator on an airplane, just waking to consciousness, "covered with a colorful mixture of spit, snot, urine, vomit, and blood," as if to suggest that what follows will be a similar portrait of unmediated regurgitation.[2] It offers a tale of abjection and redemption. Frey acknowledged changing details and shaping the narrative, but he told King that he was surprised by the controversy. He threatened to sue to *The Smoking Gun* for calling him a liar.

Months earlier, the talk-show host Oprah Winfrey had chosen *A Million Little Pieces* for her book club. She had hosted Frey on her show in October. In the fall she had also run a series of shows on "Truth in America" and "Developing Critical Literacy" for sorting through media messages. She invited journalist Frank Rich to discuss his book *The Greatest Story Ever Sold: The Decline and Fall of Truth,* which took not only the Bush administration but also American culture more broadly to task for succumbing to "truthiness" and "infotainment"; it challenged the reasoning that had led America into war with Iraq. With the Frey scandal breaking in January and her own integrity on the line, Oprah called in at the end of King's radio program to defend the author. *The Smoking Gun* had directly targeted her credibility as a cultural arbiter. It reported: "There may be a lot less to love about Frey's runaway hit, which has sold more than 3.5 million copies and, thanks to Winfrey, has sat atop *The New York Times* nonfiction paperback best seller list for the past 15 weeks." She said that she was disappointed by the controversy that had arisen in the wake of the exposé but that "the underlying message of redemption in James Frey's memoir still resonates with me, and I know it resonates with millions of other people who have read this book."[3] But public opinion continued to turn. It came out that Frey had first peddled his manuscript as a novel and that publishers had rejected it in that form. After allegations of lying were verified, a new listing appeared on Amazon.com with a publisher's note from Doubleday: "A publisher's relationship with an author is based to an extent on trust. . . . When the Smoking Gun report appeared, our first response, given that we were still learning the facts of the matter, was to support our author. Since then, we have questioned him about the allegations and have sadly come to the realization that a number of facts have been altered and incidents embellished."[4] The book was reissued with an author's note.

At the end of January, Oprah invited Frey back to her show for a reckoning. "It was a huge relief," wrote *New York Times* columnist Maureen Dowd, "after our long national slide into untruth and no consequences, into Swift boating and swift bucks, into W.'s delusion and denial, to see the Empress of Empathy icily hold someone accountable for lying."[5] Sitting opposite Frey on a soft white couch, in an elegant green jacket and gray slacks and bearing a grim expression, Oprah leaned back disapprovingly as if she wished to distance herself from the contrite author but couldn't move farther away. She demanded to know why he lied. Frey continued to insist that, though he represented an image that was "greater," "tougher," and "badder" than he actually was, the people in the book were real and the confrontations he described were essentially true. Oprah was unmoved. Although much of what he described actually happened, she now realized that he wasn't "Mr. Bravado tough guy." Nonetheless, warming toward Frey in the end, she thanked him for coming back on television "because the truth can set you free." Frey agreed "absolutely." Then she brought out Nan Talese, publisher and editor of *A Million Little Pieces,* and demanded to know what responsibility she took for the book. Talese, in a black pantsuit, sat on the opposite side of the couch, with the author between the two women, hanging his head like a schoolboy. Truth-telling experts, including Frank Rich, who said Frey's memoir was just the tip of the iceberg, Richard Cohen (a *Washington Post* columnist who had written that Oprah was "deluded"), and journalism professor Roy Peter Clark (author of the study on "critical literacy"), concluded the show with a conversation about truth and lies.

Oprah had the last word, and she cited *New York Times* book reviewer Michiko Kakutani, who a week earlier described the impulse behind the recent "memoir craze" as not just a "case about truth-in-labeling or the misrepresentations of one author: after all, there have been plenty of charges about phony or inflated memoirs in the past, most notably about Lillian Hellman's 1973 book 'Pentimento.' It is a case," she said, "about how much value contemporary culture places on the very idea of truth."[6] One indication of that valuation is that in contemporary America, the talk-show host has far greater cultural authority than the author. It is difficult to imagine Dick Cavett disciplining either Lillian Hellman or Mary McCarthy; in fact, it is much easier to imagine them disciplining him. A 1971 profile in *Time* described him as "a star-struck Nebraska kid who still keeps his nose pressed against the show-biz windowpane, almost innocently eager to talk to all the big celebrities on his very own show."[7] The shift in gender norms since the 1970s—and the far greater role of women in the media (not only as actors)—also indicates a dramatic reversal. Hellman and McCarthy may have intimidated a male talk-show host, but he was the host; Oprah makes or breaks authors' careers and dominates conversations, as her own life story (born into poverty and now the richest African American in history) serves as a foundation of her journalism. McCarthy's scandalous remarks about Hellman on Cavett and Frey's appearance on Oprah may seem book ends to a common tale, and in a sense they are. But they also indicate how murky the tale and the talk shows' involvement in it continue to be.

At a writer's conference in the summer of 2007, Nan Talese spoke about her experience on the *Oprah Winfrey Show*. She said that, though small incidents were exaggerated in the book, Oprah had manipulated Frey, Doubleday, and her to serve Oprah's own sanctimoniousness. Oprah supported the book, up through Frey's appearance on *Larry King Live*, until fans started to send her letters saying that she didn't care about the truth. Talese claimed that she had expected to participate in a panel discussion but that the show, revolving on the celebrity of Oprah herself, instead centered on a "public scourging," and that Oprah "verbally flayed [Frey] in public." It appalled Talese that at the end of the show, Oprah leaned over to Frey and said, "I know it was rough, but it was just business."[8] Talese's outrage is understandable. She is a dignified and accomplished woman in the book trade, and she felt that she had been hung out to dry. It is harder to imagine that she could be so naive as to believe that Oprah's fan base and business sense do not drive the *Oprah Winfrey Show*. Oliver

Wendell Holmes had described the public sphere as a *market-place* ninety years earlier, and that metaphor has more than taken over public conversation in America.

Kakutani insisted curiously that Frey's book is not just another misleading memoir like Hellman's *Pentimento* but a symptom of a new failure of public conversation in America. However, to inflate the Frey case and to dismiss Hellman (again) is to perpetuate, among the supposedly most literate public commentators, a failure of historical imagination. It is certainly true that the market for memoirs, indeed for all forms of confession, has exploded since the 1960s, but it is vital to understand that it was Hellman's and McCarthy's generation that charted those public dimensions of private life. At this point it is useless to lament, as Kakutani does, that we live in a relativistic culture, that "reality shows" are stage-managed and that spin doctors are an accepted part of politics, or to note, as Walter Lippmann did less emotionally in 1922, that hyperbole is an accepted part of marketing and public relations. It is, moreover, absurd for Kakutani to suggest that academic historians don't care about facts or objectivity, though they insist that the historical conditions and perspectives, which shape the historian, are also vital to consider in establishing the meanings of the facts. Truth is never something that people just discover in police reports, court records, or, as Martha Gellhorn tried to do in debunking Hellman, in train schedules. Anyone who has sat through a trial can testify to the unreliability of eye-witness accounts or even of smoking guns. The meanings of those facts, such as they are, become evident in conversation because they are attached to persons or the stories that people tell about themselves to other people.

Objectivity is something people share by balancing viewpoints, not something pure and independent that they come upon in isolation. This is neither to discount the importance of facts nor to celebrate the inherent value of opinion. The Supreme Court has had a similar problem making distinctions between facts and opinions. *Milkovich v. Lorain Journal Co.*, one of the last great libel cases to come before the Supreme Court, focused on the nature of lies and the distinction between fact and opinion. Mike Milkovich, a high school wrestling coach, sued a newspaper that had accused him of lying. The case, which made its way to the Supreme Court in 1990, six years after the Hellman case, was supposed to decide once and for all what counted as fact and what counted as opinion. It did not. Though the court found that some things were facts and some were "non-facts," it did not create "a wholesale defamation exemption for anything that might be labeled 'opinion.'" Instead it reiterated its position that the marketplace of ideas had to make space for falsehood.[9] On the one hand, the decision indicates that the law of libel cannot be structured so rigidly that people can be nailed whenever they say something false. On the other, it intimates that any decent, functioning marketplace of ideas must leave the state some room to distinguish between truth and falsehood and to hold people accountable in specific cases.

That a widely respected figure such as Hellman lied about her life rightfully offended a critic, such as McCarthy, who believed that transparency is a hallmark of civil discourse in a functioning democracy. Hellman wished to control information about herself, as Carl Rollyson complains, but that does not make her a censor or mean that she was hypocritical when she defended freedom of expression. Job applicants now routinely ask their friends to remove photographs from their Facebook accounts in case a potential employer tries to discover what they do in their spare time. Like a job application, public conversation requires not only a measure of transparency but also selectivity. Related to the problem of uncoupling fact from opinion is the reality that separating the private from the public person has also become increasingly urgent and difficult. But private and public conversations involve different values. Without mutual respect people would be unlikely to stick around for the former, but without competition and full-throated debate the larger society would fracture and decay. The Hellman-McCarthy case is significant in large part because it illustrates a crisis in both areas. On the one hand, it marks the end of a generation that engaged in such vociferous argument, yet, on the other, the case itself, spawned by a hyperbolic talking point on TV and a punishing lawsuit without any more direct reply, heralded the age in which we find ourselves with James Frey, Oprah Winfrey, Rush Limbaugh, and dysfunctional governments on local, state, and national levels.

At Lillian Hellman's funeral on July 3, 1984, her friend and neighbor on Martha's Vineyard the author John Hersey said a few words at Chilmark Cemetery. McCarthy had also criticized Hersey's *Hiroshima* on the *Dick Cavett Show,* and Hellman had called Hersey immediately afterward to invite him also to sue for libel. He had gracefully declined. In his eulogy, Hersey quipped, "Dear Lillian, you are a finished woman, now." Recognizing perhaps that Hellman was very angry at being finished, he added, "I mean 'finished' in its better sense. You shone with a high finish of integrity, decency, uprightness. You have given us this anger to remember and to use in a bad world."[10] Thinking of the person in the terms of her own writing both subverts and reinforces the distinction between the woman and her books. Of course, many would have disagreed with Hersey, but his words acknowledge that it is hard to be done with Hellman, no matter how she may be finished.

I would like to finish with one more story, borrowed from the central chapter of *An Unfinished Woman,* which is a diary entry from her 1944 trip to Moscow, a text within the text. It in turn centers on a tragicomic episode known as "the trouble," which involves the "transshipment of a Russian prostitute":

> There had been a long box in the lobby of the Metropole marked, in Russian, COFFIN OF A CHILD FOR TRANSSHIPMENT. The box carried whatever are the proper papers for a coffin and a Stockholm receiving address. It got through the Leningrad customs until a train official got curious about some odd-looking holes in the box. He poked them with some kind of instrument that went, unexpectedly through to another series of holes. Strange sounds began to be heard, and when the coffin was broken open there was a trunk inside the coffin and a Russian girl in whatever form of hysteria you get from being in a trunk that is in a coffin.[11]

The child's coffin contains a peculiar and rich collection of metaphors for Hellman's book, for the private-public figure Lillian Hellman, and for writing itself. An earlier chapter, which described her first abortion when she was working for a publisher, had already made an analogy between losing a manuscript and losing a baby. Here the baby has returned.

But, like the printed word, this body is in transit. It is *bound*, in more sense than one, carrying papers, requiring translation, an object passing from one set of hands to another through the customs house of language. But something unexpected happens. The body is not dead after all. A man, distrusting the writing, begins to probe, inserting his troubling instrument into the coffin's holes. What he finds is not the dead body of the baby but the living body of a woman, and not just any woman but a woman whose sex is for sale, a prostitute. With probing, strange sounds emerge, like the "funny noises" that come from the bedroom of the allegedly lesbian schoolteachers in *The Children's Hour*, followed by full-scale "hysteria" when the box is opened. What he finds is more than he bargained for.

We may or may not wish to read this vignette as an allegory of the reader who tries to put his finger on the female author. "The key to Lillian Hellman's character," writes Rollyson, "to what made her a legend in her own time, was her sense of herself as a grande dame."[12] Nailing Hellman with a word or a phrase, as McCarthy also attempted on the *Dick Cavett Show*, is a reflex of her own life and writing. If we look at Hellman and the conflicts she provoked with fresh eyes, we can discover our own troubling impulses. To say so is not to absolve the historical Lillian Hellman of her poisonous tendencies and lies. But she won't be found in the text any more than the baby in the coffin. The story might seem only a clever way of representing such diverse topics as the prostitution of the author and the evasion of authority, hidden sexuality versus an intrusive reading, migration and the transgression of borders, the Cold War ideology of containment (this is a *Soviet* prostitute after all) and the globalizing force of commerce. However, we find precisely the same trope with some variations in *Pentimento,* Hellman's second effort at life-writing.

The child's coffin reappears in *Pentimento* after a comical literary evening with the poets Theodore Roethke and Robert Lowell and a story about Roethke's manic wordplay on the name of Lionel and/or Diana Trilling: "Isn't it thrilling there's another Trilling?" Four or five days after the poetry reading, Hellman's housekeeper, Helen, called Hellman home from the library to examine a strange shipment that had just arrived.

> "A child's coffin has come to the house."
> *"A child's coffin?"*
> "In a pine box. Dripping."
> Indeed there was a pine box in the hall, it was the size of a small child, it was dripping, and most of the red lettering of the sender had been washed away. One could still read, "Mother Joa—" and numbers that still had two eights in them.[13]

Inside, again, there is no baby, but this time a decaying salmon that is supposed to represent the joint pseudonym Roethke had proposed for Hellman and himself: Irving K. Salmon. What is the point of this silly tale about an author's name and a dripping box, which upon opening proves to hold not the promised body, whether of the author or anyone else, but a slippery fish? For one thing, it troubles our desire to lay hands on the author, to pin down what is important about her life. The fish signifies not only the author's absence but also the fact that this author—Irving K. Salmon—is a crazy fiction to begin with, reminiscent of a tale about the one that got away.

With the illegible name of a mother (Mother Joa—) and a curious ellipsis in a narrative about female reproduction, Hellman is playing a game with us. Wouldn't it be thrilling if there were another Trilling, another critic, perhaps, with what Trilling called a liberal imagination? Whether an aborted literary allusion, possibly to Steinbeck's Ma Joad or to the author-narrator Lillian Hellman or to nothing outside the book's own language, she will not be finished as long as we continue to attempt filling in the gaps, talking about her and what she amounts to, which is words for a conversation.

Notes

Introduction

Epigraphs: Stephen Breyer, *Active Liberty: Interpreting Our Democratic Constitution* (New York: Alfred A. Knopf, 2005), 66; Lillian Hellman, *Pentimento: A Book of Portraits* (Boston: Little, Brown, 1973), 32–33.

1. Irving Howe quoted in Michiko Kakutani, "Hellman-McCarthy Libel Suit Stirs Old Antagonisms," *New York Times,* March 19, 1980, C21.

2. In a letter of March 21, 1980, to her lawyer Ben O'Sullivan, McCarthy wrote, "Thinking over the list of my champions (Podhoretz & Co.), I feel disturbed. What has happened, obviously, is that the whole business as seen by the press has been a lining-up of political sides. This really is her doing. In fact, my remark on the Cavett Show wasn't political overtly or covertly." Mary McCarthy Papers, Archives and Special Collections, Vassar College Libraries.

3. Walter Lippmann, *Public Opinion* (1922; rpt., New York: Simon and Schuster, 1997), 5, 82, 110.

4. Mary McCarthy, "The Novels That Got Away," *New York Review of Books,* November 25, 1979.

5. Lippmann, *Public Opinion,* 110.

6. Lillian Hellman, *An Unfinished Woman* (Boston: Little, Brown, 1969), 37, 33.

7. Lillian Hellman, *Scoundrel Time* (Boston: Little, Brown, 1976), 93.

8. Dick Cavett and Christopher Porterfield, *Cavett* (New York: Harcourt Brace Jovanovich, 1974), 328, 90–92.

9. Mary McCarthy, *Memories of a Catholic Girlhood* (New York: Harcourt, 1957), 29.

10. See Edith H. Walton, review of *The Company She Keeps,* by Mary McCarthy, *New York Times,* May 24, 1942.

11. Alfred Kazin, *New York Jew* (New York: Vintage, 1979), 102.

12. Alfred Kazin, "Provincetown, 1940: Bertram Wolfe, Mary Mc-Carthy, Philip Rahv," in *Alfred Kazin's America: Critical and Personal Writings,* ed. Ted Solotaroff (New York: HarperCollins, 2003), 161.

13. Carol Gelderman, *Mary McCarthy: A Life* (New York: St. Martin's, 1988), 146.

14. Susan Sontag, *Reborn: Journals and Notebooks, 1947–1963* (New York: Farrar, Straus and Giroux, 2008), 297.

15. Mary McCarthy to Hannah Arendt, December 19, 1967, in *Between Friends: The Correspondence of Hannah Arendt and Mary McCarthy, 1949–1975,* ed. Carol Brightman (New York: Harcourt Brace Jovanovich, 1995), 206.

16. Diana Trilling, *The Beginning of the Journey: The Marriage of Lionel and Diana Trilling* (New York: Harcourt Brace, 1993), 262.

17. Mary McCarthy, *Intellectual Memoirs: New York, 1936–1938* (New York: Harcourt Brace Jovanovich, 1992), 22–23.

18. Trilling, *Beginning of the Journey,* 304.

19. McCarthy, *Intellectual Memoirs,* 94.

20. The meeting is described in Carol Brightman, *Writing Dangerously: Mary McCarthy and Her World* (New York: Clarkson Potter, 1992), 298–99; and Gelderman, *Mary McCarthy,* 153.

21. See Brightman, Introduction to *Between Friends,* x.

22. Hannah Arendt to Mary McCarthy, March 10, 1949, in Brightman, *Between Friends,* 1.

23. Brightman, *Between Friends,* 275.

24. Mike Celizic, "Elizabeth Edwards: John 'Made One Mistake,'" *Today,* May 19, 2009, http://today.msnbc.msn.com/id/30681150/; Stephen M. Silverman, "Elizabeth Edwards Talks about the Fragile State of Her Marriage," *People,* May 5, 2009, http://www.people.com/people/article/0,,20276640,00.html.

25. Transcript from *Good Morning America* interview with Young regarding Edwards: http://www.livedash.com/transcript/good_morning_america/714/KGO/Monday_February_1_2010/147062. For Young's account of Edwards's lies on the campaign trail see Andrew Young, *The Politician: An Insider's Account of John Edwards's Pursuit of the Presidency and the Scandal That Brought Him Down* (New York: St. Martin's, 2010), 180, 198, 202–4, 222–24, 286, 291.

26. People v. Croswell, 3 Johns. Cas. 337 N.Y. 1804, *reprinted in* N.Y. Common Law Rep. App. 717–41 (1883); Gertz v. Robert Welch, Inc., 418 U.S. 323 (1974). See also Daniel J. Solove, *The Future of Reputation: Gossip, Rumor, and Privacy on the Internet* (New Haven: Yale University Press, 2008).

27. Hellman, *Scoundrel Time*, 154–55.

28. Irving Howe, "Lillian Hellman and the McCarthy Years," in *Selected Writings, 1950–1990* (San Diego: Harcourt Brace Jovanovich, 1990), 345–46.

29. William Wright, "Why Lillian Hellman Remains Fascinating," *New York Times*, November 3, 1996, H9. For critical biographies, see William Wright, *Lillian Hellman: The Image, the Woman* (New York: Simon and Schuster, 1986); Carl Rollyson, *Lillian Hellman: Her Legend and Her Legacy* (New York: St. Martin's, 1988); and Joan Mellen, *Hellman and Hammett: The Legendary Passion of Lillian Hellman and Dashiell Hammett* (New York: HarperCollins, 1996). For the biographical apologia, see Deborah Martinson, *Lillian Hellman: A Life with Foxes and Scoundrels* (New York: Counterpoint, 2005). Hellman's lover Peter Feibleman gives a sympathetic portrait in *Lilly: Reminiscences of Lillian Hellman* (New York: Morrow, 1988). For the continuing debate, see Carl Rollyson, "The Lives and Lies of Lillian Hellman," *New York Sun*, November 25, 2005.

30. "Clinton Camp: Obama's Record, Just Words," *PoliticusUSA*, March 27, 2008, http://www.politicususa.com/en/Clinton-3-27.

31. Lillian Hellman, "Author Jabs the Critic," *New York Times*, December 15, 1946, X3.

32. Louis Brandeis and Samuel Warren, "The Right to Privacy," *Harvard Law Review* 4, no. 5 (1890): 193–220.

33. Breyer, *Active Liberty*, 66.

34. See McCarthy, *Memories*, 11, 65, 124, 136.

35. Clyde Haberman, "The Stalemate in Albany, 5 Years On," *New York Times*, June 8, 2009.

Chapter 1. Libel and Life-Writing

Epigraphs: Time, Inc. v. Hill, 385 U.S. 374, 388–89 (1967). Arthur Kober responds to actress Bankhead's depiction of Hellman in a diary entry, January 23, 1940, Arthur Kober Papers, Wisconsin Historical Society, Madison.

1. See "Dick Cavett," in Alex McNeil, *Total Television: A Comprehensive Guide to Programming from 1948 to the Present*, 3rd ed. (New York: Penguin, 1991), 196.

2. Dick Cavett and Christopher Porterfield, *Cavett* (New York: Harcourt Brace Jovanovich, 1974), 91–92.

3. Cyclops, "*Life* TV Review: Late-Night Hope for the Republic: Dick Cavett," *Life*, December 10, 1971, 12. For accounts of the Maddox episode, see Associated Press, "'Insulted' by Cavett, Maddox Walks Out," *Milwaukee Journal*, December 19, 1970, 1:3; and "'Bigot' Remark Forces Maddox to Leave Show," *Jet*, January 7, 1971, 60.

4. All references to Mary McCarthy's appearance on the *Dick Cavett Show* are taken from video footage of the episodes (Daphne #817) provided by courtesy of Dick Cavett.

5. Rita Wade, e-mail message to author, April 14, 2010.

6. Cavett and Porterfield, *Cavett*, 76.

7. Ann Terry, "Notes and Comments" for Dick Cavett, October 16, 1979, Mary McCarthy Papers, Archives and Special Collections, Vassar College Libraries (hereinafter cited as McCarthy Papers).

8. Joan Dupont, "Mary McCarthy: Portrait of a Lady," *Paris Metro*, February 1978, 15, 16.

9. Diana Trilling quoted in William Wright, *Lillian Hellman: The Image, the Woman* (New York: Simon and Schuster, 1986), 373.

10. Rita Wade, e-mail message to author, April 14, 2010.

11. Mary McCarthy, "The Genial Host," in *The Company She Keeps* (1942; rpt., New York: Harcourt, 1970), 151.

12. Carol Brightman, *Writing Dangerously: Mary McCarthy and Her World* (New York: Clarkson Potter, 1992), 325–26.

13. Mary McCarthy to Dwight Macdonald, July 24, 1979, McCarthy Papers.

14. Mary McCarthy, *Town and Country*, 1944, rpt. in *Film Comment*, January–February 1976.

15. John Phillips and Anne Hollander, "The Art of the Theater I: Lillian Hellman–An Interview" (1964), in *Conversations with Lillian Hellman*, ed. Jackson R. Bryer (Jackson: University Press of Mississippi, 1986), 60.

16. Peter Feibleman, *Lilly: Reminiscences of Lillian Hellman* (New York: Morrow, 1988), 284.

17. Lillian Hellman, *Scoundrel Time* (Boston: Little, Brown, 1976), 93.

18. Lee Gershwin quoted in Carl Rollyson, *Lillian Hellman: Her Legend and Her Legacy* (New York: St. Martin's, 1988), 4.

19. Rosemary Mahoney, *A Likely Story: One Summer with Lillian Hellman* (New York: Doubleday, 1998), 28, 51.

20. Lillian Hellman, *Pentimento: A Book of Portraits* (Boston: Little, Brown, 1973), 21.

21. The Hellman eulogies, delivered on July 3, 1984, at Martha's Vineyard, are collected in Feibleman, *Lilly*.

22. Susan Sontag quoted in Frances Kiernan, *Seeing Mary Plain: A Life of Mary McCarthy* (New York: W. W. Norton, 2000), 678, 683.

23. Norman Mailer quoted in Brightman, *Writing Dangerously*, 606.

24. William Alfred quoted in Rollyson, *Lillian Hellman*, 368.

25. Lillian Hellman, *An Unfinished Woman* (Boston: Little, Brown, 1969), 256.

26. Stephen Gillers, cochairman, Committee for Public Justice, Testimony before US Senate, Hearings on the Nomination of Sandra Day O'Connor of Arizona to Serve as an Associate Justice of the Supreme Court of the United States, September 11, 1981, http://www.gpoaccess.gov/congress/senate/judiciary/sh-j-97-51/390-395.pdf. Roger Wilkins, Letter to the Editors, *New York Review of Books*, January 28, 1971.

27. "New Jersey Briefs," *New York Times*, October 29, 1973.

28. Nixon v. Sampson, 389 F. Supp. 107, 114 (D.D.C. 1975). See also Anthony Ripley, "U.S. Judge Rules Nixon Documents Belong to Nixon," *New York Times*, February 1, 1975; "Appeals Court Will Move Quickly on Nixon Records," *New York Times*, February 2, 1975; and "Summary of Judge's Ruling on the Nixon Documents, *New York Times*, February 1, 1975.

29. Rollyson, *Lillian Hellman*, 7.

30. Mary McCarthy to Ira Glasser, May 1, 1986, McCarthy Papers.

31. Wright, *Lillian Hellman*, 9.

32. Martha Gellhorn, "Close Encounters of the Apocryphal Kind," *Paris Review* 79 (Spring 1981): 280–301.

33. See David Laskin, *Partisans: Marriage, Politics, and Betrayal among the New York Intellectuals* (Chicago: University of Chicago Press, 2000), 16.

34. Dick Cavett, "Lillian, Mary, and Me," *New Yorker*, December 16, 2002, 34.

35. Cavett, "Lillian, Mary, and Me."

36. Answer of the Plaintiff to the interrogatories of Educational Broadcasting Corporation, December 14, 1981, McCarthy Papers.

37. Anthony Lewis, *Make No Law: The Sullivan Case and the First Amendment* (New York: Vintage, 1991), 34–36.

38. Lillian Hellman, "Complaint" against Mary McCarthy, Dick Cavett, and Educational Broadcasting Corporation, February 14, 1980, McCarthy Papers.

39. Robert Kraus, "The Plaintiff's Hour," *Harper's,* March 2003, 14.

40. Hellman, "Complaint."

41. Herbert Mitgang, "Miss Hellman Suing a Critic for 2.25 Million," *New York Times,* February 16, 1980, 12.

42. Hellman, "Complaint."

43. McCarthy, "Answers to Plaintiff's First Interrogatories," October 20, 1980, McCarthy Papers.

44. Justice Harold Baer Jr., Hellman v. McCarthy, 10 Med. L. Rep. 1789, 1790 (N.Y. Sup. Ct., May 29, 1984) (decision on summary judgment).

45. Nora Ephron, *Imaginary Friends: A Play with Music* (New York: Samuel French, 2002), 73.

46. Garrison v. Louisiana, 379 U.S. 64 (1964), 85 S. Ct. 209, 13 L. Ed. 2d 125, 1 Media L. Rep. 1548.

47. Sidney Hook, "The Scoundrel in the Looking Glass," *Encounter* 48 (February 1977): 82–91.

48. Gellhorn, "Close Encounters."

49. Samuel McCracken, "'Julia' and Other Fictions by Lillian Hellman," *Commentary,* June 1984, 35–43.

50. Hellman, *Pentimento,* 112, 147.

51. See Norman L. Rosenberg, "The Law of Libel in Troubled Times," in *Protecting the Best Men: An Interpretive History of the Law of Libel* (Chapel Hill: University of North Carolina Press, 1986), 235–57, 247; Francis Murnaghan, "From Figment to Fiction to Philosophy: The Requirement of Proof of Damages in Libel Actions," *Catholic University Law Review* 22 (1972): 1–38, 4; and Rodney A. Smolla, *Suing the Press: Libel, the Media, and Power* (Oxford: Oxford University Press, 1986), 6–19.

52. Renata Adler, *Reckless Disregard: Westmorland v. CBS et al., Sharon v. Time* (New York: Alfred A. Knopf, 1986), 29.

53. Floyd Abrams, e-mail message to author, May 3, 2010.

54. Smolla, *Suing the Press,* 62.

55. Stephen Gillers, e-mail message to author, March 6, 2008.

56. Smolla, *Suing the Press,* 63.

57. Norman Mailer, "An Appeal to Lillian Hellman and Mary McCarthy," *New York Times,* May 11, 1980, BR1.

58. Lillian Hellman, *The Children's Hour,* in *The Collected Plays* (Boston: Little, Brown, 1961), 43.

59. Rosenberg, *Protecting the Best Men,* 207.

60. McCarthy to Ben Sullivan, April 21, 1980, McCarthy Papers.

61. Hellman v. McCarthy, N.Y.L.J., May 29, 1984, at 7, col. 2–3 (Sup. Ct. N.Y. Co.) (decision on summary judgment).

62. Stephen Gillers, e-mail message to author, January 29, 2010.

63. Hellman v. McCarthy.

64. Hellman v. McCarthy.

65. I am indebted to Benjamin Zipursky for explaining to me many of the fine points of libel law and for his valuable assessment of Justice Harold Baer's decision on summary judgment.

66. Floyd Abrams, e-mail message to author, May 3, 2010.

67. Howe, "Lillian Hellman and the McCarthy Years," 341.

68. Mary McCarthy, "Material for Answering Interrogatory 15 (for B. O'S)," McCarthy Papers.

69. See Norman Podhoretz, *Ex-Friends: Falling Out with Allen Ginsberg, Lionel and Diana Trilling, Lillian Hellman, Hannah Arendt, and Norman Mailer* (New York: Free Press, 1999), 117; Daniel J. Kornstein, "The Case against Lillian Hellman: A Literary Legal Defense," *Fordham Law Review* 57 (1988–89): 683–724; Rollyson, *Lillian Hellman,* 512–24; and Paul Johnson, "Lies, Damned Lies and Lillian Hellman," in *Intellectuals* (London: Weidenfeld, 1988), 288–305, 288–89.

70. See George E. Marcus, *The Sentimental Citizen: Emotion in Democratic Politics* (University Park: Pennsylvania State University Press, 2002), 119–32; and Philip Fisher, *The Vehement Passions* (Princeton, NJ: Princeton University Press, 2002), 1–12, 171–98.

71. Mary McCarthy, *Birds of America* (New York: Harcourt Brace Jovanovich, 1971), 343.

72. See Immanuel Kant, *Critique of Judgment,* trans. Werner S. Pluhar (Indianapolis, IN: Hackett, 1987), 86–90.

73. Nancy Franklin, "Working Girl: A British Take on the World's Oldest Profession," *New Yorker,* June 30, 2008, 82–83.

74. McCarthy Deposition, August 12, 1981, 42, McCarthy Papers.

75. Mary McCarthy, "The Fact in Fiction," in *On the Contrary: Articles of Belief, 1946–1961* (New York: Farrar, Straus and Cudahy, 1961), 250.

76. McCarthy quoted in Carol Gelderman, *Mary McCarthy: A Life* (New York: St. Martin's, 1988), 329.

77. Mary McCarthy, *Memories of a Catholic Girlhood* (New York: Harcourt, 1957), 70.

78. Gelderman, *Mary McCarthy,* xvi.

79. Mary McCarthy, "Ghostly Father, I Confess," in *The Company She Keeps* (1942; rpt., New York: Harcourt, 1970), 264.

80. Mary McCarthy to Benjamin O'Sullivan, May 11, 1984, McCarthy Papers.

81. See Wallulis v. Dymowski, 323 Or. 337, 918 P.2d 755 Or., 20 June 1996, and Foster v. Churchill, 87 N.Y.2d 744, 642 N.Y.S.2d 583 [1996], respectively; emphasis added.

82. Diana Trilling to William Jovanovich (her and McCarthy's publisher), November 16, 1980, McCarthy Papers.

83. McCarthy to O'Sullivan, November 29, 1980, McCarthy Papers.

84. Mary McCarthy, *A Charmed Life* (New York: Harcourt, Brace, 1955), 58–59, emphasis in original.

85. In *Pahler v. Slayer,* a case in which a death metal band was sued for inciting violence, the Court regarded "figurative" language as incapable of amounting to a direct incitement, as it would not be taken seriously: "The Court must distinguish between artistic, figurative descriptions of violence and actual incitement to commit violence against a specific target." Not Reported in Cal. Rptr. 2d, 2001 WL 1736476, Cal. Super., 2001.

86. McCarthy to O'Sullivan, March 21, 1980, McCarthy Papers.

87. See Hellman, *Scoundrel Time,* 78, and *Pentimento,* 174, among many examples.

88. Joan Mellen, e-mail message to author, March 1, 2008.

89. Hellman, *Unfinished Woman,* 130.

90. Arendt to McCarthy in *Between Friends: The Correspondence of Mary McCarthy and Hannah Arendt, 1949–1975,* ed. Carol Brightman (New York: Clarkson Potter, 1992), 292.

Chapter 2. Language Lessons

Epigraphs: "Kill the Compromise," *Harvard Crimson,* November 19, 1935; Lillian Hellman, *Another Part of the Forest: A Play in Three Acts* (1946; New York: Dramatists Play Service, 1974), 54.

1. Lillian Hellman, *New York Post,* July 1, 1939.

2. Margaret Case Harriman, *Take Them Up Tenderly: A Collection of Profiles* (New York: Alfred A. Knopf, 1944), 99.

3. Lawrence A. Cremin, "The Revolution in American Secondary Education, 1893–1918," *Teachers College Record* 56 (1955): 295, 307. See also William G. Wraga, "The Progressive Classicism of Alexander James Inglis," *Classical Journal* 99 (2003): 59–69; and G. W. Wharton, "High School

Architecture in the City of New York," *School Review: A Journal of Secondary Education* 11 (1903): 456–85.

4. A revised edition of Allen and Greenough's *New Latin Grammar* (1888) was issued in 1903, and in 1909 the future progressive educator Alexander James Inglis, with his colleague from the Horace Mann High School Charles McCoy Baker, published *High School Course in Latin Composition*. For a history of Latin, see George A. Kennedy, "The History of Latin Education," *Helios* 14 (1987): 7–16; and K. F. Kitchell Jr., "The Great Latin Debate: The Futility of Utility?" in *Latin for the 21st Century: From Concept to Classroom,* ed. Richard A. LaFleur (Glenview, IL: Scott Foresman–Addison Wesley, 1998), 1–14; and Alexander James Inglis's dissertation, *The Rise of High School Latin in Massachusetts,* Teachers College Contribution to Education, no. 45 (New York, 1911). For Hellman's report cards, see Carl Rollyson, *Lillian Hellman: Her Legend and Her Legacy* (New York: St. Martin's, 1988), 27.

5. Wraga, "Progressive Classicism of Inglis," 59.

6. J. B. Greenough et al., eds., *Allen and Greenough's New Latin Grammar for Schools and Colleges* (Boston: Ginn, 1903), 163.

7. Lillian Hellman, *An Unfinished Woman* (Boston: Little, Brown, 1969), 9.

8. William James, *"Pragmatism" and "The Meaning of Truth"* (Cambridge, MA: Harvard University Press, 1975), 97, emphasis in original.

9. See Rollyson, *Lillian Hellman,* 394–97.

10. Jerome Wiesner, eulogy for Hellman, July 3, 1984, rpt. in Peter Feibleman, *Lilly: Reminiscences of Lillian Hellman* (New York: Morrow, 1988), 360–61.

11. Hellman, *Unfinished Woman,* 94, 188.

12. Mary McCarthy, *Memories of a Catholic Girlhood* (New York: Harcourt, 1957), 18, 103.

13. McCarthy, *Memories,* 155, 154, 144.

14. Elizabeth Hardwick calls McCarthy a "Latin student" in her preface to McCarthy's *Intellectual Memoirs: New York, 1936–1938* (New York: Harcourt Brace, 1992), xix, and elsewhere parodied McCarthy's Latinate verbal obsessions. Hardwick, "The Gang," *New York Review of Books,* September 26, 1963.

15. Mary McCarthy, "Language and Politics," in *Occasional Prose: Essays* (New York: Harcourt, 1985), 93–94. See also McCarthy, "Lies," *New York Review of Books,* August 9, 1973, 19–21.

16. Archibald MacLeish, "What Is English?" in *A Continuing Journey: Essays and Addresses* (Boston: Houghton Mifflin, 1967), 254.

17. MacLeish, "What Is English?" 257, 259.

18. MacLeish, "What Is English?" 257.

19. In *Perfect Enemies: The Religious Right, The Gay Movement, and the Politics of the 1990s* (New York: Crown, 1996), John Gallagher and Chris Bull focus on the word "unnatural" (a key word in Hellman's *Children's Hour*) in classroom battles of the 1960s. See also Michael Cobb, *God Hates Fags: The Rhetorics of Religious Violence* (New York: New York University Press, 2006), 124–25; and Madiha Didi Khayatt, *Lesbian Teachers: An Invisible Presence* (Albany: State University of New York Press, 1992). A conservative website billed as the "guide to gay and lesbian politics on the web" lists over fifty common right-wing arguments. See http://www.turnleft .com/out/knowthy_arguments.html.

20. A 1954 article uses this phrase as an epigraph: "*Omnibus ad quos, hae litterae perverint, salutem in domino sempiternam, nos praeses et socii huius universitatis. . . .* It's diploma Latin; in other words, it's the sheepskin myth." See Martin Staples Shockley, "The Sheepskin Myth," *Journal of Higher Education* 25 (1954): 481–87. See also Christopher A. Francese, "A Degree in English," *New York Times,* May 15, 2009.

21. Mary McCarthy Papers, Archives and Special Collections, Vassar College.

22. Walter A. Jessup, "Languages and the Founding Fathers," *Modern Language Journal* 20 (1936): 435.

23. Thomas Jefferson to John Brazier, August 14, 1819, in *The Writings of Thomas Jefferson: Memorial Edition,* 20 vols., ed. Andrew A. Lipscomb and Albert Ellery Bergh (Washington, DC: Thomas Jefferson Memorial Association, 1903–4), 15:209. Later he writes to Brazier that classical languages are "a solid basis to most, and an ornament to all the sciences" (15:211). See also Jefferson's letter to Thomas Cooper, October 7, 1814 (*Writings of Jefferson,* 14:200).

24. Jeremiah Day and James Luce Kingsley, "Original Papers in Relation to a Course in Liberal Education," *American Journal of Science and Arts* 15 (January 1829), 297–351.

25. Jack C. Lane, "The Yale Report of 1828 and Liberal Education: A Neorepublican Manifesto," *History of Education Quarterly* 27 (1987): 338.

26. James Joyce, *Ulysses* (1922; rpt., New York: Penguin, 2000), 169. Joseph Farrell, "The Uses of Latinity in Modern Literature" (unpublished manuscript, University of Toronto, November 11, 2006).

27. Kenneth Burke, *A Grammar of Motives* (Berkeley: University of California Press, 1945), 161, 516.

28. Joseph F. Zelenski, "Articulation between Colleges and High Schools: Something Old or Something New? A Historical Perspective, 1828–1987," *Community College Review* 16, no. 1 (1988): 34–37. See William J. Bennett, *To Reclaim a Legacy: A Report on the Humanities in Higher Education* (Washington, DC: National Endowment for the Humanities, 1984); James B. Conant, *The American High School Today: A First Report to Interested Citizens* (New York: McGraw-Hill, 1959); H. R. Douglas, *Trends and Issues in Secondary Education* (Washington, DC: Center for Applied Research in Education, 1962). Edward A. Krug, *Salient Dates in American Education, 1635–1964* (New York: Harper and Row, 1966).

29. Mary McCarthy, *How I Grew* (San Diego: Harcourt Brace Jovanovich, 1987), 6.

30. See Wayne C. Booth, *The Rhetoric of Rhetoric: The Quest for Effective Communication* (Malden, MA: Blackwell, 2004), 8.

31. Neil Postman, *The Disappearance of Childhood* (New York: Delacorte, 1982).

32. Nicholas Sammond, *Babes in Tomorrowland: Walt Disney and the Making of the American Child, 1930–1960* (Durham, NC: Duke University Press, 2005), 7.

33. See Alistair MacIntyre, *After Virtue: A Study in Moral Theory*, 2nd ed. (University of Notre Dame Press, 1984); Basil Mitchell, *Morality, Religious and Secular: The Dilemma of the Traditional Conscience* (Oxford: Clarendon Press, 1980); and George Steiner, *After Babel: Aspects of Language and Translation* (Oxford: Oxford University Press, 1975).

34. E. D. Hirsch Jr., *Cultural Literacy: What Every American Needs to Know* (Boston: Houghton Mifflin, 1987), xii. Hirsch continues his argument for the importance of a shared curriculum in fostering the American citizenry in *The Making of Americans: Democracy and Our Schools* (New Haven: Yale University Press, 2009).

35. Jefferson to Brazier, 15:209.

36. Mike Eskanazi, "The New Case for Latin," *Time*, December 2, 2000.

37. Tracy Lee Simmons, *Climbing Parnassus: A New Apologia for Greek and Latin* (Wilmington, DE: ISI Books, 2002), xvi, 164–65.

38. Winnie Hu, "A Dead Language That's Very Much Alive," *New York Times*, October 7, 2008.

39. To stimulate the new stoicism, Maureen Dowd offers her own column in Latin. For instance, "Gubernatrix (prope Russia) Palina, spectans candidaciam MMXII, post multam educationem cum Kissingro et post multam parodiam de Sabbatis Nocte Vivo atque de Tina Feia, ferociter

vituperat Obamam, ut supralupocidit (aerial shooting wolves) in Hyperborea." Dowd, "Are We Rome? Tu Betchus!" *New York Times,* October 12, 2008.

40. Harry Mount, "A Vote for Latin," *New York Times,* December 3, 2007. For a similar take on Latin, see Simmons, *Climbing Parnassus.*

41. McCarthy, "Lies."

42. Lewis Funke, "Interview with Lillian Hellman" (1968), in *Conversations with Lillian Hellman,* ed. Jackson R. Bryer (Jackson: University Press of Mississippi, 1986), 87.

43. Lillian Hellman, *The Children's Hour,* in *The Collected Plays* (Boston: Little, Brown, 1961), 6.

44. Neil Postman and Charles Weingartner, *Teaching as a Subversive Activity* (New York: Delacorte, 1969), 82–83. See also their chapter "Languaging," 98–132. And see Margaret Naumburg, *The Child and the World: Dialogues in Modern Education* (New York: Harcourt Brace, 1928).

45. John Dewey, *The Middle Works, 1899–1924,* ed. Jo Ann Boydston, 5 vols. (Carbondale: Southern Illinois University Press, 1967–72), 1:34.

46. Dewey, *Middle Works,* 1:297.

47. McCarthy, *Memories,* 24–25.

48. Robert S. Lynd and Helen Merrell Lynd, *Middletown in Transition: A Study in Cultural Conflicts* (New York: Harcourt, Brace, 1937), 222; Sammond, *Babes in Tomorrowland,* 153. The utilitarian trend was commented on in *Parents' Magazine* and such books as G. Hardy Clark, MD, *A System of Character Training of Children* (n.p.: Seaside, 1921).

49. Irvin Stock, *Mary McCarthy* (Minneapolis: University of Minnesota Press, 1968), 5.

50. Lillian Hellman, *Watch on the Rhine,* in *Collected Plays,* 224.

51. Hellman, *Unfinished Woman,* 29.

52. Lillian Hellman, *The Lark,* in *Collected Plays,* 555.

53. Roman Jakobson, "The Speech Event and the Functions of Language," in *On Language,* ed. Linda R. Waugh and Monique Monville-Burston (Cambridge, MA: Harvard University Press, 1990), 70.

54. Lillian Hellman, *Pentimento: A Book of Portraits* (Boston: Little, Brown, 1973), 128–29.

55. Greenough, *Allen and Greenough's New Latin Grammar,* 163.

56. Lillian Hellman, *Three: An Unfinished Woman, Pentimento, Scoundrel Time* (Boston: Little, Brown, 1979), 644.

57. Hellman, *Children's Hour,* 31.

58. Jeffrey Stout, *Ethics after Babel: The Languages of Morals and Their Discontents* (Boston: Beacon, 1988), 191.

59. Hellman, *Children's Hour*, 5.

60. Hellman, *Another Part of the Forest*, in *Collected Plays*, 393, 383.

61. Hellman, *Children's Hour*, 7.

62. Shakespeare, *The Merchant of Venice*, 5.1.99.

63. Rollyson, *Lillian Hellman*, 69.

64. Hellman, *Children's Hour*, 13, 17, 30, 62.

65. See John Dewey, "Horace Mann Today," and Dewey and Goodwin Watson, "The Forward View: A Free Teacher in a Free Society," both in *The Later Works*, vol. 11, ed. Jo Ann Boydston (Carbondale: Southern Illinois University Press, 1987), 387–90, 534–47.

66. Hellman, *Children's Hour*, 33.

67. Hellman, *Children's Hour*, 11.

68. In "Author Jabs the Critic," a riposte to *Times* theater critic Brooks Atkinson, Hellman says, "If I said that I don't know what your critic means when he writes that my plays are contrived I might easily sound as if I were quibbling about words. And yet the truth is I don't know what he means." *New York Times*, December 15, 1946, 3–4.

69. Harry Gilroy, "The Bigger the Lie," in *The Children's Hour: Acting Edition* (New York: Dramatists Play Service, 1953), 3.

70. James, *"Pragmatism" and "The Meaning of Truth,"* 31–32.

71. Oscar Wilde, "The Decay of Lying," in *Collins Complete Works of Oscar Wilde: Centenary Edition* (New York: HarperCollins, 1999), 1082, 1072.

72. Hellman, *Children's Hour*, 66.

73. Fred Gardner, "An Interview with Lillian Hellman" (1968), in *Conversations with Lillian Hellman*, ed. Jackson R. Bryer (Jackson: University Press of Mississippi, 1986), 110.

74. Hellman, *Children's Hour*, 58.

75. Funke, "Interview," 86.

76. In *Scoundrel Time*, she writes, "My belief in liberalism was mostly gone" (113).

77. Dewey, *Later Works*, 11:259.

78. This libelous book-within-the-book is quoted in *Harry Potter and the Deathly Hallows* (New York: Arthur A. Levine Books, 2007). For the public controversy, see Philip Marchand, "Dumbledore Gay from the Start? Here for Authors' Fest, J. K. Rowling Answers Questions about Wizard's 'Tragic Infatuation,'" *Toronto Star*, October 24, 2007.

79. See Edward Rothstein, "Is Dumbledore Gay? Depends on Definitions of 'Is' and 'Gay,'" *New York Times*, October 29, 2007; Lisa Bornstein, "The Trouble with 'Harry'; Dumbledore Gay? Even That Is Matter for Interpretation," *Rocky Mountain News*, October 27, 2007; and Tabatha Southey, "Wait, Weren't All the Wizards Gay?" *Globe and Mail*, October 27, 2007.

80. See Lawrence Downes, "The Pope Opens a Portal to Eternity, via the 1950s," *New York Times*, July 29, 2007; http://www.ratzingerfanclub.com/blog/2005/07/pope-benedict-xvi-and-harry-potter.html; and http://www.lifesite.net/ldn/2005/jul/05071301.html. The popularity of the Harry Potter books has also been responsible for the resurgence of interest among schoolchildren in Latin. Some of the books are now translated into Latin: *Harrius Potter et Philosophi Lapis* (New York: Bloomsbury, 2003).

81. Whittaker Chambers, *Witness* (New York: Regnery, 1952), 143–44.

82. Plato, *The Symposium of Plato*, trans. B. Jowett (Boston: International Pocket Library, 1983), 80.

83. Richard Lanham, *The Motives of Eloquence: Literary Rhetoric in the Renaissance* (New Haven: Yale University Press, 1976), 1–35.

84. Malcolm X and Alex Haley, *The Autobiography of Malcolm X* (1964; rpt., New York: Ballantine, 1999), 216, 387, 346–47.

85. Daniel J. Kornstein, "The Case against Lillian Hellman: A Literary/Legal Defense," *Fordham Law Review* 57 (April 1989): 689.

Chapter 3. Words of Love

Epigraphs: Lillian Hellman, *An Unfinished Woman: A Memoir* (Boston: Little, Brown, 1969), 39; Mary McCarthy, *A Charmed Life* (New York: Harcourt, Brace, 1955), 312.

1. Hellman, *Unfinished Woman*, 40.

2. Hellman, *Unfinished Woman*, 35.

3. See Lillian Hellman, *Watch on the Rhine* and *The Lark*, in *The Collected Plays* (Boston: Little, Brown, 1961), 234, 598, respectively.

4. Reuel Wilson, e-mail message to author, July 14, 2010.

5. Tess Slesinger, *The Unpossessed* (1934; rpt., New York: New York Review of Books, 2002), 295, 301.

6. Roy Lucas, "Federal Constitutional Limitations on the Enforcement and Administration of State Abortion Statutes," *North Carolina Law Review* 46 (June 1968): 730–78.

7. See Paul S. Boyer, *"Purity in Print": The Vice-Society Movement and Book Censorship in America* (New York: Charles Scribner's Sons, 1968), 185–86; Donald Friede, "Getting Started," *New York Times,* April 23, 1927; and Morris L. Ernst and Alan U. Schwartz, *Censorship: The Search for the Obscene* (New York: Macmillan, 1964).

8. Philip E. Gerber, "E. E. Cummings's Season of the Censor," *Contemporary Literature* 29, no. 2 (1988): 177–200.

9. E. E. Cummings, *Him* (New York: Boni and Liveright, 1927), 143, 146. See also Allison Carruth, "The Space Stage and the Circus: E. E. Cummings's *Him* and Frederick Kiesler's *Raumbühne*," *Modern Drama* 51 (2008): 463–64.

10. See Morris L. Ernst and Alan U. Schwartz, "On Banning a Theme," in *Censorship,* 71–79. People v. Friede, 133 Misc. 611, 233 N.Y. Supp. 565 (Magis. Ct. 1929).

11. See Cass R. Sunstein, "Paradoxes of the Regulatory State," *University of Chicago Law Review* 57 (Spring 1990): 407. See also Jean L. Cohen, *Regulating Intimacy: A New Legal Paradigm* (Princeton, NJ: Princeton University Press, 2002), 1–4, 142–50.

12. Hellman, *Unfinished Woman,* 41–42.

13. Samuel Hopkins Adams, "A Word from the Writer to the Reader," *Flaming Youth* (New York: Boni and Liveright, 1923), 5.

14. Hellman, *Unfinished Woman,* 43–47.

15. Margaret Sanger, *My Fight for Birth Control* (New York: Farrar and Rinehart, 1931) 155–56.

16. David Garrow, *Liberty and Sexuality: The Right to Privacy and the Making of Roe v. Wade* (Berkeley: University of California Press, 1994), 402–4. McCorvey candidly describes herself as a liar in *I Am Roe: My Life: Roe v. Wade, and Freedom of Choice* (New York: Perennial, 1995). Susan Brownmiller comments that McCorvey "had cooked up a tale about gang rape on a dark rural road in Georgia, a story that could not have gotten her a legal abortion in Texas even if it had been true." Brownmiller, *In Our Time: Memoir of a Revolution* (New York: Dial, 1999), 120.

17. N. E. H. Hull and Peter Charles Hoffer, *Roe v. Wade: The Abortion Rights Controversy in American History* (Lawrence: University Press of Kansas, 2001), 148.

18. See Cohen, *Regulating Intimacy,* 1–21.

19. Lillian Hellman, *Pentimento: A Book of Portraits* (Boston: Little, Brown, 1973), 169.

20. Hellman, *Unfinished Woman,* 29.

21. Lee Gershwin, Hellman's intimate friend, told Hellman's biographer Carl Rollyson that she had seven. Mary McCarthy herself told Carol Brightman that she had "a quite a lot" of abortions in an interview, "Mary McCarthy, Still Contrary," *Nation*, May 19, 1984, 616.

22. Tit. 18. Crimes and Criminal Procedure. Ch. 71. Obscenity. Section 1461. Mailing obscene or crime-inciting matter. Ch. 258 17 Stat. 598 *enacted* March 3, 1873.

23. William S. Burroughs's *Naked Lunch* was the object of the last major American censorship battle over a novel involving the Comstock Laws; it lasted from roughly 1959, when the novel appeared, to 1966. Michael Barry Goodman, *Contemporary Literary Censorship: The Case History of Burroughs'* Naked Lunch (Metuchen, NJ: Scarecrow Press, 1981).

24. Sanger, *My Fight for Birth Control*, 84. See James Reed, *The Birth Control Movement and American Society: From Private Vice to Public Virtue* (Princeton, NJ: Princeton University Press, 1978), 95.

25. Sedition Act, sec. 3, *U.S. Statutes at Large* (Washington, DC, 1918), 40:553.

26. Abrams v. United States, 250 U.S. 627–31 (1919).

27. See Anthony Lewis, *Freedom for the Thought That We Hate* (New York: Basic Books, 2007), 62.

28. Margaret Sanger, "Comstockery in America," *International Socialist Review* (1915): 46–49.

29. See the *Pictorial Review* and Sanger biography.

30. Sanger, *My Fight for Birth Control*, 130.

31. Quotations from the *Sun*, letters from Reed and from Archer, Murray, Wells, et al. to the president are reprinted in Sanger, *My Fight for Birth Control*, 137–38.

32. Norman Redlich, "Are There 'Certain Rights . . . Retained by the People'?" *New York University Law Review* 37 (1962): 787–812, esp. 805, 811.

33. Justice Hugo Black wrote in dissent: "One of the most effective ways of diluting or expanding a constitutionally guaranteed right is to substitute for the crucial word or words of a constitutional guarantee another word or words, more or less flexible and more or less restricted in meaning." It is precisely the metaphorical form of the decision to which Judge Robert Bork objected at the time of his nomination to the Supreme Court: "I certainly would not accept emanations and penumbras as analysis, which is I think less an analysis than a metaphor." See Interview with Robert Bork, September 5, 1985, in *Ninth Justice: The Fight for Bork*, ed. Patrick B. McGuigan and Dawn M. Weyrich (Washington, DC: Free Congress Research and Education Foundation, 1990), 285–303, esp. 293.

34. John Hart Ely, "The Wages of Crying Wolf: A Comment on *Roe v. Wade*," *Yale Law Review* 82 (1973): 920–49; Garrow, *Liberty and Sexuality*, 610–11.

35. Stanley Fish, "The Law Wishes to Have a Formal Existence," in *There's No Such Thing as Free Speech . . . and It's a Good Thing, Too* (New York: Oxford University Press, 1994), 141–79.

36. Louis Brandeis and Samuel Warren, "The Right to Privacy," *Harvard Law Review* 4, no. 5 (1890): 192–220.

37. William L. Prosser, "Privacy," *California Law Review* 48 (1960): 383; Michael Sandel, "Moral Argument and Liberal Toleration: Abortion and Homosexuality," *California Law Review* 77 (1989): 525.

38. Tillie Olsen, "Silences" (1962), in *Silences* (New York: Delacorte, 1978), 8 (emphasis in original), 10.

39. Lillian Hellman, *Scoundrel Time* (Boston: Little, Brown, 1976), 53–54.

40. Hellman, *Scoundrel Time*, 58.

41. Hellman, *Scoundrel Time*, 92, 93.

42. Hellman, *Scoundrel Time*, 99–100.

43. In a letter to Dwight Macdonald just months before her appearance on the *Dick Cavett Show*, McCarthy fumed about Hellman's HUAC testimony. Mary McCarthy to Dwight Macdonald, July 24, 1979, Mary McCarthy Papers, Archives and Special Collections, Vassar College Libraries (hereinafter cited as McCarthy Papers).

44. Miller's biographer Martin Gottfried shows numerous instances in Miller's testimony of untruthfulness, evasiveness, and backtracking. See Martin Gottlieb, *Arthur Miller: His Life and Work* (New York: Da Capo, 2003), 290–93.

45. Arthur Miller, *Timebends: A Life* (New York: Grove, 1987), 387–406.

46. Melville B. Nimmer, "The Right of Publicity," *Law and Contemporary Problems* 19 (1954): 203.

47. Tallulah Bankhead, *Tallulah: An Autobiography* (1952; rpt., Jackson: University of Mississippi Press, 2004), 26.

48. Nathan Glazer, "An Answer to Lillian Hellman," *Commentary*, June 19, 1976, 36–39, emphasis added.

49. Her most famous line ("I cannot and will not cut my conscience to fit this year's fashions") is echoed in his ("I might have every rational reason to conform to the fashion of the time except for a single overriding consideration: I simply could not believe that anything I knew or any individual I could name was in the remotest sense a danger

to democracy in America"). Hellman, *Scoundrel Time,* 93; Miller, *Time-bends,* 397.

50. Watkins v. United States, 354 U.S. 178 (1957), id. at 199.

51. Deborah Nelson, *Pursuing Privacy in Cold War America* (New York: Columbia University Press, 2002), 15–19.

52. William O. Douglas, *The Right of the People* (New York: Arena Books, 1958), 63–64, 57.

53. Matt Coles, "The ACLU: Then and Now," February 28, 2002, http://www.aclu.org/hiv/gen/11531res20020228.html.

54. Lillian Hellman, *The Collected Plays* (Boston: Little, Brown, 1971), 518 (*The Autumn Garden*), 593 (*The Lark*), 716 (*Toys in the Attic*).

55. Brandeis used this phrase in the "Right to Privacy" article, and it wends its way through his jurisprudence. See his dissent in Olmstead v. United States, 227 U.S. 438, 478 (1928).

56. See Anthony Lewis, *Make No Law: The Sullivan Case and the First Amendment* (New York: Vintage Books, 1991), 184–86. Time, Inc. v. Hill, 385 U.S. 374, 388–89 (1967); Garment, "Annals of the Law: The Hill Case," *New Yorker,* April 17, 1989, 90, 98, 104, 109. Bernard Schwartz, *The Unpublished Opinions of the Warren Court* (New York: Oxford University Press, 1985), 240–303; Laura Kalman, *Abe Fortas: A Biography* (New Haven: Yale University Press, 1990), 262–63.

57. Mary McCarthy to Ben O'Sullivan, "Material for Answering Interrogatory 15," McCarthy Papers.

58. Hellman, *Pentimento,* 13, 16.

59. Hellman, *Pentimento,* 27, 29.

60. Hellman, *Pentimento,* 42.

61. See Pamela S. Bromberg, "Establishing the Woman and Constructing a Narrative in Lillian Hellman's Memoirs," in *Critical Essays on Lillian Hellman,* ed. Mark W. Estrin (Boston: G. K. Hall, 1989), 119–23; Linda Wagner-Martin, "Lillian Hellman: Autobiography and Truth," in Estrin, *Critical Essays on Lillian Hellman,* 131–32; and Sidonie A. Smith and Marcus K. Billson, "Lillian Hellman and the Strategy of the Other," in *Women's Autobiography: Essays in Criticism,* ed. Estelle C. Jelinek (Bloomington: Indiana University Press, 1980), 163–79.

62. Hellman, *Pentimento,* 47.

63. This episode is reported in Joan Mellen, *Hellman and Hammett: The Legendary Passion of Lillian Hellman and Dashiell Hammett* (New York: HarperCollins, 1996), 16–125, 144. Mellen cites interviews between herself and Philip D'Arcey, as well as with Alvin Sargent, Hellman, and Dan Rather (this last makes no reference to an abortion). See

also Dashiell Hammett, *Selected Letters* (Washington, DC: Counterpoint, 2001), 62, 120.

64. Arthur Kober diary, July 19, 1937, Arthur Kober Papers, Wisconsin Historical Society, Madison.

65. Mellen, *Hellman and Hammett*, 126.

66. Hellman, *Pentimento*, 129. In *An Unfinished Woman*, she recalls meeting a woman, while traveling in Spain in 1937, who had a pregnancy that "she had fixed herself" (99).

67. Robert Bork, "Neutral Principles and Some First Amendment Problems," *Indiana Law Journal* (Fall 1971): 170–77.

68. Edgar Allan Poe, "The Purloined Letter," in *Great Short Works of Edgar Allan Poe*, ed. G. R. Thompson (New York: Harper and Row, 1970), 442, emphasis in original.

69. Mary McCarthy herself told Carol Brightman that she had "a quite a lot" of abortions in an interview, "Mary McCarthy, Still Contrary," *Nation*, May 19, 1984, 616.

70. Mary McCarthy, *The Company She Keeps* (1942; rpt., New York: Harcourt, 1970), 20.

71. Mary McCarthy, *Intellectual Memoirs: New York, 1936–1938* (New York: Harcourt, Brace, 1992), 62.

72. McCarthy *Intellectual Memoirs*, 61–62.

73. McCarthy, *Intellectual Memoirs*, 66; Carol Brightman, *Writing Dangerously: Mary McCarthy and Her World* (New York: Clarkson Potter, 1992), 167. In a letter to her lawyer Ben O'Sullivan, after Hellman had sued her, McCarthy wrote, "I know that Hellman *tried* to have an affair with Philip Rahv and failed—he told me about it—but I don't see how that can help my case, alas." McCarthy to O'Sullivan, April 21, 1980, McCarthy Papers, emphasis in original.

74. See Susan Brownmiller, *In Our Time: Memoir of a Revolution* (New York: Dial, 1999), 7; and Hull and Hoffer, *Roe v. Wade*, 109–10.

75. Brownmiller refers to this debut issue in her memoir: "Eager to make a mark in the reproductive rights debate, the editors [of *Ms.*] borrowed a tactic from feminists in France and came up with a declaration, 'We Have had Abortions,' addressed to the White House. . . . Three years earlier both the declaration, and *Ms.* itself would have been inconceivable." *In Our Time*, 131–32. *Ms.* ran a similar petition in 2006. http://www.msmagazine.com/radar/2006-07-24-we-had-abortions.asp.

76. Carol Brightman, "Mary, Still Contrary," *Nation*, May 19, 1984, 611–18, rpt. in *Conversations with Mary McCarthy*, ed. Carol Gelderman (Jackson: University Press of Mississippi, 1991), 244–45.

77. Brightman, "Mary, Still Contrary," 236.

78. See Michael Sandel, *Liberalism and the Limits of Justice,* 2nd ed. (Cambridge: Cambridge University Press, 1998), x.

79. Hannah Arendt, *The Human Condition* (Chicago: University of Chicago Press, 1958), 32, 73.

80. Mary McCarthy, "Philosophy at Work," *New Yorker,* October 18, 1958, 198–205.

81. Hannah Arendt to Mary McCarthy, August 8, 1969, in *Between Friends: The Correspondence of Hannah Arendt and Mary McCarthy, 1949–1975,* ed. Carol Brightman (New York: Harcourt Brace, 1995), 241–44.

82. McCarthy, *Intellectual Memoirs,* 101; Brightman, *Writing Dangerously,* 620.

83. Mary McCarthy, *The Group* (New York: Harcourt, 1963), 3.

84. McCarthy, *The Group,* 8, 160.

85. Mary McCarthy, *How I Grew* (San Diego: Harcourt Brace Jovanovich, 1987), 77–78.

86. Mary McCarthy, "Acts of Love," in *Occasional Prose* (New York: Harcourt Brace Jovanovich, 1985), 187–88.

87. McCarthy, *How I Grew,* 55.

88. Mary McCarthy, *Memories of a Catholic Girlhood* (New York: Harcourt, 1957), 166.

89. Gerald Gunther, *Constitutional Law,* 11th ed. (Mineola, NY: Foundation Press, 1985), 501.

90. Quoted in Miriam Gross, "A World out of Joint," interview with Mary McCarthy, *Observer,* October 14, 1979, 35. Reprinted in Gelderman, *Conversations with Mary McCarthy,* 176. See also David Laskin, *Partisans: Marriage, Politics, and Betrayal among the New York Intellectuals* (Chicago: University of Chicago Press, 2000), 17.

91. Whalen v. Roe, 429 U.S. 589, 599–600 (1977).

92. Deborah Nelson, *Pursuing Privacy in Cold War America,* xii.

93. McCarthy, *The Group,* 39–40, 43.

94. McCarthy, *The Group,* 58–59.

95. Michael Sandel, "Moral Argument and Liberal Toleration: Abortion and Homosexuality," *California Law Review* 77 (1989): 521–38.

96. McCarthy, *The Group,* 46.

97. McCarthy, *The Group,* 72.

98. McCarthy, *The Group,* 83.

99. McCarthy, *The Group,* 88–89.

100. See Jennifer Nedelsky, "Reconceiving Autonomy: Sources, Thoughts and Possibilities," *Yale Journal of Law and Feminism* 1, no. 7

(1989): 7–36. See Regina Graycar and Jenny Morgan, *The Hidden Gender of Law*, 2nd ed. (Sydney, Australia: Foundation Press, 2002).

101. Brightman, *Writing Dangerously*, 92; Shelia Tobias, "The Group on Mary McCarthy," *New York Herald Tribune Book Review*, January 1, 1964, 9.

102. See Norman Mailer, "The Mary McCarthy Case," *New York Review of Books*, October 17, 1963, 1–3; Norman Podhoretz, quoted in Mailer, "Mary McCarthy Case," 1; Eleanor Widmer, "Finally a Lady," in *The Forties: Fiction, Poetry, Drama*, ed. Warren G. French (Deland, FL: Everett/Edwards, 1969), 101; and Brightman, *Writing Dangerously*, 460–84. Hellman says of McCarthy, "In fiction, she is a lady writer, a lady magazine writer," in John Phillips and Anne Hollander, "The Art of the Theater I: Lillian Hellman—An Interview" (1964), in *Conversations with Lillian Hellman*, ed. Jackson R. Bryer (Jackson: University of Mississippi Press, 1986), 60.

103. McCarthy, *Intellectual Memoirs*, 62–63.

104. McCarthy, *How I Grew*, 84. See Robert Gerstein, "Intimacy and Privacy," *Ethics* 89 (1978): 76–81.

105. Mary McCarthy, "Cruel and Barbarous Treatment," in *Company She Keeps*, 5–6.

106. Brightman, *Writing Dangerously*, 56.

107. See Lasky, *Partisans*, 35.

108. McCarthy, *Intellectual Memoirs*, 101–14.

109. McCarthy, *Intellectual Memoirs*, 98.

110. McCarthy, *Charmed Life*, 199.

111. McCarthy, *Charmed Life*, 208.

112. McCarthy, *Intellectual Memoirs*, 98.

113. Quoted in Lewis M. Dabney, *Edmund Wilson: A Life in Literature* (New York: Farrar, Straus and Giroux, 2005), 241.

114. McCarthy, "Cruel and Barbarous Treatment," 8.

115. See Ferdinand David Schoeman, ed., *Philosophical Dimensions of Privacy: An Anthology* (London: Cambridge University Press, 1984).

116. McCarthy, "Cruel and Barbarous Treatment," 4.

117. Paul Johnson, "Lies, Damned Lies and Lillian Hellman," *Intellectuals* (London: Weidenfeld, 1980), 299, 292.

118. Catharine A. MacKinnon, *Toward a Feminist Theory of the State* (Cambridge, MA: Harvard University Press, 1989), 185–86.

119. Diana Trilling, *The Beginning of the Journey: The Marriage of Diana and Lionel Trilling* (New York: Harcourt Brace, 1993), 412.

120. Charles Fried, "Privacy," *Yale Law Journal* 77 (1968): 475.

121. McCarthy, *Charmed Life,* 108.

122. By 1930, according to the best available estimates, there were at least eight hundred thousand illegal abortions a year in America. See Garrow, *Liberty and Sexuality,* 272.

123. Ann Rosalind Jones, "Writing the Body: Toward an Understanding of *l'Ecriture feminine,*" in *The New Feminist Criticism: Essays on Women, Literature and Theory,* ed. Elaine Showalter (New York: Pantheon, 1985), 362.

124. Hellman, *Unfinished Woman,* 35.

Chapter 4. Choice Words

Epigraphs: Simone de Beauvoir, *Les Mandarins* (Paris: Gallimard, 1954), 254; Richard Rodgers and Oscar Hammerstein II, *South Pacific,* in *Six Plays by Rodgers and Hammerstein* (New York: Random House, 1955), 319.

1. "The Moscow Trials: A Statement by American Progressives," *New Masses,* May 3, 1938, 19.

2. James T. Farrell, "Dewey in Mexico," in *John Dewey: Philosopher of Science and Freedom,* ed. Sidney Hook (New York: Dial, 1950), 351.

3. Mary McCarthy to Dwight Macdonald, July 24, 1979, Mary McCarthy Papers, Archives and Special Collections, Vassar College Libraries (hereinafter cited as McCarthy Papers).

4. The Spanish Relief Appeal Board evolved from an organization started by Dwight Macdonald's wife, Nancy, in 1953; it was chaired for some time by McCarthy in the 1950s. Years later, Macdonald asked Hellman to join. On learning of the invitation, another board member, Gabriel Javsicas, became furious and resigned, prompting McCarthy to depart as well. Carol Brightman and Carol Gelderman offer useful accounts of interpersonal frictions on the board, but there are still gaps in the record (cf. Carol Brightman, *Writing Dangerously: Mary McCarthy and Her World* [New York: Clarkson Potter, 1992], 608–9; and Gelderman, *Mary McCarthy: A Life* [New York: St. Martin's, 1988], 335). In a letter dated March 19, 1979, Dwight Macdonald wrote to McCarthy, "explaining the reason I had proposed Lillian Hellman for the SRA Board 8 or 9 years ago. . . . So I thought, and still do, she'd given up her Stalinism and her joining our board would be good for her and us. 'Scoundrel Time', a tasteless, false book was years in the future and, while I wouldn't want to add the author of such a book to our board, I don't agree w. Nancy and other Board mem-

bers we're not censors and shouldn't drop her for that reason now." McCarthy Papers. Hellman's FBI file indicates that already in 1938 she had sponsored an organization that merged North American and Medical Aid Committees to Aid Spanish Democracy (according to a booklet published by them called "Children in Concentration Camps").

5. Mary McCarthy, *The Oasis: A Novel* (1949; rpt., New York: Authors Guild Backinprint, 1999), 6.

6. Mary McCarthy, "The Man in the Brooks Brothers Shirt," in *The Company She Keeps* (1942; rpt., New York: Harcourt, 1970), 101.

7. Brightman, *Writing Dangerously*, 153.

8. Mary McCarthy, *A Charmed Life* (New York: Harcourt, Brace, 1955), 33 (emphasis in original), 191.

9. A long-running debate in the media during John McCain's presidential campaign focused on the question of whether McCain was true to himself. Among others, see Megan Garber, "John McCain and the Authenticity Trap: Why 'Let McCain Be McCain' Doesn't Wash," *Columbia Journalism Review*, July 22, 2008. Journalist Mike Barnicle asserted that McCain "has to figure out, . . . does he remain true to himself, in which [case] he would obviously have immense appeal to independents in the fall, or does he play to the band right now in the spring." http://mediamatters .org/items/200802120009.

10. Ralph Waldo Emerson, "Self-Reliance," in *Essays and Lectures* (New York: Library of America, 1983), 259, 264.

11. Hannah Arendt, "Lying in Politics," in *Crises of the Republic* (New York: Harcourt Brace, 1972), 5–6, 3.

12. Hannah Arendt, *The Origins of Totalitarianism* (New York: Harcourt, 1951), vii.

13. See Jeffrey Stout, "The Languages of Morals," in *Ethics after Babel: The Language of Morals and Their Discontents* (Boston: Beacon, 1988), 60–81.

14. Lillian Hellman, *Watch on the Rhine*, in *The Collected Plays* (Boston: Little, Brown, 1961), 234.

15. R. M. Hare, *The Language of Morals* (Oxford: Oxford University Press, 1952), 1.

16. Aristotle, *Politics*, trans. B. Jowett, in *The Complete Works of Aristotle: The Revised Oxford Translation*, ed. Jonathan Barnes, 2 vols. (Princeton, NJ: Princeton University Press, 1984), 2:1988. See also Stanley Cavell's discussion of this famous passage in *Cities of Words: Pedagogical Letters on a Register of the Moral Life* (Cambridge, MA: Harvard University Press, 2004), 24.

17. Mary McCarthy, *Charmed Life*, 180.

18. Kenneth Burke, *Attitudes toward History* (1937; rpt., Berkeley: University of California Press, 1984), 5.

19. Ann George and Jack Selzer, *Burke in the 1930s* (Columbia: The University of South Carolina Press, 2007), 56.

20. Burke, *Attitudes toward History*, 41, emphasis in original.

21. Kenneth Burke, *The Philosophy of Literary Form: Studies in Symbolic Action*, 3rd ed. (Berkeley: University of California Press, 1969), 246.

22. Lillian Hellman, *The Autumn Garden*, in *Collected Plays*, 513.

23. Leon Trotsky, "Their Morals and Ours," *New International* (February 1938): 19.

24. " 'Guests' Aiding Strike Beaten at Waldorf; Fists, Bon Mots Fly in Empire Room Fracas," *New York Times*, February 7, 1934, 1. Mary McCarthy, *The Group* (New York: Harcourt, 1963), 182–85.

25. Arthur M. Schlesinger Jr., "Whittaker Chambers and His *Witness*" (1952), in *"The Politics of Hope" and "The Bitter Heritage": American Liberalism in the 1960s* (Princeton, NJ: Princeton University Press, 2008), 230, 244.

26. Mary McCarthy, "My Confession," in *On the Contrary: Articles of Belief, 1946–1961* (New York: Farrar, Straus and Cudahy, 1961), 75, 76.

27. Whittaker Chambers, *Witness* (New York: Regnery, 1952), 744, 773.

28. Chambers, *Witness*, 982.

29. Alan Wald, *James T. Farrell: The Revolutionary Socialist Years* (New York: New York University Press, 1978), 58–84.

30. Marion Hammett and William Smith, "Inside the Trotsky 'Trial,' " *New Masses*, April 27, 1937, 10, 11. André Malraux responded to Trotsky's aspersions against himself (such as accusing Malraux of being an agent of Stalin) by calling him a liar in the *Nation* (March 27, 1937, 351). Articles in the *Nation*, however, paint a complex picture. Authors Benjamin Stolberg and Louis Fischer struggle to understand how the Trotsky-Stalin choice arose in the first place in "Trotsky in the U.S.S.R.," *Nation*, 10, 1937, 400–406.

31. McCarthy, "My Confession," 84.

32. Mary McCarthy, *The Groves of Academe* (New York: Harcourt, Brace, 1952), 301.

33. See Kenneth Burke, *Attitudes toward History*, iii, 166–75.

34. Mary McCarthy, "My Confession," 103.

35. Quoted in Farrell, "Dewey in Mexico," 362.

36. Farrell, "Dewey in Mexico," 365.

37. Agnes E. Meyer interview with John Dewey, *Washington Post,* December 9, 1937.

38. Farrell, "Dewey in Mexico," 374.

39. Farrell, "Dewey in Mexico," 376.

40. Chambers, *Witness,* 78.

41. Sidney Hook, "The Degradation of the Word," in *Sidney Hook on Pragmatism, Democracy, and Freedom: The Essential Essays,* ed. Robert B. Talisse and Robert Tempo (Amherst, NY: Prometheus, 2002), 296–306.

42. Sidney Hook, "The Scoundrel in the Looking Glass," in *Philosophy and Public Policy* (Carbondale: Southern Illinois University Press, 1980), 82–91.

43. Arthur Koestler, *The God That Failed,* ed. Richard Crossman (1949; rpt., New York: Columbia University Press, 1999), 54, 61.

44. See Goronwy Rees, "*Darkness at Noon* and the 'Grammatical Fiction,'" in *Arthur Koestler's* Darkness at Noon, ed. Harold Bloom (New York: Chelsea House, 2004), 15–30.

45. Arthur Koestler, *Darkness at Noon* (1940; rpt., New York: Scribner, 1968), 97–100.

46. Arthur Koestler, *Twilight Bar: An Escapade in Four Acts* (New York: Macmillan, 1947), 103.

47. Brightman, *Writing Dangerously,* 301.

48. Koestler, *The God That Failed,* 17, 61.

49. Arthur M. Schlesinger Jr., *The Vital Center: The Politics of Freedom* (Boston: Houghton Mifflin, 1949).

50. Lillian Hellman, *Scoundrel Time* (Boston: Little, Brown, 1976), 153.

51. *Life,* April 14, 1949. See Dwight Macdonald, "The Waldorf Conference," *politics* (Winter 1949): 32A–32D; Arthur Miller, *Timebends: A Life* (New York: Grove, 1987); Francis Stonor Saunders, *The Cultural Cold War: The CIA and the World of Arts and Letters* (New York: New Press, 1999), 45–57; and Peter Coleman, *The Liberal Conspiracy: The Congress for Cultural Freedom and the Struggle for the Mind of Postwar Europe* (New York: Free Press, 1989).

52. Miller, *Timebends,* 235.

53. Saunders, *Cultural Cold War,* 5.

54. Geoffrey Roberts, *The Unholy Alliance: Stalin's Pact with Hitler* (Bloomington: Indiana University Press, 1989), 109; A. S. Gromyko et al., eds., *Soviet Peace Efforts on the Eve of World War II,* 2nd printing (Moscow: Progress, 1976), doc. 7. See also Ivan Maisky, *Who Helped Hitler?* (London: Hutchinson, 1964).

55. Lillian Hellman, "The Time of the 'Foxes,'" *New York Times,* October 22, 1967.

56. Lillian Hellman, *The Little Foxes,* in *Collected Plays,* 199.

57. Brooks Atkinson, "Miss Bankhead Has a Play," *New York Times,* February 26, 1939, sec. 9, p. 1.

58. Hellman, *Little Foxes,* 199.

59. Hellman, "Time of the 'Foxes.'"

60. The distinction between "freedom from" and "freedom to" is much discussed. See F. H. Bradley, *Ethical Studies,* 2nd ed. rev. (Oxford: Clarendon, 1962), 55–57; a feminist treatment that centers on freedom rather than power in Janet Radcliffe Richards, "Enquiries for Liberators," in *The Skeptical Feminist: A Philosophical Enquiry* (Boston: Routledge and Kegan Paul, 1980), 66–67; and Wayne C. Booth, "Freedom of Interpretation: Bakhtin and the Challenge of Feminist Criticism," in *The Politics of Interpretation,* ed. W. J. T. Mitchell (Chicago: University of Chicago Press, 1982), 51–82.

61. Hellman, *Little Foxes,* 199.

62. Atkinson, "Miss Bankhead Has a Play."

63. *The Spanish Earth* can be viewed on YouTube. http://www .youtube.com/watch?v=ep24InPrJRQ

64. Martha Gellhorn, "Close Encounters of the Apocryphal Kind," in *Critical Essays on Lillian Hellman,* ed. Mark W. Estrin (Boston: G. K. Hall, 1989), 181.

65. Lillian Hellman, *An Unfinished Woman* (Boston: Little, Brown, 1969), 82.

66. Carl Rollyson, *Lillian Hellman: The Legend and Her Legacy* (New York: St. Martin's, 1988), 276.

67. Wright, *Lillian Hellman: The Image, the Woman* (New York: Simon and Schuster, 1986), 133.

68. Hellman charted a trip across Europe in a series of articles for the *New York Star* (November 4–5, 7–10, 1948) to see Marshal Tito.

69. Hellman reports that Roosevelt asked her several times when she had written *Watch on the Rhine* because he had been told that she had paid for "Communist" war protesters who kept a picket line around the White House before Germany attacked the Soviet Union. *Pentimento: A Book of Portraits* (Boston: Little, Brown, 1973), 195.

70. Irving Howe, "Lillian Hellman and the McCarthy Years," in *Selected Writings, 1950–1990* (San Diego: Harcourt Brace Jovanovich, 1990), 345.

71. Lillian Hellman, "Back of Those Foxes," *New York Times*, February 26, 1939, sec. 9, p. 1.

72. Lillian Hellman, *Unfinished Woman*, 87.

73. See Stephen Koch, *The Breaking Point: Hemingway, Dos Passos, and the Murder of José Robles* (New York: Counterpoint, 2005).

74. See Mary McCarthy to Ben Sullivan, McCarthy Papers. She also seems to draw upon it in "My Confession": "Jeweled lady-authors turned white and shook their bracelets angrily when I came into a soiree" (100). Also see Brightman, *Writing Dangerously*, 325–26.

75. Hellman, *Unfinished Woman*, 117.

76. Hellman, *Unfinished Woman*, 162.

77. Tallulah Bankhead, *Tallulah: My Autobiography* (1952; rpt., Jackson: University of Mississippi Press, 2004), 242.

78. Bankhead, *Tallulah*, 241.

79. Hellman, *Unfinished Woman*, 81.

80. Irving Howe quoted in *New York Times*, March 19, 1980, C21.

81. Robert Bechtold Heilman, *The Iceman, the Arsonist, and the Troubled Agent: Tragedy and Melodrama on the Modern Stage* (Seattle: University of Washington Press, 1973), 301.

82. Karl Marx and Friedrich Engels, *The Communist Manifesto*, trans. Samuel Moore (London: Penguin, 1967), 82.

83. Lillian Hellman, *New York Times*, February 26, 1939.

84. Hellman, *Little Foxes*, 195.

85. Hellman, *Little Foxes*, 199.

86. See James Livingston, *Pragmatism, Feminism, and Democracy: Rethinking the Politics of American History* (New York: Routledge, 2001), 2.

87. Margaret Case Harriman, *Take Them Up Tenderly: A Collection of Profiles* (New York: Alfred A. Knopf, 1944).

88. Hellman, *Scoundrel Time*, 113.

89. Livingston, *Pragmatism, Feminism, and Democracy*, 23–25.

90. Peter Brooks, *The Melodramatic Imagination: Balzac, Henry James, and the Mode of Excess* (New Haven: Yale University Press, 1976), 205. Brooks published a sketch of the argument of this important book in the *Partisan Review* in 1972.

91. James L. Rosenberg, "Melodrama," in *The Context and Craft of Drama*, ed. Robert W. Corrigan and James L. Rosenberg (New York: Chandler, 1964), 168.

92. Arthur Kober to Lillian Hellman, February 10, 1941, Arthur Kober Papers, Wisconsin Historical Society, Madison.

93. Hellman, *Little Foxes,* 199.

94. Lionel Trilling, "Introduction to the 1975 Edition," in *The Middle of the Journey* (New York: The New York Review of Books, 2002), xxv–xxvii.

95. Lionel Trilling, "Freud and Literature," in *The Liberal Imagination* (1950; rpt., New York: New York Review of Books, 2008), 34, 53, 56.

96. Kenneth Burke, *A Rhetoric of Motives* (1950; rpt., Berkeley: University of California Press, 1969), 10.

97. George Orwell, "You and the Atomic Bomb," *Tribune,* October 19, 1945.

98. Burke, *Rhetoric of Motives,* 22–23, emphasis in original.

99. Robert Corrigan, *Tragedy: Vision and Form* (San Francisco: Chandler, 1965), ix, xi.

100. See, e.g., Paul Boyer, *By the Bomb's Early Light: American Thought and Culture at the Dawn of the Atomic Age* (New York: Pantheon, 1985); and Alan Nadel, *Containment Culture: American Narratives, Postmodernism, and the Atomic Age* (Durham, NC: Duke University Press, 1995).

101. Gertrude Stein, *Reflection on the Atomic Bomb,* ed. Bartlett Haas (Los Angeles: Black Sparrow Press, 1973), 161.

102. Richard Shepard, "Lillian Hellman Teaching at Yale," *New York Times,* February 1, 1966. The State Department paid for Thomson's adaptation of Stein's *Four Saints in Three Acts* with an African-American cast (starring Leontyne Price). See Saunders, *Cultural Cold War,* 118–19.

103. I take this biographical sketch largely from Thomas Pogge, *John Rawls: His Life and Theory of Justice* (New York: Oxford University Press, 2007), 9–18.

104. John Rawls, "Fifty Years after Hiroshima," in *Collected Papers* (Cambridge, MA: Harvard University Press, 1999), 565.

105. Kenneth W. Thompson, *American Diplomacy and Emergent Patterns* (New York: New York University Press, 1962), x–xii.

106. Hannah Arendt, *Crises of the Republic* (New York: Harcourt Brace, 1972), 9.

107. Harry S. Truman, *Memoirs,* vol. 1 (New York: Doubleday, 1955), 349–50.

108. Harry Truman, Address to Congress, March 12, 1947, in *Memoirs.*

109. See Henry L. Stimson and McGeorge Bundy, *On Active Service in Peace and War* (New York: Harper and Brothers, 1948), 629–32; and Len Giovannitti and Fred Freed, *The Decision to Drop the Bomb* (New York: Coward-McCann, 1965), 205–8.

110. John Hersey, *Hiroshima* (New York: Vintage, 1946), 90.

111. Nadel, *Containment Culture*, 54–55.

112. Robert P. Newman, *The Cold War Romance of Lillian Hellman and John Melby* (Chapel Hill: University of North Carolina Press, 1989), 298.

113. Jean-Paul Sartre, *Les Mouches,* in *Théâtre complet* (Paris: Gallimard, 2005), 53.

114. James Agee, "The Atomic Age," *Time,* August 20, 1945.

115. Mary McCarthy, "The Fact in Fiction," in *On the Contrary,* 267.

116. Hellman, *Scoundrel Time,* 155.

117. See Gregory D. Sumner, *Dwight Macdonald and the* politics *Circle: The Challenge of Cosmopolitan Democracy* (Ithaca, NY: Cornell University Press, 1995), 2–5.

118. Carol Gelderman, *Conversations with Mary McCarthy,* 15–16; also in Gelderman, *Mary McCarthy,* 139. See also Sumner, *Macdonald and the* politics *Circle,* 26.

119. Schlesinger, *Vital Center,* 10.

120. Murray Krieger, *The Tragic Vision* (New York: Holt, Rinehart and Winston, 1960), 1.

121. Daniel Bell, *The End of Ideology* (1960; rpt., Cambridge, MA: Harvard University Press, 1988), 301–2.

122. Sidney Hook, "Pragmatism and the Tragic Sense of Life," *Commentary,* August 1960, rpt. in *Sidney Hook on Pragmatism, Democracy, and Freedom: The Essential Essays* (Amherst, NY: Prometheus, 2002), 68–90, 73. This essay is also included in Robert Corrigan's *Tragedy: Vision and Form* (San Francisco: Chandler, 1965) and attributed to an address of the same title, though not identical to the *Commentary* article, to the American Philosophical Association, October 1960.

123. Mary McCarthy, "Sartre and the McCoy," *politics* (Winter 1949), 49.

124. Newman, *Cold War Romance,* 142–50.

125. Hellman, *Scoundrel Time,* 154, 78.

126. Hellman knew the British politician and editor of *The God That Failed,* Richard Crossman, and spent an evening with him while working on the play, a month after Hammett went to jail. See *Scoundrel Time,* 153.

127. "They Will Be Good Strong Hands," Address by Lillian Hellman to the Women of America, February 10, 1948, Arthur Kober Papers.

128. Hellman, *Autumn Garden,* 466.

129. Hellman, *Autumn Garden*, 539.

130. Lillian Hellman, *Unfinished Woman*, 134. For accounts of Hammett's contribution, see Rollyson, *Lillian Hellman*, 299–301; Deborah Martinson, *Lillian Hellman: A Life with Foxes and Scoundrels* (New York: Counterpoint, 2005), 245; Joan Mellen, *Hellman and Hammett: The Legendary Passion of Lillian Hellman and Dashiell Hammett* (New York: HarperCollins, 1996), 273–78; and Harold Clurman, *All People Are Famous* (New York: Harcourt Brace Jovanovich, 1974), 247, among many others.

131. Hellman, *Autumn Garden*, 541.

132. Hellman, *Autumn Garden*, 526.

133. Hellman, *Autumn Garden*, 537.

134. Hellman, *Autumn Garden*, 538.

135. For example, Hellman filed a $500,000 suit against CBS and Samuel Goldwyn Productions in Manhattan Supreme Court in 1967 to forbid the showing of the complete movie of *The Little Foxes*. See "Lillian Hellman Files Suit over 'Little Foxes,'" *New York Times*, October 21, 1967, 17.

136. Harold Clurman, Introduction to Richard Moody, *Lillian Hellman* (New York: Pegasus, 1972), emphasis in original. See also Harold Clurman, *On Directing* (New York: Macmillan, 1972), 49–50.

137. Marvin Felheim, "*The Autumn Garden*: Mechanics and Dialectics," in *Critical Essays on Lillian Hellman*, ed. Mark W. Estrin (Boston: G. K. Hall, 1989), 53.

138. Lillian Hellman, ed., *The Selected Letters of Anton Chekhov*, trans. Sidonie Lederer (London: Hamish Hamilton, 1955), xxvi.

139. Hellman, *Autumn Garden*, 545.

140. Harold Clurman, *New Republic*, March 26, 1951.

141. Martinson, *Lillian Hellman*, 247, 243.

Chapter 5. Criticism versus Libel

Epigraphs: Justice Harold Baer Jr., Hellman v. McCarthy, N.Y.L.J., May 29, 1984, at 7, col. 2–3 (Sup. Ct. N.Y. Co.); Al Gore, *The Assault on Reason* (New York: Penguin, 2007), 11.

1. Dwight Macdonald quoted in Michiko Kakutani, "Hellman-McCarthy Libel Suit Stirs Old Antagonisms," *New York Times*, March 19, 1980, C21.

2. W. K. Wimsatt and Monroe C. Beardsley, "The Intentional Fallacy" and "The Affective Fallacy," in *The Verbal Icon: Studies in the Meaning of Poetry* (Lexington: University of Kentucky Press, 1954), xi, 21.

3. See Ann Douglas, "Periodizing the American Century: Modernism, Postmodernism, and Postcolonialism in the Cold War Context," *Modernism/Modernity* 5, no. 3 (1998): 71–98, esp. 74–75.

4. Tennessee Williams, *A Streetcar Named Desire* (New York: Signet, 1951), 100, 41, 43.

5. Robert Penn Warren, *All the King's Men* (1946; rpt., New York: Harcourt Brace Jovanovich, 1982), 436. See also Lionel Trilling, *The Middle of the Journey* (New York: Viking, 1947); and Saul Bellow, *The Victim* (New York: Vanguard, 1947).

6. Rick Perlstein, *Nixonland: The Rise of a President and the Fracturing of America* (New York: Scribner, 2008), 46.

7. Fair comment required that the facts on which the comment was based be accurate and known to the reader or listener. There was a minority view that misstatement of the facts did not remove the privilege, which Robert Sack suggests was the basis for the constitutional protection for the decision in *New York Times Co. v. Sullivan.* Robert D. Sack, *Sack on Defamation: Libel, Slander and Related Problems,* 3rd ed. (New York: Practicing Law Institute, 1999), §4.4.2–3.

8. For Supreme Court discussions of "public discourse," see Hustler Magazine, Inc. v. Falwell, 485 U.S. 46, 55 (1988); Bethel School District No. 403 v. Fraser, 478 U.S. 675, 682–83 (1986); and Robert C. Post, "The Constitutional Concept of Public Discourse: Outrageous Opinion, Democratic Deliberation, and Hustler Magazine v. Falwell," *Constitutional Domains: Democracy, Community, Management* (Cambridge, MA: Harvard University Press, 1995), 119–78.

9. Morris L. Ernst and Alexander Lindey, *Hold Your Tongue! Adventures in Libel and Slander* (New York: W. Morrow, 1932), vii.

10. Mary McCarthy said: "Others unable to answer plaintiff's intemperate charges include Clifford Odets, Morris Ernst, Lucille Watson, Tallulah Bankhead and Alan Campbell" in her answers to "Plaintiff's First Interrogatories," October 20, 1980, 21, Mary McCarthy Papers, Archives and Special Collections, Vassar College Libraries (hereinafter cited as McCarthy Papers).

11. Lillian Hellman, *Pentimento: A Book of Portraits* (Boston: Little, Brown, 1973), 195. George Jean Nathan wrote of her name appearing on the stationery of a committee to "guarantee the right of free speech to Morris Ernst," in *Theatre Book of the Year, 1943–44* (New York: Knopf, 1944), 296. Carl Rollyson refers to Ernst's visit to Pleasantville in *Lillian Hellman: Her Legend and Her Legacy* (New York: St. Martin's, 1988), 188–89.

12. See Rodney A. Smolla, *Free Speech in an Open Society* (New York: Vintage, 1992), 118; and Smolla, "Let the Author Beware: The Rejuvenation of the American Law of Libel," *University of Pennsylvania Law Review* 132 (1983): 1.

13. Post, *Constitutional Domains*, 68–88.

14. Fred Friendly, *The Good Guys, the Bad Guys and the First Amendment* (New York: Random House, 1975), xiv. See also David Bauder, "Average Home Has More TVs Than People," Associated Press, September 21, 2006; and Joseph J. Pilota et al., "Simultaneous Media Usage: A Critical Consumer Orientation to Media Planning," *Journal of Consumer Behavior* 3 (2004): 285–92.

15. Bill Mann, "Here's How You Can Strike Back against Right-Wing Cable, Radio," *Huffington Post,* August 18, 2009, http://www.huffing tonpost.com/bill-mann/heres-how-you-can-strike_b_262121.html.

16. See Robert W. Mitchell, "Remarks of the Commissioner to the Media Institute" (unpublished manuscript, January 28, 2009); Justice Byron White Opinion in Red Lion Broadcasting Co. v. Federal Communications Commission 395 U.S. 367 (1969), rpt. in *Freedom of Expression in the Supreme Court: The Defining Cases,* ed. Terry Eastland (Lanham, MD: Rowman Littlefield, 2000), 178–84; Katherine Anne Ruane, "Fairness Doctrine: History and Constitutional Issues," http://wikileaks.org/leak/crs/R40009.pdf; Timothy Brennan, "The Fairness Doctrine as Public Policy," *Journal of Broadcasting and Electronic Media* 33 (1989): 419–40; Adrian Cronauer, "The Fairness Doctrine: A Solution in Search of a Problem," *Federal Communications Law Journal* 47, no. 1 (1994); Hugh Carter Donahue, "The Fairness Doctrine Is Shackling Broadcasting," *Technology Review* 89 (November–December 1986); and Thomas W. Hazlett, "The Fairness Doctrine and the First Amendment," *Public Interest* (Summer 1989): 103–16.

17. See Ernst and Lindey, *Hold Your Tongue!,* 71; Norman Rosenberg, *Producing the Best Men: An Interpretive History of the Law of Libel* (Chapel Hill: The University of North Carolina Press, 1986), 6, 169, 171–73; and Val E. Limburg, "Fairness Doctrine," http://www.museum.tv/eotvsection.php?entrycode=fairnessdoct.

18. Sack, *Sack on Defamation,* §4.4.1. The majority opinion in *Times v. Sullivan,* which largely superseded the "fair comment" defense, notes: "Since the Fourteenth Amendment requires recognition of the conditional privilege for honest misstatements of fact, it follows that a defense of fair comment must be afforded for honest expression of opinion based upon privileged, as well as true, statements of fact. Both defenses are of

course defensible if the public official proves actual malice, as was not done here." New York Times Co. v. Sullivan, 376 U.S. 254 (1964).

19. William L. Prosser, *Handbook of the Law of Torts,* 4th ed. (St. Paul, MN: West, 1971), 737; Rosenberg, *Producing the Best Men,* 3.

20. Adams v. Frontier Broadcasting Co., 555 P.2d 556; 1976 Wyo. LEXIS 221; 2 Media L. Rep. 1166 at 566–67.

21. Hellman v. McCarthy, N.Y.L.J., May 29, 1984, at 7, col. 2–3 (Sup. Ct. N.Y. Co.) (decision on summary judgment).

22. Since 2006, Cavett has hosted a show on the TCM cable network.

23. Samuel Beckett, *Waiting for Godot: A Tragicomedy in Two Acts* (New York: Grove, 1954), 85.

24. Anand Giridharadas, "'Athens' on the Net," *New York Times,* September 12, 2009.

25. David Roberts, "'As Rude as You Like—Honest': Theatre Criticism and the Law," *New Theater Quarterly* 19, no. 3 (2003): 267.

26. PBS depends on public funding and, until recently, not on private advertising, though definitions of private advertising have been blurry in the case of public broadcasting and, throughout the administration of George W. Bush, a political hot potato. See Stephen Labaton, Lorne Manly, and Elizabeth Jensen, "Republican Chairman Exerts Pressure on PBS, Alleging Biases," *New York Times,* May 2, 2005.

27. Eric Barnouw, *Tube of Plenty: The Evolution of American Television,* 2nd rev. ed. (New York: Oxford University Press, 1990), 100–110; and Lawrence S. Wittner, *Cold War America: From Hiroshima to Watergate,* rev. exp. ed. (New York: Holt, Rinehart and Winston, 1978), 120.

28. See Ellen Schrecker, *Many Are the Crimes: McCarthyism in America* (Princeton, NJ: Princeton University Press, 1998), 397–99; and Barnouw, *Tube of Plenty,* 117–30.

29. See Friendly, *Good Guys,* 21–23.

30. Susan Jacoby, *Alger Hiss and the Battle for History* (New Haven: Yale University Press, 2009), 97–98.

31. Robert Stripling, *The Red Plot against America,* ed. Bob Considine (Drexel Hill, PA: Bell, 1949), 89–94; Allen Weinstein, *Perjury: The Hiss-Chambers Case* (New York: Random House, 1978), 17.

32. Quoted in Weinstein, *Perjury,* 13.

33. Hébert quoted in Whittaker Chambers, *Witness* (New York: Regnery, 1952), 590–91; see also Chambers, *Witness,* 589.

34. Sam Tanenhaus remarks that the televised Chambers-Hiss hearings ushered in a new age of political spectacle that would include Army–McCarthy, Watergate, Oliver North, and Clarence Thomas–Anita

Hill. Tanenhaus, *Whittaker Chambers: A Biography* (New York: Random House, 1997), 266.

35. Chambers, *Witness,* 711.

36. Chambers, *Witness,* 722.

37. Lionel Trilling, *Sincerity and Authenticity* (Cambridge, MA: Harvard University Press, 1972), 54.

38. Lillian Hellman, *Scoundrel Time* (Boston: Little, Brown, 1976), 84.

39. Gertz v. Robert Welch, Inc., 418 U.S. 343–44 (1974).

40. Rosanova v. Playboy Enterprises, Inc. (S.D. Ga., 1976), 411 F. Supp. 440, 443, *aff'd* (CA5 Ga.).

41. Katie Zernike, "Kerry Pressing Swift Boat Case Long after Loss," *New York Times,* May 28, 2006.

42. Abrams v. United States, 250 U.S. 627–31 (1919).

43. In an article for the *New York Times Magazine,* Ron Suskind described George W. Bush's hostility to open dialogue and his administration's belief that reality is constructed. In conversation with a member of Bush's staff, Suskind writes: "The aide said that guys like me were 'in what we call the reality-based community,' which he defined as people who 'believe that solutions emerge from your judicious study of discernible reality.' I nodded and murmured something about enlightenment principles and empiricism. He cut me off. 'That's not the way the world really works anymore,' he continued. 'We're an empire now, and when we act, we create our own reality. And while you're studying that reality—judiciously, as you will—we'll act again, creating other new realities, which you can study too, and that's how things will sort out. We're history's actors . . . and you, all of you, will be left to just study what we do.'" See Suskind, "Faith, Certainty and the Presidency of George W. Bush," *New York Times Magazine,* October 17, 2007.

44. See Anthony Lewis, *Make No Law: The Sullivan Case and the First Amendment* (New York: Vintage, 1992), 80–90.

45. Peck v. Tribune Co., 214 U.S. 185, 189–90 (1909). For Holmes on "private rights," see 250 U.S. at 628. For an opinion joined by Holmes and Brandeis that indicates that states retain the power to restrict libel, see Near v. Minnesota, 283 U.S. 697 (1931).

46. "Sore Loser Kerry Mulls Lawsuit against Swiftvet O'Neill," *New York Post,* Page Six column, November 18, 2004. For the potential viability of a Kerry libel suit, see Edward B. Foley and David Goldberger, "The Swift Boat Ad: A Legal Analysis," Election Law @ Moritz, http://moritzlaw.osu .edu/electionlaw/ebook/part3/campaign_false02.html.

47. Transcript of Kerry-O'Neill debate from the *Dick Cavett Show,* http://undergroundclips.com/articles/Kerry_on_Cavett_show.pdf.

48. Transcript of *Dick Cavett Show,* http://undergroundclips.com/ articles/Kerry_on_Cavett_show.pdf.

49. "Nixon: Is There Any Way We Can Screw Cavett?" on *Dr. X's Free Associations,* http://drx.typepad.com/psychotherapyblog/2008/01/ nixon-is-there.html.

50. Quotations from the episode are taken from a video of the show provided by courtesy of Dick Cavett. See also Bernard M. Timberg, *Television Talk: A History of the TV Talk Show* (Austin: University of Texas Press, 2002), 78–82.

51. Norman Mailer, *The Armies of the Night: History as Novel / The Novel as History* (New York: Penguin, 1968), 5, 54.

52. Norman Mailer, "An Appeal to Lillian Hellman and Mary McCarthy, *New York Times,* May 11, 1980.

53. Richard Poirier, Letter to the Editor, *New York Times Book Review,* June 15, 1980.

54. A copy of Mailer's unpublished letter can be found in the McCarthy Papers. See also Carol Brightman, *Writing Dangerously: Mary McCarthy and Her World* (New York: Clarkson Potter, 1992), 618–19; and John Leonard, "What Do Writers Think of Reviews and Reviewers?" *New York Times,* August 7, 1980.

55. Buckley v. Vidal, 327 F.Supp. 1051 (S.D.N.Y.1971). See also "Buckley Drops Vidal Suit, Settles with Esquire," *New York Times,* September 26, 1972, 40.

56. Rodney Smolla, "The Thinning American Skin," in *Suing the Press: Libel, the Media, and Power* (New York: Oxford University Press, 1986), 3–25.

57. Kakutani, "Hellman-McCarthy Libel Suit." See also Daniel J. Kornstein, "The Case against Lillian Hellman: A Literary Legal Defense," *Fordham Law Review* 57 (1988–89): 713.

58. Sissela Bok, *Lying: Moral Choice in Public and Private Life* (New York: Vintage Books, 1978), 4, 8.

59. Quoted in Lewis, *Make No Law,* 188.

60. Specifically, the academic institutionalization of this interdisciplinary subject has been traced to a law and literature symposium on jurisprudence published in 1976 by the *Rutgers Law Review.* See Richard Weisberg, *Poethics: And Other Strategies of Law and Literature* (New York: Columbia University Press, 1992), 3–47. J. Allen Smith, "Law and the Humanities: A Preface," *Rutgers Law Review* 29 (1976): 223–27.

61. Wilkow v. Forbes, Inc., Not Reported in F.Supp. 2d, 2000 WL 631344 N.D.Ill., 2000. Milkovich v. Lorain Journal Co., 497 U.S. 1 (1990). See Edward M. Sussman, "Milkovich Revisited: 'Saving' the Opinion Privilege," *Duke Law Journal* 41 (1991): 415–48.

62. Stephen Greenblatt, *Renaissance Self-Fashioning: From More to Shakespeare* (Chicago: University of Chicago Press, 1980), 4. For an instance and explanation of his autobiographical impulse, see the Epilogue, 255–57.

63. McCarthy to Artine Artinian, January 31, 1951, McCarthy Papers, emphasis in original.

64. McCarthy to Ortwin de Graef, March 17, 1987, McCarthy Papers.

65. Paul de Man, *Allegories of Reading: Figural Language in Rousseau, Nietzsche, Rilke, and Proust* (New Haven: Yale University Press, 1979), 282.

66. De Man, *Allegories of Reading*, 292. For other discussions of the passage, see David Lehman, *Signs of the Times: Deconstruction and the Fall of Paul de Man* (New York: Poseidon, 1991), 219–20; and Denis Donoghue, "Deconstructing Deconstruction," *New York Review of Books,* June 12, 1980.

67. See Jacques Derrida, "Like the Sound of the Sea Deep within a Shell: Paul de Man's War," *Critical Inquiry* (Spring 1988): 597. Also Lehman, *Signs of the Times*, 212.

68. Paul de Man, *Blindness and Insight: Essays in the Rhetoric of Contemporary Criticism* (Minneapolis: University of Minnesota Press, 1971), 25.

69. De Man, *Allegories of Reading*, 200.

70. James v. Gannett Co., Inc., 40 N.Y.2d 415, 419; 353 N.E.2d 834 N.Y. 1976.

71. Sack, *Sack on Defamation,* § 2.4.2.1, citing Vocational Guidance Manuals v. United Newspaper Magazine Corp., 280 A.D. 593, 116 N.Y.S.2d 429, 432 (App. Div. 1st Dep't 1952), *aff'd,* 305 N.Y. 780, 113 N.E.2d 299 (1953).

72. Celle v. Filipino Reporter Enterprises, Inc., quoting November v. Time, Inc., 209 F.3d 163, 177; 2000 U.S. App. LEXIS 6785, 13 N.Y.2d 175, 179, 194 N.E.2d 126, 128, 244 N.Y.S.2d 309 (1963).

73. Randall P. Bezanson, "The 'Meaning' of First Amendment Speech," *ETC: A Review of General Semantics* (Summer 1997): 52, 2, 133–48.

74. Richard Rorty, *Contingency, Irony, and Solidarity* (New York: Cambridge University Press, 1989), xiv–xvi.

75. Wayne C. Booth, *A Rhetoric of Irony* (Chicago: University of Chicago Press, 1974), 43–44.

76. For the recent autobiographical hoaxes, see "The Literature of Lies," *Poets and Writers* (May–June 2006): 34, 3, 10–11; and Nancy Milford, "The False Memoir," *Washington Post*, February 5, 2006.

77. Elizabeth W. Bruss, *Autobiographical Acts: The Changing Situation of a Literary Genre* (Baltimore: Johns Hopkins University Press, 1976); Philippe LeJeune, *Le Pacte autobiographique* (Paris: Seuil, 1975).

78. Lillian Hellman, *An Unfinished Woman* (Boston: Little, Brown, 1969), 192.

Conclusion

1. "A Million Little Lies: Exposing James Frey's Fiction Addiction," January 8, 2003, http://www.thesmokinggun.com/documents/celebrity/million-little-lies.

2. James Frey, *A Million Little Pieces* (New York: Doubleday, 2003), 1.

3. "Winfrey Stands behind 'Pieces' Author," http://www.cnn.com/2006/SHOWBIZ/books/01/11/frey.lkl/

4. http://www.amazon.com/Million-Little-Pieces-James-Frey/dp/0307276902/ref=sr_1_1?ie=UTF8&s=books&qid=1273582664&sr=1-1.

5. Maureen Dowd, "Oprah's Bunk Club," *New York Times*, January 8, 2006.

6. Michiko Kakutani, "Bending the Truth in a Million Little Ways," *New York Times*, January 17, 2006.

7. "Television: Dick Cavett: The Art of Show and Tell," *Time*, June 7, 1971.

8. C-SPAN's BookTV, July 31, 2007, http://www.youtube.com/watch?v=4i8v_upwWqs.

9. Milkovich v. Lorain Journal Co., 110 S.Ct. 2695, 2705 (1990). See also Rodney A. Smolla, *Free Speech in an Open Society* (New York: Vintage Books, 1992), 53, 374–75.

10. John Hersey quoted in Peter Feibleman, *Lilly: Reminiscences of Lillian Hellman* (New York: Morrow, 1988), 362.

11. Lillian Hellman, *An Unfinished Woman* (Boston: Little, Brown, 1969), 144.

12. Carl Rollyson, *Lillian Hellman: Her Legend and Her Legacy* (New York: St. Martin's, 1988), 2.

13. Lillian Hellman, *Pentimento: A Book of Portraits* (Boston: Little, Brown, 1973), 216–17.

Index